CYBERIA

# CYBERIA

Life in the Trenches of Hyperspace

Douglas Rushkoff

HarperSanFrancisco
*A Division of* HarperCollins*Publishers*

CYBERIA: *Life in the Trenches of Hyperspace.*
Copyright © 1994 by Douglas Rushkoff. All rights
reserved. Printed in the United States of America. No
part of this book may be used or reproduced in any
manner whatsoever without written permission except
in the case of brief quotations embodied in critical
articles and reviews. For information address
HarperCollins Publishers, 10 East 53rd Street,
New York, NY 10022.

FIRST EDITION

Library of Congress Cataloging-in-Publication Data
Rushkoff, Douglas.
Cyberia : life in the trenches of hyperspace / Douglas
Rushkoff.
p. cm.
Includes bibliographical references and index.
ISBN 0–06–251010–X
1. Subculture—California—San Francisco.
2. Technology—Social aspects—California—
San Francisco.   3. Computers—Social aspects—
California—San Francisco.   4. Cybernetics—
California—San Francisco.   5. Hallucinogenic
drugs—California—San Francisco.   6. San Francisco
(Calif.)—Social life and customs.
I. Title.
HQ2044.U62S47  1994          93–26184
306'.1—dc20                  CIP

94  95  96  97  98  ❖  HAD  10  9  8  7  6  5  4  3  2  1

This edition is printed on acid-free paper that meets the
American National Standards Institute Z39.48 Standard.

For my dad

# contents

## Part V

# acknowledgments

Thanks to the people in this book. You opened your lives to me and I've attempted to depict you accurately—which means as *I* experienced you, and little more. There's no such thing as non-fiction, only points of view.

Thanks to George Gleason, who served as my first real link to Cyberia, introducing me to an online and offline community of dedicated seekers. Officially, he was my assistant on the research end of this project. Actually, he was my tour guide to a startlingly new landscape.

Thanks to Mark Hellesto, who, under the pretense of transcribing interviews, saved me from despair, carpal-tunnel syndrome, and maybe even Lucifer incarnate.

Thanks to Pat Wells and Ruta Fox for telling me to write, Walter Kirn for showing me I could, Al Zuckerman for getting me in the business, David Vigliano for taking the torch, Claudine Murphy and Leslie Rossman for getting me noticed, Mary South for finding me an ego, Fran Fisher for turning my text into English, and Tom Grady for providing me with a publishing house I can call home.

Thanks to the WELL, Terence McKenna, Ralph Abraham, Timothy Leary, Rupert Sheldrake, Genesis P. Orridge, Caresse, Genesse, Earth Girl, Jody Radzik, Mark Heley, Diana, Preston, Greenfire, Craig Neidorf, David Troup, Marc de Groot, John Barlow, Howard Rheingold, David Gans, The Writers Conference, Jaida, Gracie & Zarkov, R.U. Sirius, Jas Morgan, Sarah Drew, *Mondo 2000,* John Morganthaler, Lila Mellow-Whipkit, Bruce Sterling, RoseX, William Gibson, Phiber Optik, and many, many others for your road maps. Here's another.

CYBERIA

# introduction

## Surfing the Learning Curve of Sisyphus

On the most rudimentary level there is simply terror of feeling like an immigrant in a place where your children are natives—where you're always going to be behind the 8-ball because they can develop the technology faster than you can learn it. It's what I call the learning curve of Sisyphus. And the only people who are going to be comfortable with that are people who don't mind confusion and ambiguity. I look at confusing circumstances as an opportunity—but not everybody feels that way. That's not the standard neurotic response. We've got a culture that's based on the ability of people to control everything. Once you start to embrace confusion as a way of life, concomitant with that is the assumption that you really don't control anything. At best it's a matter of surfing the whitewater.

—John Barlow, lyricist for the Grateful Dead and cofounder of the Electronic Frontiers Foundation

"Are we in the bowl yet?" the boy asks, feeling the first effects of the drug.

"I think so," answers his friend, also a sophomore at U.C. Berkeley, who punches a few keys on his computer, releasing a brilliant paisley landscape onto the monitor. "We're over the event horizon. Now it's just a matter of time."

The questioner panics. "So we're in it, then? We're in the attractor?"

"Are you talking about the acid, the computer, or the universe?"

A pause. The swirling computer-generated pictures are reflected in the boys' eyes. "All of 'em, I guess."

"I grok," agrees the operator.

Two college students at three in the morning, tripping on the drug Ecstasy as they create fractal images on a computer in their dorm room. Their topic of conversation? The end of our dimension, of course.

Having turned the concepts of a new math called chaos theory into a working model for reality, the boys experience their existence as a field of interdependent equations. Humanity floats through this field, and can get pulled into one equation or another, just as a planet or solar system can get sucked into a black hole. These equations—called chaos attractors—are like bowls. Once we pass over the lip of the bowl—the event horizon—there's no way to go but inside. We're sucked off the plane of reality as we know it, and down into another one. Everything changes.

The boys don't just think this, they feel it—and in many ways at once: their consciousness is being drawn into an intense psyche-delic trip, their computer picture is about to shift into a new multi-dimensional representation of an equation, and their world is changing around them faster than they can articulate or even imag-ine. And these are the people who grok this turf. Welcome to Cyberia.

Time seems to be speeding up. New ideas and technologies have accelerated our culture into an almost unrecognizable reality, and those on the frontier tell us that this is only the beginning. The dif-ferent ways in which our culture is changing can be understood as different aspects of a single renaissance. Inspired by the computer, chaos math, chemicals, and creativity, this renaissance has been interpreted by many as an evolutionary leap for humanity into another dimension. Whether or not this is true, those who can comprehend, or "grok," the nature of this shift will be better pre-pared to survive the twenty-first century.

The easiest access to this hyperdimensional realm is through tech-nology. Now that PCs are linked through networks that cover the globe and beyond, many people spend real time out there in "cyberspace"—the territory of digital information. This apparently boundless universe of data breaks all the rules of physical reality. People can interact regardless of time and location. They can fax "paper" over phone lines, conduct twenty-party video-telephone conversations with participants in different countries, and even "touch" one another from thousands of miles away through new technologies such as virtual reality. All this and more can happen in cyberspace.

Cyberspace has also gained a metaphorical value for many other kinds of experiences. Drugs, dance, spiritual techniques, chaos math, and pagan rituals all bring people into similar regions of consciousness, where the limitations of time, distance, and the body are meaningless. People move through these regions as they might move through computer programs or video games—unlimited by the rules of a linear, physical reality.

For example, many computer programs and data libraries are structured as webs, a format that has come to be known as "hypertext." To learn about a painter, a computer user might start with a certain museum. From the list of painters, he may select a particular portrait. Then he may ask for biographical information about the subject of the portrait, which may reveal a family tree. He may follow the family tree up through the present, then branch off into data about immigration policies to the United States, the development of New York real estate, or even a grocery district on the Lower East Side. In a hypertext video game, a player might be a detective searching a room. In the room is a chest of drawers. Select a drawer. The drawer opens, inside is a note. Point to the note, and text appears. Read the note, see a name. Select the name, see a picture. One item in the picture is a car. Select the car, go for a ride through the neighborhood. See an interesting house, go inside. . . .

But an acid trip, a new cyberpunk novel, a quick-cut MTV video, or a night at a "house music" club can provide the same hypertext-style experience. The rules of linear reality no longer apply. Meanwhile, as evidenced by quantum physics and chaos math, numbers and particles have ceased to behave with the predictability of linear equations. Instead, they jump around in a discontinuous fashion, disappearing, reappearing, suddenly gaining and losing energy. Our reality, scientists are concluding, can no longer be explained by the simple, physical, time-based rules of law and order. Everything is connected, somehow, but not in the way we thought. There is another, greater, less obvious, invisible territory, of which the physical reality we've grown to know and love is only one aspect.

We need a new word to express this boundless territory. The kids in this book call it Cyberia.

Cyberia is the place a businessperson goes when involved in a phone conversation, the place a shamanic warrior goes when traveling out of body, the place an "acid house" dancer goes when experiencing the bliss of a techno-acid trance. Cyberia is the place alluded to by the mystical teachings of every religion, the theoretical tangents of every science, and the wildest speculations of every imagination. Now, however, unlike any other time in history, Cyberia is thought to be within our reach. The technological strides of our postmodern culture, coupled with the rebirth of ancient spiritual ideas, have convinced a growing number of people that Cyberia is the dimensional plane in which humanity will soon find itself.

We may in fact be at the brink of a renaissance of unprecedented magnitude, heralded by the 1960s, potentiated by the computer and other new technologies, mapped by chaos math and quantum physics, fueled by psychedelic drugs and brain foods, and manifesting right now in popular culture as new music, fiction, art, entertainment, games, philosophy, religion, sex, and lifestyle. These changes are being implemented and enjoyed by a group of young people we'll call the cyberians, who are characterized primarily by a faith in their ability to consciously rechoose their own reality—to design their experience of life.

Theoretical mathematicians and physicists were the first to predict this designer reality. Their ability to observe phenomena, they now believe, is inextricably linked to the phenomena themselves. Having lost faith in the notion of a material explanation for existence, these scientists have begun to look at the ways reality conforms to their expectations, mirroring back to them a world changed by the very act of observation. As they rely more and more on the computer, their suspicions are further confirmed: This is not a world reducible to neat equations and pat answers, but an infinitely complex series of interdependencies, where the tiniest change in a remote place can have systemwide repercussions. When computers crunch data from real-world observations, they do not produce simple, linear graphs of an orderly existence but instead churn out phase maps and diagrams whose spiraling intricacy resembles that of an ancient mosaic, a coral reef, or a psychedelic hallucination. When the entire procession of historical, biological, and cosmological events is reanalyzed in the light of modern mathematical discoveries like the fractal and feedback loops, it points toward this era—the turn of the century—as man's leap out of history altogether and into the timeless dimension of Cyberia.

Inklings of what this dimension may be like come to us through the experience of computer hackers and psychedelic tripsters, who think of themselves not as opposite ends of the spectrum of human activity but as a synergistic congregation of creative thinkers bringing the tools of high technology and advanced spirituality into the living rooms of the general public. Psychedelics can provide a shamanic experience for any adventurous consumer. This experience leads users to treat the accepted reality as an arbitrary one, and to envision the possibilities of a world unfettered by obsolete thought systems, institutions, and neuroses. Meanwhile, the cybernetic experience empowers children of all ages to explore a new, digital landscape. Using only a personal computer and a modem, anyone can now access the datasphere (a web of telecommunications and computer networks stretching around the world and into outer space). New computer interface technologies such as virtual reality promise to make Cyberia a place where we can take not only our minds but our bodies along for the ride.

Cyberians interpret the development of the datasphere as the hardwiring of a global brain. This is to be the final stage in the development of "Gaia," the living being that is the Earth, for which humans serve as the neurons. As computer programmers and psychedelic warriors together realize that "all is one," a common belief emerges that the evolution of humanity has been a willful progression toward the construction of Cyberia, the next dimensional home for consciousness.

The spiritual implications of these technological and conceptual advances are not to be reckoned with in church, but rather on the dance floor, which, like the Mayan temple, serves as a shamanic common ground where participants from all corners of Cyberia may come together to celebrate the heightening of the human experience and resonate, in bliss, with the acceleration of time.

The cyberian experience finds its expression in new kinds of arts and entertainment that rely less on structure and linear progression than on textural experience and moment-to-moment awareness. Role-playing games, for example, have no beginning or end, but instead celebrate the inventiveness of their players, who wind their way through complex fantasies together, testing strategies that they may later use in their own lives, which have in turn begun to resemble the wild adventures of their game characters. Similarly, the art and literature of Cyberia have abandoned the clean lines and smooth surfaces of *Star Trek* and *2001: A Space Odyssey* in favor of the grimy, posturban realism of *Batman, Neuromancer,* and *Bladerunner,* in which computers do not simplify human issues but expose and even amplify the obvious faults in our systems of logic and social engineering.

Not surprisingly, the reaction of traditionalists to this expression has been harsh and marked by panic. Cyberians question the very reality on which the ideas of control and manipulation are based; and as computer-networking technology gets into the hands of more cyberians, the hypnotic spell of years of television and its intense public relations is broken. The result is that the population at large gains the freedom to reexamine previously accepted policies and prejudices. Using media "viruses," politically inclined cyberians launch into the datasphere, at lightning speed, potent ideas that openly challenge hypocritical and illogical social structures, thus rendering them powerless.

A new scientific paradigm, a new leap in technology, and a new class of drug created the conditions for what many believe is the renaissance we are observing today. Parallels abound between our era and renaissances of the past: the computer and the printing press, LSD and caffeine, the holograph and perspective painting, the wheel and the spaceship, agriculture and the datasphere. But cyberians see this era as more than just a rebirth of classical ideas. They believe the age upon us now might take the form of categorical upscaling of the human experience onto uncharted, hyperdimensional turf.

Our technologies do give us the benefit of instant access to the experiences of all who went before us and the ability to predict much of what lies ahead. We may indeed be approaching one of those rare moments on the spiral staircase of human history when we can see all the way up and all the way down at the same time. If this is the case, and the cyberians are correct, then perhaps the only thing we must do now—before we slip even further into the chaos attractor at the end of time—is learn to cope with the change.

We may soon conclude that the single most important contribution of the 1960s and the psychedelic era to popular culture is the notion that we have chosen our reality arbitrarily. The mission of the cyberian counterculture of the 1990s, armed with new technologies, familiar with cyberspace and daring enough to explore unmapped realms of consciousness, is to rechoose reality consciously and purposefully. Cyberians are not just actively exploring the next dimension; they are working to create it.

As the would-be colonizers of Cyberia, they have developed new ways of speaking, creating, working, living, and loving. They rebel against obsolete systems of language, thought, and government and may be at the forefront of a significant new social movement. Their impact is not limited to Silicon Valley, college campuses, or the pages of science fiction. They are changing our world, and they are doing so with a particular vision.

This book is meant to provide a guided tour through that vision: Cyberia. It is an opportunity to take part in, or at least catch up with, a movement that could be reshaping reality. The cyberian explorers we will meet in the next chapters have been depicted with all their human optimism, brilliance, and frailty. Like the first pioneers of any new world, they suffer from the same fears, frustrations, and failures as those who stay behind and watch from the safety of familiarity. These are not media personalities but human beings, developing their own coping mechanisms for survival on the edges of reality.

Whether or not we are destined for a wholesale leap into the next dimension, there are many people who believe that history as we know it is coming to a close. It is more than likely that the aesthetics, inventions, and attitudes of the cyberians will become as difficult to ignore as the automatic teller machine and MTV. We all must cope, in one way or another, with the passage of time. It behooves us to grok Cyberia.

Most people think it's far out if we get virtual reality up and running. This is much more profound than that. This is the real thing. We're going to find out what "being" is. It's a philosophical journey and the vehicles are not simply cultural but biology itself. We're closing distance with the most profound event that a planetary ecology can encounter, which is the freeing of life from the chrysalis of matter. And it's never happened before—I mean the dinosaurs didn't do this, nor did the procaryotes emerging. No. This takes a billion years of forward moving evolution to get to the place where information can detach itself from the material matrix and then look back on a cast-off mode of being as it rises into a higher dimension.

—Terence McKenna, author, botanist, and psychedelic explorer

# 1

# Computers: Revenge of the Nerds

# chapter one

## Navigating the Datastream

Craig was seven when he discovered the "catacombs." His parents
had taken him on a family visit to his uncle, and while the adults sat
in the kitchen discussing the prices of sofas and local politics, young
Craig Neidorf—whom the authorities would eventually prosecute as
a dangerous, subversive hacker—found one of the first portals to
Cyberia: a video game called *Adventure.*

Like a child who wanders away from his parents during a tour
of the Vatican to explore the ancient, secret passages beneath the
public walkways, Craig had embarked on his own video-driven
visionquest. As he made his way through the game's many screens
and collected magical objects, Craig learned that he could use
those objects to "see" portions of the game that no one else could.
Even though he had completed whatever tasks were necessary in
the earlier parts of the game, he was drawn back to explore them
with his new vision. Craig was no longer interested in just winning
the game—he could do that effortlessly. Now he wanted to get
inside it.

"I was able to walk through a wall into a room that did not
exist," Craig explains to me late one night over questionably accessed phone lines. "It was not in the instructions. It was not part
of the game. And in that room was a message. It was a message
from the creator of the game, flashing in black and gold. . . . "

Craig's voice trails off. Hugh, my assistant and link-artist to the
telephone net, adjusts his headset, checks a meter, then acknowledges with a nod that the conversation is still being recorded satis-
factorily. Craig would not share with me what the message said—
only that it motivated his career as a cyberian. "This process—
finding something that wasn't written about, discovering something that I wasn't supposed to know—it got me very interested.
I searched in various other games and tried everything I could think

of—even jiggling the power cord or the game cartridge just to see what would happen. That's where my interest in playing with that kind of thing began . . . but then I got an Apple."

At that point, Cyberia, which had previously been limited to the other side of the television screen, expanded to become the other side of the computer screen. With the help of a telephone connection called a "modem," Craig was linked to a worldwide system of computers and communications. Now, instead of exploring the inner workings of a packaged video game, Craig was roaming the secret passages of the datasphere.

By the time he was a teenager, Craig Neidorf had been arrested. Serving as the editor of an "on-line magazine" (passed over phone lines from computer to computer) called *Phrack,* he was charged with publishing (legally, "transporting") a dangerous, $79,000 program document detailing the workings of Bell South's emergency 911 telephone system (specifically, the feature that allows them to trace incoming calls). At Neidorf's trial, a Bell South employee eventually revealed that the "program" was actually a three-page memo available to Bell South customers for less than $30. Neidorf was put on a kind of probation for a year,[1] but he is still raising money to cover his $100,000 legal expenses.

But the authorities and, for most part, adult society are missing the point here. Craig and his compatriots are not interested in obtaining and selling valuable documents. These kids are not stealing information—they are surfing data. In Cyberia, the computer serves as a metaphor as much as a tool; to hack through one system to another and yet another is to discover the secret rooms and passageways where no one has ever traveled before. The web of interconnected computer networks provides the ultimate electronic neural extension for the growing mind. To reckon with this technological frontier of human consciousness means to reevaluate the very nature of information, creativity, property, and human relations.

Craig is fairly typical of the young genius-pioneers of this new territory. He describes the first time he saw a hacker in action:

"I really don't remember how he got in; I was sitting there while he typed. But to see these other systems were out there was sort of interesting. I saw things like shopping malls—there were heating computers you could actually call up and look at what their temperature settings were. There were several of these linked together. One company ran the thermostat for a set of different subscribers, so if it was projected to be 82 degrees outside, they'd adjust it to a certain setting. So, back when we were thirteen or so, we talked about how it might be neat to change the settings one day, and make it too hot or too cold. But we never did."

But they could have, and that's what matters. They gained access. In Cyberia, this is funhouse exploration. Neidorf sees it as "like when you're eight and you know your brother and his friends have a little treehouse or clubhouse somewhere down in the woods, and you and your friends go and check it out even though you know your brother would basically kill you if he found you in there." Most of these kids get into hacking the same way as children of previous generations daringly wandered through the hidden corridors of their school basements or took apart their parents' TV sets. But with computers they hit the jackpot: There's a whole world there—a whole new reality, which they can enter and even change. Cyberia. Each new opening leads to the discovery of an entirely new world, each connected to countless other new worlds. You don't just get in somewhere, look around, find out it's a dead end, and leave. Tom Sawyer and Becky Thatcher were fascinated by a few winding caves; cyberkids have broken through to an infinitely more complex and rewarding network. Each new screen takes them into a new company, institution, city, government, or nation. They can pop out almost anywhere. It's an endless ride.

As well as being one of the most valuable techniques for navigating cyberspace, hacking the vast computer net is the first and most important metaphor in Cyberia. For the first time, there is a technical arena in which to manifest the cyberian impulses. These impulses range from pure sport to spiritual ecstasy and from redesigning reality to downright subversion.

## Crashing the System

David Troup gained his fame in the computer underground for a program he wrote called The Bodyguard, which helps hackers maintain their chain of connections through a long series of systems breaches. Through another ingeniously exploited communications system glitch, we spoke as he relaxed on his living room couch in

Minnesota. From the sound of his voice I knew he was using a speaker phone, and I heard several of his friends milling about the room, popping open beers, and muttering in agreement with Troup, their local hero.

"The fun of hacking lies in the puzzle solving. Finding out what lies around that next corner, around the next menu or password. Finding out just how twisted you can get. Popping out of a computer-based network into a phone-based network and back again. Mapping networks that go worldwide. We watched a system in Milwaukee grow from just two systems into a huge network. We went with them. By the end, we probably had a more detailed map of their network than they did."

The Bodyguard has become an indispensable part of the hacker's daytrip survival kit. "It's kind of a worm [a tunneling computer virus] that hacks along with you. Say I'm cruising through fifteen Unixes [computers that run Unix software] to get at some engineering firm. Every time I go onto a Unix, I will upload my Bodyguard program. What it does is watch me and watch the system. It's got the names of the system operators. If a system operator ["sysop," the watch-dog for illegal penetrants] or somebody else who has the ability to check the system logs on [enters the network through his own computer], the Bodyguard will flash an error flag [warning! danger!] and terminate you at that point. It also will send you a number corresponding to the next place down the hierarchy of machines that you've penetrated. You'll have your last connection previous to the one where you got canned. It will then reconnect you to where you were, without using the system that knocked you off. It'll recreate the network for you. It takes about four or five minutes. It's nice because when you're deep in a group of systems, you can't watch everything. Your Bodyguard gets you off as soon as a sysop signs on, before he even knows you're there. Even if they just log in, you hit the road. No need to take any chances."

While the true hacker ethic is not to destroy anything, most young people who get themselves into a position where it's possible to inflict damage find it hard to resist doing so. As Troup explains, "Most kids will do the most destructive thing they know how to do. There's nothing in there that they need, or want, or even understand how to use. Everybody's crashed a system now or then."

Someone at Troup's end coughs in disagreement and paranoia. David corrects himself. No need to admit he's ever done anything illegal, now, is there? "I'd say 90 percent of everybody. Everybody's got that urge, you know? 'God, I've got full system control—I could just do a recursive rm [a repeated cycle to begin removing things] and kiss this system goodbye.' More likely, someone will create a small bug like putting a space before everyone's password [making it impossible for anyone to log on] and see how long it takes the system operator to figure it out." The passwords will appear correct when the system operator lists them—except that each one will have a tiny space before it. When the sysop matches the user's password with the one that the computer says the user should have, the operator won't notice the extra space before the computer's version.

This is the "phony phone call" to the nth power. Instead of pranking one person on the other end, the hacker incapacitates a big company run by "nasty suits." Hard to resist, especially when it's a company known to keep tabs on *us*. The events that frightened Troup out of hacking for a while concerned just such a company. "TRW is the Holy Grail target for hackers. They're into everything, which is why everyone wants to get into them. They claimed to be impenetrable, which is half the reason why everyone wants to get in. The more you look into it, the more security holes they have. They aren't so bad." One of Troup's friends in the background chortles with pride. "It's difficult, because you have to cover your tracks, but it's not impossible. Just time-consuming," Troup explains.

"I remember TRW used to have those commercials that just said 'TRW, making the world a better tomorrow.' That's all they did. They were getting us used to seeing them. Because they were into everything. They sent Tiger Teams [specialized computer commando squads who establish security protocol in a system] into every system the government has, either to improve the system's security or to build it in the first place. They have back doors into everything they've ever worked on. They can assume control over anything they want to. They're big. They're bad. And they've got more power than they should have, which is why we were after them. They had Tiger Teams into airport security, aerospace security. And the government gets software from TRW, upgrades from TRW [also, potentially, with back doors].

"When we got all the way up to the keyhole satellite, we said 'That's enough.' We have really good resources. We have people that can pose as nonpeople—they have Social Security numbers, tax IDs, everything. But we all got kind of spooked by all this. We had a continuation of our plan mapped out, but we decided not to go through with it. We ditched all the TRW stuff we had. I gave it to a friend who buried it underwater somewhere along the Atlantic shelf. If I tell him to get it back, he will, but if I tell him to get it back using a slightly different phrase, he will disappear . . . for obvious reasons."

Most purposeful hacking is far less romantic, and done simply to gain access to systems for their computing power. If someone is working on a complex program or set of computations, it's more convenient to use some corporation's huge system to carry out the procedure in a few minutes or hours than to tie up one's own tiny personal computer for days. The skill comes in getting the work done before the sysop discovers the intrusion. As one hacker explains to me through an encrypted electronic mail message, "They might be on to you, but you're not done with them yet—you're still working on the thing for some company or another. But if you've got access to, say, twenty or thirty Unix systems, you can pop in and out of as many as you like, and change the order of them. You'll always appear to be coming from a different location. They'll be shooting in the dark. You're untraceable."

This hacker takes pride in popping in and out of systems the way a surfer raves about ducking the whitewater and gliding through the tube. But, just as a surfer might compete for cash, prizes, or beer endorsements, many young hackers who begin with Cyberia in their hearts are quickly tempted by employers who can profit from their skill. The most dangerous authoritarian response to young cyberian hackers may not be from the law but from those hoping to exploit their talents.

With a hacker I'll call Pete, a seventeen-year-old engineering student at Columbia University, I set up a real-time computer conference call in which several other hackers from around the country could share some of their stories about a field called "industrial hacking." Because most of the participants believe they have several taps on their telephone lines, they send their first responses through as a series of strange glyphs on the screen. After Pete establishes the cryptography protocol and deciphers the incoming messages, they look like this (the names are mine):

#1: *THE PURIST*
INDUSTRIAL HACKING IS DARKSIDE HACKING. COMPANY
A HIRES YOU TO SLOW DOWN, DESTROY, SCREW UP, OR
STEAL FROM COMPANY B'S R&D DIVISION [RESEARCH AND
DEVELOPMENT]. FOR EXAMPLE, WE COULD SET UP ALL
THEIR MATH WRONG ON THEIR CADCAMS [COMPUTER AIDED
DESIGN PROGRAMS] SO THAT WHEN THEY LOOK AT IT ON
THE COMPUTER IT SEEMS FINE, BUT WHEN THEY TRY TO
PUT THE THING TOGETHER, IT COMES OUT ALL WRONG.
IF ALL THE PARTS OF AN AIRPLANE ENGINE ARE
MACHINED 1MM OFF, IT'S JUST NOT GOING TO WORK.

#2: *THE PRANKSTER*
THERE WAS A GUY IN FLORIDA WHO WORKED ON A CADCAM
SYSTEM WHICH USED PIRATED SOFTWARE. HE WAS SMART,
SO HE FIGURED OUT HOW TO USE IT WITHOUT ANY
MANUALS. HE WORKED THERE FOR ABOUT A YEAR AND A
HALF BUT WAS FIRED UNFAIRLY. HE CAME TO US TO GET
THEM SHUT DOWN. WE SAID "SURE, NO PROBLEM."
CADCAM SOFTWARE COMPANIES SEND OUT LOTS OF DEMOS.
WE GOT AHOLD OF SOME CADCAM DEMOS, AND WROTE A
SIMPLE ASSEMBLY PROGRAM SO THAT WHEN THE PERSON
PUTS THE DISK IN AND TYPES THE "INSTALL" OR
"DEMO" COMMAND, IT WIPES OUT THE WHOLE HARD DISK.
SO WE WRAPPED IT UP IN ITS PACKAGE, SENT IT OUT
TO A FRIEND IN TEXAS OR WHEREVER THE SOFTWARE
COMPANY WAS REALLY FROM, AND HAD HIM SEND IT TO
THE TARGETED COMPANY WITH A LEGIT POSTMARK AND
EVERYTHING. SURE ENOUGH, SOMEONE PUT THE DEMO IN,
AND THE COMPANY HAD TO END UP BUYING OVER $20,000
WORTH OF SOFTWARE. THEY COULDN'T SAY ANYTHING
BECAUSE THE SOFTWARE WE WIPED OUT WAS ILLEGAL
ANYWAY.

*THE PURIST*
THAT'S NOTHING. THAT'S A PERSONAL VENDETTA.
INDUSTRIAL HACKING IS BIG BUSINESS. MOST
CORPORATIONS HAVE IN-HOUSE COMPUTER CONSULTANTS
WHO DO THIS SORT OF THING. BUT AS A FREELANCER
YOU CAN GET HIRED AS A REGULAR CONSULTANT BY ONE
OF THESE FIRMS-SAY MCDONNELL DOUGLAS-GET INTO A

VICE PRESIDENT'S OFFICE, AND SHOW THEM THE SPECS
OF SOME LOCKHEED PROJECT, LIKE A NEW ADVANCED
TACTICAL FIGHTER WHICH HE HAS NOT SEEN, AND SAY,
"THERE'S MORE WHERE THIS CAME FROM." YOU CAN GET
THOUSANDS, EVEN MILLIONS OF DOLLARS FOR THIS KIND
OF THING.

### #3: *THE THEORIST*
DURING THE BIG CORPORATE TAKEOVER CRAZE,
COMPANIES THAT WERE ABOUT TO BE TAKEN OVER
BEGAN TO NOTICE MORE AND MORE THINGS BEGIN TO GO
WRONG. THEIR PAYROLL WOULD GET SCREWED UP, THEIR
ELECTRONIC MAIL MESSAGES AREN'T GOING THROUGH,
THEIR PHONE SYSTEM KEEPS DYING EVERY NOW AND THEN
IN THE MIDDLE OF THE DAY. THIS IS PART OF THE
TAKEOVER EFFORT.
   SOMEONE ON THE BOARD OF DIRECTORS MAY HAVE SOME
BUDDY FROM COLLEGE WHO WORKS IN THE COMPUTER
INDUSTRY WHO HE MIGHT HIRE TO DO AN ODD JOB NOW
AND AGAIN.

### *THE PURIST*
I LIKE INDUSTRIAL HACKING FOR THE IDEA OF DOING
IT. I STARTED ABOUT A YEAR OR SO AGO. AND WILLIAM
GIBSON BROUGHT ROMANCE INTO IT WITH NEUROMANCER.
IT'S SO DO-ABLE.

### #4: *THE PRO*
WE GET HIRED BY PEOPLE MOVING UP IN THE
POLITICAL SYSTEMS, DRUG CARTELS, AND OF COURSE
CORPORATIONS. WE EVEN WORK FOR FOREIGN COMPANIES.
IF TOYOTA HIRED US TO HIT FORD, WE'D HIT FORD A
LITTLE BIT, BUT THEN TURN AROUND AND KNOCK THE
HELL OUT OF TOYOTA. WE'D RATHER PICK ON THEM THAN
US.
   MOST INDUSTRIAL HACKERS DO TWO HACKS AT ONCE.
THEY GET INFORMATION ON THE COMPANY THEY'RE
GETTING PAID TO HIT, BUT THEY'RE ALSO HACKING
INTO THE COMPANY THAT'S PAYING THEM, SO THAT IF
THEY GET BETRAYED OR STABBED IN THE BACK THEY'VE
GOT THEIR BUTTS COVERED. SO IT'S A LOT OF WORK.
THE PAYOFFS ARE SUBSTANTIAL, BUT IT'S A TON OF
WORK.
   IN A REAL TAKEOVER, 50 PERCENT OF THE HACKING IS
PHYSICAL. A BUNCH OF YOU HAVE TO GO AND GET JOBS
AT THE COMPANY. YOU NEED TO GET THE INFORMATION
BUT YOU DON'T WANT TO LET THEM ON TO WHAT YOU'RE
DOING. THE WARGAMES-STYLE AUTOMATIC DIALER WILL

GET DISCOVERED SCANNING. THEY KNOW WHAT THAT IS;
THEY'VE HAD THAT HAPPEN TO THEM MANY TIMES
BEFORE.

I REMEMBER A JOB THAT I DID ON A LOCAL TV
STATION. I WENT IN POSING AS A STUDENT WORKING ON
A PROJECT FOR A COMMUNICATIONS CLASS. I GOT A
TOUR WITH AN ENGINEER, AND I HAD A NOTEBOOK AND
BUSILY WROTE DOWN EVERYTHING HE SAID. THE GUY
TOOK ME BACK WHERE THE COMPUTERS WERE. NOW IN
ALMOST EVERY COMPUTER DEPARTMENT IN THE UNITED
STATES, WRITTEN ON A PIECE OF MASKING TAPE ON THE
PHONE JACK OR THE MODEM ITSELF IS THE PHONE
NUMBER OF THAT MODEM. IT SAVES ME THE TIME AND
TROUBLE OF SCANNING 10,000 NUMBERS. I'M ALREADY
WRITING NOTES, SO I JUST WRITE IN THE NUMBER, GO
HOME, WAIT A WEEK OR SO, AND THEN CALL THEM UP
(YOU DON'T CALL THEM RIGHT AWAY, STUPID). YOUR
LOCAL TELEPHONE COMPANY WON'T NOTICE YOU AND THE
COMPANY YOU'RE ATTACKING WON'T NOTICE YOU. YOU
TRY TO BE LIKE A STEALTH BOMBER. YOU SNEAK UP ON
THEM SLOWLY, THEN YOU KNOCK THE HELL OUT OF THEM.
YOU TAKE THE MILITARY APPROACH. YOU DO SIGNALS
INTELLIGENCE, HUMAN INTELLIGENCE; YOU'VE GOT YOUR
SPECIAL OPS SOLDIER WHO TAKES A TOUR OR GETS A
JOB THERE. THEN HE CAN EVEN TAKE A TOUR AS AN
EMPLOYEE-THEN HE'S TRUSTED FOR SOME REASON-JUST
BECAUSE HE WORKS THERE, WHICH IS THE BIGGEST
CROCK OF SHIT.

DISCONNECT

Someone got paranoid or someone's line voltage changed
enough to suggest a tap, and our conversation had been automatically terminated.

Pete stores the exchange on disk, then escorts me out onto the
fire escape of his apartment for a toke and a talk. He can see I'm a
little shaken up.

"That's not really hacking," he says, handing me the joint. I thank
him with a nod but opt for a Camel Light. "That's cracking. Hacking
is surfing. You don't do it for a reason. You just do it." We watch a
bum below us on the street rip a piece of cardboard off an empty
refrigerator box and drag it away—presumably it will be his home
for tonight.

"That guy is hacking in a way," I offer. "Social hacking."

"That's bullshit. He's doing it for a reason. He stole that cardboard because he needs shelter. There's nothing wrong with that, but he's not having such a good time, either."

"So what's real hacking? What's it about?"

Pete takes a deep toke off his joint and smiles. "It's tapping in to the global brain. Information becomes a texture . . . almost an experience. You don't do it to get knowledge. You just ride the data. It's surfing, and they're all trying to get you out of the water. But it's like being an environmental camper at the same time: You leave everything just like you found it. Not a trace of your presence. It's like you were never there."

Strains of Grateful Dead music come from inside the apartment. No one's in there. Pete has his radio connected to a timer. It's eleven o'clock Monday night in New York, time for David Gans's radio show, *The Dead Hour.* Pete stumbles into the apartment and begins scrounging for a cassette. I offer him one of my blank interview tapes.

"It's low bias but it'll do," he says, grabbing the tape from me and shoving it into a makeshift cassette machine that looks like a relic from the Korean War. "Don't let the case fool you. I reconditioned the whole thing myself. It's got selenium heads, the whole nine yards." Satisfied that the machine is recording properly, he asks, "You into the Dead?"

"Sure am." I can't let this slip by. "I've noticed lots of computer folks are into the Dead . . . and the whole subculture." I hate to get to the subject of psychedelics too early. However, Pete doesn't require the subtlety.

"Most of the hackers I know take acid." Pete searches through his desk drawers. "It makes you better at it." I watch him as he moves around the room. "Look at this." He shows me a ticket to a Grateful Dead show. In the middle of the ticket is a color reproduction of a fractal.

"Now, you might ask, what's a computer-generated image like that doing on a Dead ticket, huh?"

# chapter two

## Operating from Total Oblivion

The fractal is the emblem of Cyberia. Based on the principles of chaos math, it's an icon, a metaphor, a fashion statement, and a working tool all at the same time. It's at once a highly technical computer-mathematics achievement and a psychedelic vision, so even as an image it bridges the gap between these two seemingly distant, or rather "discontinuous," corners of Cyberia. Once these two camps are connected, the real space defined by "Cyberia" emerges.

Fractals were discovered in the 1960s by Benoit Mandelbrot, who was searching for ways to help us cope, mathematically, with a reality that is not as smooth and predictable as our textbooks describe it. Conventional math, Mandelbrot complained, treats mountains like cones and clouds like spheres. Reality is much "rougher" than these ideal forms. No real-world surface can accurately be described as a "plane," because no surface is absolutely two-dimensional. Everything has nooks and crannies; nothing is completely smooth and continuous. Mandelbrot's fractals—equations which grant objects a fractional dimensionality—are revolutionary in that they accept the fact that reality is not a neat, ordered place. Now, inconsistencies ranging from random interference on phone lines to computer research departments filled with Grateful Deadheads all begin to make perfect sense.

Mandelbrot's main insight was to recognize that chaos has an order to it. If you look at a natural coastline from an airplane, you will notice certain kinds of mile-long nooks and crannies. If you land on the beach, you will see these same shapes reflected in the rock formations, on the surface of the rocks themselves, and even in the particles making up the rocks. This self-similarity is what brings a sense of order into an otherwise randomly rough and strange terrain. Fractals are equations that model the irregular but stunningly self-similar world in which we have found ourselves.

But these dicontinuous equations work differently from traditional math equations, and challenge many of our assumptions about the way our reality works. Fractals are circular equations: After you get an answer, you plug it back into the original equation again and again, countless times. This is why computers have been so helpful in working with these equations. The properties of these circular equations are stunningly different from those of traditional, linear equations. The tiniest error made early on can amplify into a tremendous mistake once the equation has been "iterated" thousands of times. Think of a wristwatch that loses one second per hour. After a few days, the watch is only a minute or so off. But after weeks or months of iterating that error, the watch will be completely incorrect. A tiny change anywhere in a fractal will lead to tremendous changes in the overall system. The force causing the change need not be very powerful. Tremendous effects can be wrought by the gentlest of "feedbacks."

Feedback makes that loud screeching sound whenever a microphone is brought close to its own speaker. Tiny noises are fed back and iterated through the amplification system thousands of times, amplified again and again until they are huge, annoying blasts of sound. Feedback and iteration are the principles behind the now-famous saying, "When a butterfly flaps its wings in China, it can cause a thunderstorm in New York." A tiny action feeds back into a giant system. When it has iterated fully, the feedback causes noticeable changes. The idea has even reached the stock market, where savvy investors look to unlikely remote feedbacks for indications of which way the entire market might move once those tiny influences are fully iterated. Without the computer, though, and its ability to iterate equations, and then to draw them as pictures on a screen, the discovery of fractals would never have been possible.

Mandelbrot was at IBM, trying to find a pattern underlying the random, intermittent noise on their telephone lines, which had been causing problems for their computer modems. The fact that the transmission glitches didn't seem to follow many real pattern would have rendered a classical mathematician defenseless. But Mandelbrot, looking at the chaotic distribution of random signals, decided to search for signs of self-similarity—that is, like the coastline of a beach, would the tiny bursts between bursts of interference look anything like the large ones? Of course they would. Inside each burst of interference were moments of clear reception. Inside each of those moments of clear reception were other bursts of interference and so on. Even more importantly, the pattern of their intermittency was similar on each level.

This same phenomenon—self-similarity—can be observed in many systems that were previously believed to be totally irregular and unexplainable, ranging from the weather and the economy to the course of human history. For example, each tiny daily fluctuation in the weather mirrors the climatic record of the history of the planet. Each major renaissance in history is itself made up of smaller renaissance events, whose locations in time mirror the overall pattern of renaissances throughout history. Every chaotic system appears to be adhering to an underlying order of self-similarity.

This means that our world is entirely more interdependent than we have previously understood. What goes on inside any one person's head is reflected, in some manner, on every other level of reality. So any individual being, through feedback and iteration, has the ability to redesign reality at large. Mandelbrot had begun to map the landscape of Cyberia.

## A Brief Kiss

The terrace of the Applied Sciences Building overlooks what students at University of California at Santa Cruz call "Elf Land"—a dense section of woods where psychedelically enhanced humans meet interdimensional beings. Back in the corridor of the building, posters of computer-generated fractal images depicting the "arithmetic limits of iterative nonlinear equations" line the walls. The pictures nearest the terrace look like the ferns on the floor of the forest. The ones farther back look more like the arrangements of the trees above them. Posters still farther seem like aerial maps of the forest, seen from above.

The mathematician residing in this self-similar niche of academia and psychedelia is Ralph Abraham, who broke through to Cyberia on his own, and in a very different manner. He abandoned Princeton University in favor of U.C. Santa Cruz in 1968, during what he calls "the apex of the counterculture." It was while taking psychedelics in huge barn "be-ins" with his newfound friends that

Abraham became familiar with what people were calling the "emotional reality" of numbers, and this led him to the hills and caves of the Far East where he spent several years meditating and hallucinating. On returning to the university and his computer, he embarked with renewed vigor into hyperspace to churn out the equations that explain his hallucinations and our existence.

While it seems so unlikely to the modern mind that psychedelics could contribute to real progress in mathematics and science, cyberians, for the most part, take this connection for granted. "In the sixties," Abraham explains, "a lot of people on the frontiers of math experimented with psychedelic substances. There was a brief and extremely creative kiss between the community of hippies and top mathematicians. I know this because I was a purveyor of psychedelics to the mathematical community. To be creative in mathematics, you have to start from a point of total oblivion. Basically, math is revealed in a totally unconscious process in which one is completely ignorant of the social climate. And mathematical advance has always been the motor behind the advancement of consciousness. What's going on now is at least as big a thing as the invention of the wheel."[2]

The "brief kiss" Abraham witnessed was the marriage of two powerful intellectual communities, both of which had touched Cyberia—one theoretically and the other experientially. And as cyberian mathematicians like Abraham tripped out further, they saw how this kiss was itself a fractal event, marking a point in human history from which the underlying shape or order of existence—the very "roughness" of reality—could be inferred. They had conceived and birthed their own renaissance.

Abraham has since dedicated himself to the implications of this rebirth. He sees the most important, seemingly sudden, and non sequitur events in human history—of which the kiss above is one—as part of an overall fractal curve. "It's happened before. The Renaissance was one. Christianity is one. The troubadors in the south of France; agriculture; the new concept of time that came along with the Old Testament—they are all actually revivals. But they are more than revivals. It's sort of a spiral model where there's a quantum leap to a new level of organization and complexity."

Today, Abraham is in his Santa Cruz office, wearing a sweatshirt, drawstring pants, and Birkenstocks. He does not sport a slide rule or pocket protector. He is Cyberia's Village Mathematician, and his words are reassuring to those who are living in a world that has already taken this quantum leap. Just as the fractal enabled Mandelbrot to comfort IBM executives about the ultimately orderly nature of their line interference, Abraham uses fractals to show how this uncharted island in history on which we have found ourselves fits into a larger picture.

"There is this fractal structure of discontinuity. If you look at the biggest discontinuities in human history, you will see they all seem to have very similar structures, suggesting a mathematical model behind the evolution of civilization."

Abraham argues that cyberian interest in the pagan, psychedelic, spiritual, and tribal is not in the least contradictory to the advances in computer technology and mathematics. Historically, he points out, renaissance periods have always involved a resurgence of archaic elements along with the invention of new technologies and mathematical systems. The success of Cyberia, according to the bearded technosage, will depend on our ability to put these disparate elements together. "We have emphasized integration and synthesis, trying to put everything together in one understanding, using mathematical models only as one tool. We are also open to various pagan elements like astrology, telepathy, the paranormal, and so on. We're an interesting network."

For younger cyberians, Abraham's network provides an invaluable template by which they can direct their own activities. As Ralph would say, he "groks" their experience; he understands how these kids feel responsible for reshaping not only their own reality but the course of human history.

"We have to consciously interact with the creation of the future in order for it to be other than it was." In past renaissances, each creative birth, each intimation of what we can call "fractal reality," was buried by a tremendous counterrevolutionary force. "What happened with the Renaissance? Within 200 or 250 years, it was dead again." Society refused to cope with Cyberia then. But the invention of the computer coupled with the undeniable usefulness and profound beauty of the fractal has made today's renaissance impossible to resist.

## Valley of the Nerds

Two men are staring into a computer screen at Apple's research and development branch. While the first, a computer nerd straight out of Central Casting, mans the keyboard, beside him sits the other, John Barlow, lyricist for the Grateful Dead, psychedelics explorer, and Wyoming rancher. They watch the colorful paisley patterns representing fractal equations swirl like the aftervisions of a psychedelic hallucination, tiny Martian colonies forming on an eerie continental coastline. The computer operator magnifies one tiny piece of the pattern, and the detail expands to occupy the entire screen. Dancing microorganisms cling to a blue coral reef. The new patterns reflect the shape of the original picture. He zooms in again and the shapes are seen again and again. A supernova explodes into weather system, then spirals back down to the pods on the leaf of a fern plant. The two men witness the creation and recreation of universes.

Barlow scratches his whiskers and tips his cowboy hat. "It's like looking at the mind of God."

The nerd corrects him: "It *is* the mind of God."

And as the latest kiss between the worlds of science and spirituality continues, the fractal finds its way into the new American psychedelic folklore—as evidenced by that fractal-enhanced Grateful Dead ticket.

It's the morning after a Dead show, in fact, when the young man who designed that famous concert ticket unveils his latest invention for a small group of friends gathered at his Palo Alto home. Dan Kottke, who was one of the original Apple engineers, left the company and sold off his stock to launch his career as an independent computer graphic designer. He has just finished the prototype for his first effort: a small light-up LED device that flashes words and pictures. He plugs it in and the group watches it go through its paces. It's not as trippy as a fractal, but it's pretty mesmerizing all the same. So is Kottke, who approaches the psychedelic-spiritual search with the same patience and discipline he'd use to assemble an intricate circuit board.

"When I was a freshman in college," he carefully removes the wires from the back of his invention, "I would take psychedelics and sit by myself for a whole day. What I arrived at was that cosmic consciousness was a completely normal thing that one day everyone would arrive at, if they would just sit and think clearly."

Kottke, like many of the brilliant people at his home today, sees Cyberia as a logical result of psychedelics and rationality. "That's how I became friends with Steve Jobs. We used to take psychedelics together and talk about Buddhist philosophy. I had no idea he was connected with Woz [Steve Wozniak] or selling blue boxes [telephone dialers that allow you to make free calls] at the time. We just talked about transcendentalism and Buddhism and listened to Bob Dylan. It must have been his alter ego."

Until Jobs and Wozniak created the Apple personal computer, cyberian computer exploration was limited to the clunky and essentially unusable Altair brand. "It appealed to the soldering iron kinds of hackers," explains Dan, "but not the spiritual kind." So the very invention of the personal computer, then, was in some ways psychedelic-influenced. Maybe that's why they called it Apple: the fruit of forbidden knowledge brought down to the hands of the consumer through the garage of a Reed College acid head? In any case, the Apple gave computing power and any associated spiritual insights to the public and, most important, to their children.

It's easy to understand why kids are better at learning to use computers than adults. Just like in the immigrant family who comes to America, it is the children who learn the new language first and best. When mainframe computers appeared in high schools around the country, it was the students, not the administrators, who became the systems operators. This set into motion a "revenge of the nerds" on a scale we haven't yet fully comprehended. But when the computer industry was born and looking desperately for skilled programmers and developers, these kids were too young to be hired. The companies turned instead to the acid heads.

"When your brain is forming," explains Kottke, using his long fingers to draw pictures in the oriental rug, "it makes axons that are long, linear things, feeling their way to some part of the brain very far away to get connected. Your consciousness develops the same way. The middle teen years are about making connections between things in your mind like computers and psychedelics and fractals and music." Everyone is staring at the impression Dan's fingers have left in the rug, relating the pattern he's drawn to the design of the colorful weave underneath.

Kottke's soft voice grounds the group in reality once again. "But this kind of thinking is very easily discouraged. The quelling of creativity is like a virus that gets passed down generation to generation. Psychedelics can break that cycle." So, according to firsthanders like Kottke, everything old becomes new again, and the psychedelics user's mind is rejuvenated to its original ability to wander and wonder. The frames and systems of logic one has been using to organize experience fall away. What better language to adopt than computer language, which is also unfettered by prejudices, judgments, and neuroses?

"Consciousness is binary," poses Kottke, from a casual lotus position. "It's essentially digital." At least this is the way computers "think." When information is stored digitally rather than in a picture, on a record, or even in a book of words, it is broken down into a series of yes/no's or dot/dashes. Things must be spelled out explicitly. The computer functions purely in duality but, unlike the human mind, has no interpretive grid.

One of the primary features of the psychedelic experience as it relates to the human computer hardware, believes Ron Lawrence, a Macintosh expert from Los Angeles who archives Tim Leary's writing, is that it "reformats the hard disk and clears out the ram." That is, one's experience of life is reevalutated in an egoless context and put into a new order. One sees previously unrecognizable connections between parallel ways of thinking, parallel cultures, ideologies, stories, systems of logic, and philosophies. Meanwhile, trivial cares of the moment are given the opportunity to melt away (even if in the gut-wrenching crucible of intense introspection), and the tripper may reenter everyday life without many of the cognitive traps that previously dominated his interpretation of reality. In other words, the tripper gains the ability to see things in an unprejudiced manner, like the computer does.

Just like the great chaos mathematicians, great programmers must be able to come from "a point of total oblivion" in order to fully grok cyber language, and in the mid-1970s and early 1980s, psychedelics users were the only qualified, computer-literate people available to rapidly growing companies trying to develop software and hardware before their competitors. In the field of pure research, no one cares what an employee looks like or what kinds of drugs he eats—it's creative output that matters. Steve Jobs felt this way, which is why his Macintosh project at Apple was staffed mostly by tie-dye-wearing young men. Today, even executives at the more establishment-oriented computer companies have been forced to include psychedelics-influenced developers in their ranks.

Chris Krauskopf, manager of the Human Interface Program at Intel, admits, "Some of the people here are very, very, very bright. They were bored in school, and as a result they hung out, took drugs, and got into computers."[3] Luckily for them, the drug tests that defense contractors such as Intel are required to give their employees cannot detect psychedelics, which are taken in microdoses. As for marijuana tests, well, it's gotten pretty easy to predict when those are coming, and a phone call or two from personnel executives to the right people in Research and Development can easily give, say, forty-eight hours' notice. . . .

A high-level personnel executive from a major Southern California defense contractor admits that the company's biggest problem now is that "alternative culture members" are refusing to work for them. In a secret, off-the-record lunch talk, the rather elderly gentleman said, between sips of Earl Grey, that the "long-hairs we've hired have the ability to attack computer problems from completely different angles. It would be interesting to take the plans of a stealth bomber and trace back each innovation to the computer it was drawn on. I bet the tie-dyes would win out over the pocket-protectors every time." According to him, the company's biggest problem now is finding programmers willing to work for a defense industry contractor. "They're all against the idea of making weapons. We may not be able to meet our production schedule— we may lose contracts—because we can't get enough of them to work for us."

Marc de Groot, a programmer and virtual-reality designer from San Francisco, understands why companies in the defense industry might depend on cyberians. "My question to you is: Which is the less moral of the two propositions: doing drug testing on your employees, or doing defense contracting in the first place? That's the real question: Why are a bunch of acid heads working for a company that makes weapons?" De Groot's two-bedroom apartment in the hills is modestly appointed with furniture that looks like leftovers from his college dorm room. Trouble is, de Groot didn't go to college. After three tries, he realized he could learn more about computers by working for his university as a programmer than by taking its classes, so he dropped out as a student and dropped back in as an employee.

"I think that people who like to expand their minds with things like higher math and computers and media are fundamentally the same people who would want to expand their minds with anything available. But this is a very bad political climate for talking about all this. You can't mix a thing like drugs with any intellectual endeavor and have it stay as credible." Yet, de Groot's apartment—which has one small bedroom dedicated to life's comforts and the rest filled with computer hardware—shows many signs of the alternative culture he prefers to keep out of the public eye. Dan Kottke's fractal Grateful Dead ticket is pinned to the wall next to the computer on which de Groot designed sound systems for VPL, the leading "virtual reality" interface design firm.

Psychedelics are a given in Silicon Valley. They are an institution as established as Intel, Stanford, marriage, or religion. The infrastructure has accommodated them. Word of which companies are "cool" and which are not spreads about as rapidly as Dead tickets. De Groot finds his "user-friendly" employment opportunities on the WELL, an acronym for Whole Earth 'Lectronic Link, or on other bulletin board services (BBSs).

"One of the articles that goes around on a regular basis is a list of all the companies that do urine testing in the Silicon Valley. So you can look it up ahead of time and decide that you don't want to apply. Computer programmers have set up this information service because they know that a lot of their friends and they themselves use these drugs."

De Groot pauses. He is careful not to implicate himself, but his emotions are running high. "And even more than that, people who don't use the drugs are outraged because of the invasion of privacy. They just feel like it's an infringement on civil liberties. And I think they're right. I have a friend who applied simultaneously at Sun Micro Systems and Xerox Park, Palo Alto Research Center. And he found out—and he's someone who uses drugs—he found out that Xerox Park was gonna do a urine test so he dried out and he went in and did the urine test and passed and then they offered him the job, and he said, 'I'm not taking the job because you people do urine testing and I'm morally opposed to it,' and he went to work for Sun. Sun does not do urine testing. They're very big on *not* doing it. I think it's great."

Not surprisingly, Sun Micro Systems' computers run some of the most advanced fractal graphics programs, and Intel—which is also quite "Deadhead-friendly," is an industry leader in experimental technologies like virtual reality. The companies that lead in the Valley of the Nerds are the ones that recognize the popularity of psychedelics among their employees. Still, although they have contributed to or perhaps even created the computer revolution, psychedelics-using cyberians feel like a persecuted sect in an oppressive ancient society that cannot see its own superstitious paranoia. As an engineer at a Microsoft research facility complains, drug testing makes her feel like the "target victim of an ancient voodoo spell."

From the cyberian perspective, that's exactly what's going on; so computer programmers must learn not to give any hair or bodily fluids to their employers. The confiscated parts are being analyzed in scientific "rituals" that look into the employee's past and determine whether she has engaged in her own rituals—like smoking pot—that have been deemed heretical by the dominating religious body. In this case, that dominating body is the defense industry, and the heretics are pot smokers and psychedelics users, who have demonstrated a propensity to question the justifiability of the war machine.

# chapter three

Persecution of psychedelics users has fostered the development of
a cyberian computer subculture. De Groot is a model citizen of the
cyber community and dedicates his time, money, and equipment to
fostering the "Global Electronic Village." One system he developed,
which takes up almost half his apartment, is an interface between a
ham radio and a computer.

**33**

He eats an ice cream from the shop downstairs as he explains
how his intention in building the interface was to "provide ham
radio operators with access to the electronic mail services of UNIX
systems to other sites on the Internet. My terminal is up twenty-
four hours a day. It was never done before, it was fun to do, it gave
me the ability to learn about electronic mail, and it provided a service." No profit? "You could make money off of it, I suppose, but
my specific concern was to advance the state of the radio art."

It's hard to keep in mind that young men like de Groot are not
just exploring the datasphere but actively creating the networks
that make it up. This is not just a hobby or weekend pastime; this
is the construction of the future.

De Groot views technology as a way to spread the notion of interconnectedness. "We don't have the same distance between us anymore. Camcorders have changed everything. Whenever something
happens in the world, chances are that someone's around with a
camcorder to tape it. We're all neighbors in a little village, as it
were." Even de Groot's more professional endeavors have been
geared toward making computers more accessible to the community at large. The success of the cyberian paradigm is dependent on
regular people learning to work with the technologies developed by
vanguard, countercultural entrepreneurs and designers.

"If you don't adhere to the new paradigm then you're not going
to survive." De Groot puts down his ice cream spoon to make the

point. "It's sink or swim. People who refuse to get involved with computers now are hurting themselves, not anybody else. In a very loose sense, they are at a disadvantage survival-wise. Their ability to have a good-quality life will be lessened by their reluctance to get with the program."

Getting with the program is just a modem away. This simple device literally plugs a user in to cyberspace. Cyberspace, or the data-sphere, consists of all the computers that are attached to phone lines or to one another directly. If a computer by itself can be likened to a cassette deck, having a modem turns it into a two-way radio. After the first computer nets between university and military research facilities went up, scientists and other official subscribers began to "post" their most recent findings to databases accessible to everyone on the system. Now, if someone at, say, Stanford discovers a new way to make a fission reactor, scientists and developers around the world instantly know of the find. They also have a way of posting their responses to the development for everyone to see, or the option of sending a message through electronic mail, or "E-mail," which can be read only by the intended recipient. So, for example, a doctor at Princeton sees the posting from Stanford. A list of responses and commentary appears after the Stanford announcement, to which the Princeton doctor adds his questions about the validity of the experiment. Meanwhile, he E-mails his friends at a big corporation that Stanford's experiment was carried out by a lunatic and that the corporation should cease funding that work.

The idea of networking through the computer quickly spread. Numerous public bulletins boards sprang up, as well as information services like Compuserve and Prodigy. Information services are large networks of databanks that a user can call through the modem and access everything from stock market reports and Macintosh products updates to back issues of newspapers and *Books in Print.* Ted Nelson, the inventor of hypertext, an early but unprecented user-friendly way of moving through files, has been working for the past decade or so on the ultimate database, a project aptly named "Xanadu." His hope is to compile a database of—literally—everything, and all of the necessary software to protect copyrights, make royalty payments, and myriad other legal functions. Whether or not a storehouse like Xanadu is even possible, the fact that someone is trying, and being supported by large, Silicon Valley businesses like Autodesk, a pioneer in user-interface and cyberspace technology, legitimizes the outlook that one day all data will be accessible from any node—any single computer—in the matrix. The implications for the legal community are an endless mire of property, privacy, and information issues, usually boiling down to one of the key conflicts between pre- and postcyberian mentality: Can data be owned, or is it free for all? Our ability to process data develops faster than our ability to define its fair use.

The best place to watch people argue about these issues is on public bulletin boards like the Whole Earth 'Lectronic Link. In the late 1970s, public and private bulletin board services sprang up as a way for computer users to share information and software over phone lines. Some were like clubs for young hackers called kødz kidz, who used BBSs to share anything from Unix source code to free software to recently cracked phone numbers of corporate modems. Other BBSs catered to specialized users' groups, like Macintosh users, IBM users, software designers, and even educators. Eventually, broad-based bulletin board services, including the WELL, opened their phone lines for members to discuss issues, create E-mail addresses, share information, make announcements, and network personally, creatively, and professionally.

The WELL serves as a cyber-village hall. As John Barlow explains, "In this silent world, all conversation is typed. To enter it, one forsakes both body and place and becomes a thing of words alone. You can see what your neighbors are saying (or recently said), but not what either they or their physical surroundings look like. Town meetings are continuous and discussions rage on everything from sexual kinks to depreciation schedules."[4]

The discussions on the WELL are organized into conferences. These conferences are broken down into topics, which themselves are made up of individual responses. For example, there's a conference called EFF, which is dedicated to discussing issues related to Electronic Frontiers Foundation, a group that is attempting to develop legal frameworks for cyberactivities. If you browse the topics on the EFF conference, you will see a list of the conversations now going on. (Now is a tricky word. It's not that users are continuously plugged in to the conference and having a real-time discussion.

Conversations occur over a period of days, weeks, or months.) They might be about "Copyright and Electronic Mail," or "Sentencing of Hackers," or even "Virtual Sex!"

Once you pick a topic in which to participate, you read an opening statement that describes the topic or issues being discussed. It may be as simple as, "I just read *The Turbulent Mirror* by Briggs and Peat. Is anyone interested in discussing the implications of chaos math on Western philosophy?" or, "I'm thinking of buying a hydroponic system for growing sensemilla. Any advice?" Other interested participants then enter their responses, one after the other, which are numbered in the order entered. Conversations can drift into related or unrelated areas or even lead to the creation of new topics. All participants are required to list themselves by name and user identification (userid) so that someone may E-mail a response directly to them rather than post it on the topic for everyone to see. The only rule on the WELL is, "you own your own words," which means that anything someone posts onto the WELL remains his own property, so to speak, and that no one may exploit another user's words without permission.

But the WELL is not a dry, computery place. Once on the WELL, there's a tangible feeling of being "plugged in" to a cyber community. One develops a cyber personality unencumbered by his looks and background and defined entirely by his entries to topics. The references he makes to literature, the media, religion, his friends, his lifestyle, and his priorities create who he is in cyberspace. One can remain on the sidelines watching others make comments, or one can dive in and participate.

## Cyberspace as Chaos

The danger of participation is that there are hundreds or even thousands of potentially critical eyes watching every entry. A faulty fact will be challenged, a lie will be uncovered, plagiarism will be discovered. Cyberspace is a truth serum. Violations of cyber morality or village ethics are immediately brought to light and passed through the circuits of the entire datasphere at lightning speed. A store with a bad returns policy that cheats a WELL user has its indiscretions broadcast globally within minutes. Information about crooked politicians, drug conspiracies, or other news stories that might be censored from sponsored media outlets finds an audience in cyberspace.

The cyber community has been made possible by the advent of the personal computer and the telecommunications network. Other major contributors include television and its satellite system as well as the appearance of consumer-grade video equipment, which has made it more than likely for police indiscretions to occur within shooting range of a camcorder. The cyber revolution has made the world a smaller place. Just as a company called TRW can expose anyone's economic history, links like the WELL, UseNet, or even CNN can expose TRW, too. Access to cyberspace—formerly reserved for the military or advanced scientific research—now alters the context in which many individuals relate to the world.

Members of the Global Village see themselves as part of a fractal event. The virtual community even incorporates and promotes many of the principles of chaos mathematics on social and political levels. A tiny, remote voice criticizing the ethics of a police action or the validity of an experimental result gets heard and iterated throughout the net.

Ultimately, the personal computer and its associated technologies may be our best access points to Cyberia. They even serve as a metaphor for cyberians who have nothing to do with computers but who look to the net as a model for human interaction. It allows for communication without the limitations of time or space, personality or body, religion or nationality. The vast computer-communications network is a fractal approach to human consciousness. It provides the means for complex and immediate feedback and iteration, and is even self-similar in its construction, with giant networks mirroring BBSs, mirroring users' own systems, circuit boards, and components that themselves mirror each participant's own neural biocircuitry. In further self-similarity, the monitors on some of these computers depict complex fractal patterns mirroring the psychedelics-induced hallucinations of their designers, and graphing—for the first time—representations of existence as a chaotic system of feedback and iteration.

The datasphere is a hardwiring of the planet itself, providing ways of distributing and iterating information throughout the net. To join in, one needs only to link up. Or is it really that easy?

## Arbitrating Anarchy

David Gans, host of *The Grateful Dead Hour* (the national radio program that our Columbia University hacker taped a few nights ago) is having a strange week. The proposal he's writing for his fourth Grateful Dead book is late, he still has to go into the studio to record his radio show, his band rehearsal didn't get out until close to dawn, and something odd is occurring on the WELL this morning. Gans generally spends at least several hours a day sitting in his Oakland studio apartment, logged onto the WELL. A charter member of the original WELL bulletin board, he's since become host of dozens of conferences and topics ranging from the Grateful Dead to the Electronic Frontiers Foundation. In any given week, he's got to help guide hundreds or even thousands of computer interchanges. But this week there are even more considerations. An annoying new presence has made itself known on the WELL: a user calling himself "Stink."

Stink showed up late one night in the Grateful Dead conference, insisting to all the Deadheads that "Jerry Garcia stinks." In the name of decorum and tolerance, the Deadheads decided among themselves to ignore the prankster. "Maybe he'll get bored and go away," Gans repeatedly suggested. WELLbeings enjoy thinking of the WELL as a loving, anarchic open house, and resort to blocking someone out completely only if he's truly dangerous. Stealing passwords or credit card numbers, for example, is a much more excommunicable deed than merely annoying people with nasty comments.

But today David Gans's electronic mailbox is filled with messages from angry female WELLbeings. Stink has begun doing "sends"— immediate E-mail messages that appear on the recipient's screen with a "beep," interrupting whatever she is doing. People usually use sends when they notice that a good friend has logged on and want to experience a brief, "live" interchange. No one "sends" a stranger. But, according to Gans's E-mail, females logged on to the WELL are receiving messages like "Wanna dance?" or "Your place or mine?" on their screens, and have gotten a bit irked. Anonymous phone calls can leave a girl feeling chilly, at the very least. This is somehow an even greater violation of privacy. From reading the girl's postings, he knows her name, the topics she enjoys, how she feels about issues; if he's a hacker, who knows how much more he knows?

David realizes that giving Stink the silent treatment isn't working. But what to do? He takes it to the WELL staff, who, after discussing the problem with several other distressed topic hosts, decide to put Stink into a "problem shell." Whenever he tries to log on to the WELL, he'll receive a message to call the main office and talk to a staff member. Until he does so, he is locked out of the system.

Stink tries to log on and receives the message, but he doesn't call in. Days pass. The issue seems dead. But topics about Stink and the implications of his mischievous presence begin to spring up all over the WELL. Many applaud the banishment of Stink, while others warn that this is the beginning of censorship. "How," someone asks, "can we call ourselves an open, virtual community if we lock out those who don't communicate the way we like? Think of how many of us could have been kicked off the WELL by the same logic?" "What are we, Carebears?" another retorts. "This guy was sick!"

David lets the arguments continue, defending the WELL staff's decision-making process where he can, stressing how many painful hours were spent deliberating on this issue. Meanwhile, though, he begins to do some research of his own and notices that Stink's last name—not a common one—is the same as another user of the WELL called Bennett. David takes a gamble and E-mails Bennett, who tells him that he's seen Stink's postings but that there's no relation.

But the next day, there's a new, startling addition to a special "confession" conference: Bennett admits that he is Stink. Stink's WELL account had been opened by Bennett's brother but never used. Bennett reopened the account and began using it as a joke, to vent his "alter ego." Free of his regular identity, he could be whoever he wanted and act however he dared with no personal repercussions. What had begun as a kind of thought experiment or acting exercise had soon gotten out of hand. The alter ego went out of control. Bennett, it turns out, was a mild-mannered member of conferences like Christianity, and in his regular persona had even consoled a fellow WELLbeing after her husband died. Bennett is not a hacker-kid; he has a wife and children, a job, a religion, a social conscience, and a fairly quiet disposition. He begs for the forgiveness of other WELLbeings and says he confessed because he felt so guilty lying to David Gans about what had happened. He wants to remain a member of the cyber community and eventually regain the trust of WELLbeings.

Some WELLbeings believe Bennett and forgive him. Others do not. "He just confessed because he knows you were on to him, David. Good work." Some suggest a suspension, or even a community service sentence: "Isn't there some administrative stuff he can do at the WELL office as penance?"

But most people just wonder out loud about the strange cyber experience of this schizoid WELLbeing, and what it means for the Global Village at large. Was Bennett like this all the time and Stink merely a suppressed personality, or did Cyberia affect his psyche adversely, creating Stink where he didn't exist before? How vulnerable are the rest of us when one goes off his virtual rocker? Do the psychology and neurosis of everyday real-life human interactions need to follow us into cyberspace, or is there a way to leave them behind? Just how intimate can we get through our computers, and at what cost?

# chapter four

# Interfacing with the Technosphere

The evolution of computer and networking technology can be seen as a progression toward more user-friendly interfaces that encourage hypertext-style participation of both the computer illiterate and those who wish to interact more intimately in Cyberia than can be experienced by typing on a keyboard. DOS-style printed commands were replaced by the Macintosh interface in the late 1970s. Instead of typing instructions to the computer, users were encouraged to click and drag icons representing files across their screens and put them wherever they wanted, using the now-famous mouse. But this has all changed again with the development of virtual reality, the computer interface that promises to bring us into the matrix—mind, body, and soul.

41

VR, as it's called, replaces the computer screen with a set of 3-D, motion-sensitive goggles, the speaker with a set of 3-D headphones, and the mouse with a glove or tracking ball. The user gains the ability to move through a real or fictional space without using commands, text, or symbols. You put on the goggles, and you see a building, for example. You "walk" with your hand toward the doorway, open the door, and you're inside. As you do all this, you see the door approaching in complete perspective. Once you open the door, you see the inside of the building. As you turn your head to the left, you see what's to the left. As you look up, you see the ceiling. As you look to the right, let's say, you see a painting on the wall. It's a picture of a forest. You walk to the painting, but you don't stop. You go into the painting. Then you're in the forest. You look up, see the sun through the trees, and hear the wind rustle through the leaves. Behind you, you hear a bird chirping.

Marc de Groot (the Global Village ham radio interface) was responsible for that "behind you" part. His work involved the creation of 3-D sound that imitates the way the body detects whether a sound is coming from above, below, in front, or behind. To him, VR is a milestone in human development.

"Virtual reality is a way of mass-producing direct experience. You put on the goggles and you have this world around you. In the beginning, there were animals, who had nothing but their experience. Then man came along, who processes reality in metaphors. We have symbology. One thing stands for another. Verbal noises stand for experience, and we can share experience by passing this symbology back and forth. Then the Gutenberg Press happened, which was the opportunity to mass-produce symbology for the first time, and that marked a real change. And virtual reality is a real milestone too, because we're now able for the first time to mass-produce the direct experience. We've come full circle."

Comparisons with the Renaissance abound in discussions of VR. Just as the 3-D holograph serves as our cultural and scientific equivalent of the Renaissance's perspective painting, virtual reality stands as a 1990s computer equivalent of the original literacy movement. Like the printing press did nearly five hundred years ago, VR promises pop cultural access to information and experience previously reserved for experts.

De Groot's boss at VPL, Jaron Lanier, paints an even rosier picture of VR and its impact on humanity at large. In his speaking tours around the world, the dredlocked inventor explains how the VR interface is so transparent that it will make the computer disappear. "Try to remember the world before computers. Try to remember the world of dreaming, when you dreamed and it was so. Remember the fluidity that we experienced before computers. Then you'll be able to grasp VR." But the promise of virtual reality and its current level of development are two very different things. Most reports either glow about future possibilities or rag on the crudeness of today's gear. Lanier has sworn off speaking to the media for precisely that reason.

"There's two levels of virtual reality. One is the ideas, and the other is the actual gear. The gear is early, all right? But these people from *Time* magazine came in last week and said, 'Well, this stuff's really overblown,' and my answer's like, 'Who's overblowing it?'— you know? It reminds me of an interview with Paul McCartney in the sixties where some guy from the BBC asked him if he did any illegal activities, and he answered, 'Well, actually, yes.' And the reporter asked 'Don't you think that's horrible to be spreading such things to the youth of the country?' and he said, 'I'm not doing that. *You're* doing that.' "[5]

But the press and the public can't resist. The promise of VR is beyond imagination. Sure, it makes it possible to simulate the targeting and blow-up of an Iraqi power plant, but as a gateway to Cyberia itself, well . . . the possibilities are endless. Imagine, for example, a classroom of students with a teacher, occurring in real time. The students are from twelve different countries, each plugged in to a VR system, all modemed to the teacher's house. They sit around a virtual classroom, see one another and the teacher. The teacher explains that today's topic is the Colosseum in ancient Rome. She holds up a map of ancient Rome and says, "Let's go." The students fly over the skyline of the ancient city, following their teacher. "Stay together now," she says, pointing out the Colosseum and explaining why it was positioned across town from the Forum. The class lands at the main archway to the Colosseum. "Let's go inside . . . " You get the idea.

More amazing to VR enthusiasts is the technology's ability to provide access to places the human body can't go, granting new perspectives on old problems much in the way that systems math provides planners with new outlooks on currents that don't follow predictable patterns.

Warren Robinett, manager of the Head-Mounted Display Project at the University of North Carolina, explains how the strength of VR is that it allows the user to experience the inside of a cell, an anthill, or the shape of a galaxy:

"Virtual reality will prove to be a more compelling fantasy world than Nintendo, but even so, the real power of the Head-Mounted Display is that it can help you perceive the real world in ways that were previously impossible. To see the invisible, to travel at the speed of light, to shrink yourself into microscopic worlds, to relive experiences—these are the powers that the head-mounted display offers you. Though it sounds like science fiction today, tomorrow it will seem as commonplace as talking on the telephone."[6]

One of these still fictional interface ideas is called "wireheading." This is a new branch of computer technology where designers envision creating hardware that wires the computer directly to the brain. The user literally plugs wires into his own head, or has a microchip and transmitter surgically implanted inside the skull. Most realistic visions of wireheading involve as-yet unvented biological engineering techniques where brain cells would be coaxed to link themselves to computer chips, or where organic matter would be grafted onto computer chips which could then be attached to a person's nerve endings. This "wetware," as science fiction writers call it, would provide a direct, physical interface between a human nervous system on one side, and computer hardware on the other. The computer technology for such an interface is here; the understanding of the human nervous system is not.

Although Jaron Lanier's company is working on a "nerve chip" that would communicate directly with the brain, he's still convinced that the five senses provide the best avenues for interface.

"There's no difference between the brain and the sense organs. The body is a continuity. Perception begins in the retina. Mind and body are one. You have this situation where millions of years of evolution have created this creature. What is this creature aside from the way it interfaces with the rest of creation? And how do you interface? Through the sense organs! So the sense organs are almost a better defining point than any other spot in the creature. They're central to identity and define our mode of being. We're visual, tactile, audio creatures. The whole notion of bypassing the senses is sort of like throwing away the actual treasure."[7]

Still, the philosophical implications of a world beyond the five senses are irresistible, and have drawn into the ring many worthy contenders to compete for the title of VR spokesperson. The most vibrant is probably Timothy Leary, whose ride on the crest of the VR wave has brought him back on the scene with the zeal of John the Baptist preparing the way for Christ, or a Harvard psychology professor preparing the intelligentsia for LSD.

"Just as the fish donned skin to walk the earth, and man donned a space suit to walk in space, we'll now don cyber suits to walk in Cyberia. In ten years most of our daily operations, occupational, educational, and recreational, will transpire in Cyberia. Each of us will be linked in thrilling cyber exchanges with many others whom we may never meet in person. Fact-to-face interactions will be reserved for special, intimate, precious, sacramentalized events."[8]

Leary sees VR as an empowerment of the individual against

the brainwashing forces of industrial slavedriving and imperialist expansion:

"By the year 2000, the I.C. (inner city) kid will slip on the Eye-Phone, don a form-fitting computer suit, and start inhabiting electronic environments either self-designed or pulled up from menus. At 9:00 A.M. she and her friend in Tokyo will meet in an electronic simulation of Malibu Beach for a flirtatious moment. At 9:30 A.M. she will meet her biology teacher in an electronic simulation of the heart for a hands-on 'you are there' tutorial trip down the circulatory system. At 10:00 A.M. she'll be walking around medieval Verona with members of her English literature seminar to act out a scene from *Romeo and Juliet.* At 11:00 A.M. she'll walk onto an electronic tennis court for a couple of sets with her pal in Managua. At noon, she'll take off her cyberwear and enjoy a sensual, tasty lunch with her family in their nonelectronic kitchen."[9]

What was that part about Malibu Beach—the flirtatious moment? Sex, in VR? Lanier readily admits that VR can provide a reality built for two: "It's usually kind of shocking how harmonious it is, this exposure of a collective energy between people. And so a similar thing would happen in a virtual world, where there's a bunch of people in it, and they're all making changes at once. These collective changes will emerge, which might be sort of like the Jungian level of virtual reality." Users will literally "see" what the other means. Lanier's trick answer to the question of sex is, "I think everything in virtual reality is sexual. It's eroticizing every moment, because it's all, like, creative." But that answer doesn't satisfy true cyber fetishists. If a cyber suit with full tactile stimulation is possible, then so should be cyber sex! A conversation about teledildonics, as it's been called, gets VR enthusiasts quite heated up.

## Loading Worlds

We're at Bryan Hughes's house, headquarters of the Renaissance Foundation, a group dedicated to fostering the growth of the VR interface for artists and educators. Bryan has just unpacked some crates from Chris Krauskopf at Intel, which include a computer, a VR system designed by Eric Gullichsen called Sense8, and the prototype of a new kind of helmet-goggles combination. As Bryan searches through the crates for an important piece of connective hardware, the rest of us, who have been invited to try out the potentially consumer-grade VR, muse on the possibilities of virtual sex.

Dan, an architecture student at Berkeley with a penchant for "smart drugs," begins. "They're working on something called 'smart skin,' which is kind of a rubber for your whole body that you slip into, and with gel and electrodes it can register all your body movements and at the same time feed back to you any skin sensations it wants you to feel. If you pick up a virtual cup, it will send back to you the feeling of the texture of the cup, the weight, everything."

"So this skin could also imitate the feeling of . . . ?" I venture.

"A girl," answers Harding, a graphic designer who makes handouts, T-shirts, and flyers for many of the acid house clubs in the Bay Area. "It would go like this: you either screw your computer, or screw someone else by modem. If you do your computer, you just call some girl out of its memory. Your cyber suit'll jack you off. If you do it the phone-sex way, the girl—or guy or anything out there, actually—there could be a guy who's virtual identity is a girl or a spider even—"

"You could look like—be anyone you wanted—" Dan chimes in. "And then—"

Harding nods. "Every command you give the computer as a movement of your body is translated onto her suit as a touch or whatever, then back to your suit for the way her body feels, the way she reacts, and so on."

"But she can make her skin feel like whatever she wants to. She can program in fur, and that's what she'll feel like to you."

My head is spinning. The possibilities are endless in a sexual designer reality. . . . But then I begin to worry about those possibilities. And—could there be such a thing as virtual rape? Virtual muggings or murder through tapped phone lines? . . . These scenarios recede into the distant future as Bryan comes back into the room. The chrome connector he has been searching for is missing, so we'll have to make do with masking tape.

We each take turns trying on the new VR helmet. Using the latest sonar technology, it senses the head position of the operator through a triangular bar fitted with tiny microphones. The triangle must be mounted on a pole several feet above the helmet-wearing user—a great idea except the little piece that connects the triangle thing to the pole is missing. But Bryan's masking tape holds the many-thousand-dollar strip of hardware safely, and I venture into the electronic realm.

The demo tour is an office. No virtual sex. No chirping birds. But it looks 3-D enough. Bryan hands me the joystick that is used in this system instead of VPL's more expensive glove controller. Bryan's manner is caring, almost motherly. He's introduced thousands to VR at conventions with Tim Leary across the country and even in Japan, yet it's as if he's still sensitive to the fact that this is my "first time." It seems more like a video game than anything else, and I flash on Craig Neidorf wandering through mazes, looking for magical objects. Then Bryan realizes that I haven't moved, and gently coaxes me to push forward on the joystick. My body jolts as I fly toward the desk in front of me. Bryan watches my progress through a TV monitor next to the computer, which displays a two-dimensional version of what I'm seeing.

"That's right," he encourages, "it only needs a little push." I ease back on the virtual throttle and guide myself around the room. "You can move your head," he suggests with calm reassurance. As I turn my head, the world whizzes by in a blur, but quickly settles down. "The frame rate is still slow on this machine." That's what accounts for the strobelike effect as I swivel my head too quickly. The computer needs to create a new picture every time I move, and the illusion of continuity—essentially the art of animation—is dependent on flashing by as many pictures per second as possible. I manage to work my way around the desk and study a painting on the wall. Remembering what I've been told about VR, I walk into the painting. Nothing happens. Everything turns blue.

"He walked into the painting," remarks one of the peanut gallery watching my progress. "Push reset."

"That's not one of the ones you can walk into," Bryan tells me as he punches some commands into the computer. "Let's try a different world."

'LOADING WORLD 1203.WLD'

blinks on the screen as the hard drive grinds a new set of pictures into the RAM of the machine.

Now I'm in an art gallery, and the paintings do work. I rush toward a picture of stars and galaxies, but I overshoot it. I go straight up into the air (there is no ceiling here), and I'm flying above the museum now, looking at the floor below me. With Bryan's guidance, I'm back on the ground. "Why don't you go into the torus," he suggests. "It's neat in there." A torus is a three-dimensional shape from systems math, the model for many different chaos attractors. Into the doughnut-shaped VR object I go.

Even the jaded VR veterans gather around to see what the torus looks like from inside. I steer through the cosmic shape, which is textured in what looks like a galactic geometry of clouds and light. As I float, I feel my body making the movements, too. The illusion is working, and an almost out-of-body sensation takes over. I dive then spiral up. The stars swirl. I've got it now and this world is mine. I glide forward and up, starting a loop de loop when—

Blue.

"Shit." Bryan punches in some commands but it's no use. There's a glitch in the program somewhere.

But while it lasted, the VR experience was like getting a glimpse of another world—one which might not be too unlike our own. The illusion of VR worked better the more I could control my movement. As scientists have observed, the more dexterity a person experiences in a virtual world, the sharper he will experience the focus of the pictures. The same computer image looks clearer when you can move your head to see different parts. There is no real reason for this phenomenon. Lanier offers one explanation:

"In order to see, you have to move your head. Your head is not a passive camera mount, like a tripod or something holding your eyes up. Your head is like a spy submarine: it's always bobbing and looking around, performing a million little experiments a second, lining things up in the environment. Creating your world. That level of interactivity is essential to the most basic seeing. As you turn on the head-tracking feature in the Head-Mounted Display [the feature that allows you to effect where you're looking] there's a subjective increase in the resolution of the display. A very clear demonstration of the power of interactivity in the lowest level of perception." [10]

And a very clear demonstration of the relationship of human perception to the outside world, casting further doubt on the existence of any objective physical reality. In Cyberia at least, reality is directly dependent on our ability to actively participate in its creation.

Designer reality must be interactive rather than passive. The user must be part of the iterative equation. Just as Craig Neidorf was most fascinated by the parts of his *Adventure* video game that were not in the instructions, cyberians need to see themselves as the source of their own experience.

## Get Virtual with Tim!

Friday. Tim Leary's coming to town to do a VR lecture, and the Renaissance Foundation is throwing him a party in cooperation with *Mondo 2000* magazine—the voice of cyber culture. It's down-stairs at Big Heart City, a club south of Market Street in the new warehouse/artist district of San Francisco, masterminded by Mark Renney, cyber culture's interface to the city's politicians and in-vestors. Entrance with or without an invite is five dollars—no ex-ceptions, no guest list. Cheap enough to justify making everyone pay, which actually brings in a greater profit than charging fifteen dollars to outsiders, who at an event like this are outnumbered by insiders. Once past the gatekeepers, early guests mill about the large basement bar, exchanging business cards and E-mail ad-dresses, or watching Earth Girl, a colorfully dressed cyber hippy, set up her Smart Drugs Bar, which features an assortment of drinks made from neuroenhancers dissolved into fruit juice.

Tim arrives with R.U. Sirius, the famously trollish editor of *Mondo 2000,* and is immediately swamped by inventors, enthusiastic heads, and a cluster of well-proportioned college girls. Everyone ei-ther wants something from Tim or has something for Tim. Leary's eyes dart about, looking for someone or something to act as a buffer zone. R.U., having vanished into the crowd, is already doing some sort of media interview. Tim recognizes me from a few parties in LA, smiles, and shakes my hand. "You're, umm—"

I finish for him as he pulls me to his side.

The septuagenarian Leary manages to process the entire crowd of givers and takers—with my and a few others' help—in about ten minutes. A guy from NASA has developed 3-D slides of fractal pic-tures. Leary peaks through the prototype viewfinder, says "Wow!" then hands it to me. "This is Doug. He's writing a book. What do you think, Doug?" Then he's on to the next one. An interview for Japanese TV? "Sure. Call me at the hotel. Bryan's got the number." "Never been down to Intel—it's the greatest company in the world.

E-mail me some details!" Tim is "on," but on edge, too. He's mastered the art of interfacing without engaging, then moving on without insulting, but it seems that this frequency of interactions per minute is taking a heavy toll on his nervous system. He spews superlatives ("That's the best 3-D I've ever seen!"), knowing that overkill will keep the suitors satisfied longer. He reminds me of the bartender at an understaffed wedding reception, who gives the guests extra strong drinks so they won't come back for more so soon.

As a new onslaught of admirers appears behind the flank just processed, Bryan Hughes's gentle arm finds Tim's shoulder. "The system's ready. Why don't you come try it?"

In the next room, Bryan has set up his VR gear. Tim is escorted past a long line of people patiently waiting for their first exposure to cyberspace, and he's fitted into the gear. Next to him and the computer stands a giant video projection of the image Tim is seeing through his goggles. I can't tell if he's blown away or just selling the product—or simply enjoying the fact that as long as he's plugged in he doesn't have to field any more of the givers and takers. As he navigates through the VR demo, the crowd oohs and ahhs his every decision. Let's get virtual with Tim! Tim nears the torus. People cheer. Tim goes into the torus. People scream. Tim screams. People clap. Tim dances and writhes like he's having an orgasm.

"This is sick," says Troy, one of my connections to the hacker underworld in the Bay Area, whom I had interviewed that afternoon. "We're going now. . . . " Troy had offered to let me come along with him and his friends on a real-life "crack" if I changed the names, burned the phone numbers, etc., to protect their anonymity.

## Needles and PINs

Troy had me checked out that afternoon through the various networks, and I guess I came up clean enough, or dirty enough to pass the test. Troy and I hop into his van, where his friends await us. Simon and Jack, a cracker and a videographer respectively, are students at a liberal arts college in the city. (Troy had dropped out of college the second week and spent his education loan on army surplus electronics equipment.)

Troy puts the key in the ignition but doesn't crank the engine. "They want you to smoke a joint first."

"I really don't smoke pot anymore," I confess.

"It proves you're not a cop," says Jack, whose scraggly beard and lumberjack build suddenly trigger visions of myself being hacked or even cracked to death. I take the roach from Simon, the youngest of the trio, who is clad in an avocado green polyester jumpsuit. With the first buzz of California sensemilla, I try to decide if his garb is an affectation for the occasion or legitimate new edge nerdiness but the van suddenly lurches into gear and takes off out of the alley behind the club, the sounds of Tim Leary and Big Heart City winding further onto the takeup reel of my pocket cassette recorder.

I'm stoned by the time we get to the bank. It's on a very nice street in Marin County. "Bank machines in better neighborhoods don't have cameras in them," Jack tells me as we pull up.

Simon has gone over the scheme twice, but he won't let me tape his voice; and I'm too buzzed to remember what he's saying. (Plus, he's speaking about twice the rate of normal human beings—due in part to the speed he injected into his thigh.) What he's got in his hands now is a black plastic box about the size of two decks of cards with a slit going through it. Inside this box is the magnetic head from a tape deck, recalibrated somehow to read the digital information on the back of bank cards. Simon affixes some double-stick black tape to one side of the box, then slides open the panel door of the van and goes to the ATM machine. Troy explains to me how the thing works:

"Simon's putting our card reader just over the slot where you normally put your card in. It's got a RAM chip that'll record the ID numbers of the cards as they're inserted. It's thin enough that the person's card will still hit the regular slot and get sucked into the machine."

"Won't people notice the thing?" I ask.

"People don't notice shit, anymore," says Jack, who is busy with his video equipment. "They're all hypnotized."

"How do you get their PIN number?" I inquire.

"Watch." Jack chuckles as he mounts a 300mm lens to his Ikegami camera. He patches some wires as Simon hops back into the van. "I'll need your seat."

I switch places with Jack, who mounts his camera on a tiny tripod, then places it on the passenger seat of the van. Troy joins me in the back, and Jack takes the driver seat.

"Switch on the set," orders Jack, as he plugs something into the cigarette lighter. A Sony monitor bleeps on, and Jack focuses in on the keypad of the ATM machine. Suddenly, it all makes sense.

It's a full forty minutes until the arrival of the first victim at the machine—a young woman in an Alpha Romeo. When she gets to the machine, all we can see in the monitor is her hair.

"Shit!" blurts Simon. "Move the van! Quick!"

"We'll get the next one," Troy reassures calmly.

After a twenty-minute readjustment of our camera angle, during which at least a dozen potential PIN "donors" use the ATM, we're at last in a position to see around the operators' hair, shoulders, and elbows to the numbers on the keypad. Of course, this means no one will show up for at least half-an-hour. The pot has worn off and we're all hungry.

A police car cruises by. Instinctively, we all duck. The camera sits conspicuously on the passenger seat. The cop doesn't even slow down.

"They wouldn't even know what to look for," cracks Simon.

A stream of ATM patrons finally passes through, and Troy dutifully records the PIN numbers of each. I don't think any of us likes having to actually see the victims in person. If they were merely magnetic files in a hacked system, the deed might feel less evil. But these are flesh bodies. I propose this to Troy, but Simon tells me to shut up. My presence seems to magnify their guilt.

We remain in silence until the flow of bankers thins to a trickle and then dies away completely. It is about 1:00 A.M. As Simon retrieves his hardware from the ATM, Troy finally acknowledges my question.

"This way we know who to take from and who not to. Like that Mexican couple. We won't do their account. They wouldn't even understand the withdrawal on their statement and they'd probably be scared to say anything about it to the bank. And a couple of hundred bucks makes a real difference to them. The guys in the Porsche? Fuck 'em."

We're back at Simon's by about two o'clock. He downloads his card reader's RAM chip into the PC. Numbers flash on the screen as

Simon and Jack cross-reference PIN numbers with each card. Once they have a complete list, Simon pulls out a white plastic machine called a "securotech" or "magnelock" or something like that. A Lake Tahoe hotel that went out of business last year sold it to a surplus electronic supply house, along with several hundred plastic cards with magnetic strips that were used as keys to the hotel's rooms. By punching numbers on the keypad of the machine, Simon can "write" the appropriate numbers to the cards.

Troy shows me a printout of information they got off a bulletin board last month; it details which number means what: a certain three numbers refer to the depositor's home bank, branch, account number, etc. Within two hours, we're sitting around a stack of counterfeit bank cards and a list of PIN numbers. Something compels me to break Troy's self-satisfied grin.

"Which one belongs to the Mexican couple?"

"The fourth one," he says with a smirk. "We won't use it."

"I thought it was the fifth one," I say in the most ingenuous tone I've got. "Couldn't it be the fifth one?"

"Fine," Suddenly Troy grabs the fourth and fifth cards from the stack and throws them across the room. "Happy?"

I hold my replies to myself. These guys could be dangerous.

But no more dangerous or daring than exploits of Cyberia's many other denizens, with whom we all, by choice or necessity, are becoming much more intimate. If Cyberia is to be a place where traditional boundaries lose their meaning, then so do the cushions of economic security, social status, and even locks and keys. This is a new terrain, and those who know it best right now are not all mild-mannered nerds or corporate chairmen seeking to preserve the status quo. Most of these cyberians are out to change the way the rest of us live, whether we like it or not. We have just peered through the first window into Cyberia—the computer monitors, digital goggles, and automatic teller screens that provide instant access to the technosphere. But, as we'll soon see, Cyberia is made up of much more than information networks. It can also be accessed personally, socially, artistically, and, perhaps easiest of all, chemically.

# 2

# Drugs: The Substances
# of Designer Reality

# chapter five

## Seeing Is Beholding

Terence McKenna—considered by many the successor to Tim Leary's psychedelic dynasty—couldn't make it to Big Heart City Friday night for the elder's party. The bearded, lanky, forty-somethingish Irishman was deep into a Macintosh file, putting the finishing touches on his latest manuscript about the use of mind-altering plants by ancient cultures. But by Saturday evening he was ready to descend from his small mountaintop ranch house to talk about the virtual reality that has his fans so excited.

We're backstage with McKenna at a rave where he'll be speaking about drugs, consciousness, and the end of time. He's gotten famous, on the West Coast at least, as a sort of public relations manager for the plant kingdom. Part human, part gnome, and part mushroom, McKenna speaks from experience. This experience just happens to be an intimate connection with mind-altering vegetation, so his words sprawl like kudzu over the consciousness. If you listen to McKenna, that is, really listen, you can't help but get wrapped up in his rap. The luckiest of friends and mentees hang out with him in his dressing room as he prepares to go on.

"VR really is like a trip," one boy offers McKenna in the hopes of launching the Celtic Bard into one of his lyrical diatribes. Terence ponders a moment and then he's off.

"I link virtual reality to psychedelic drugs because I think that if you look at the evolution of organism and self-expression and language, language is seen to be some kind of process that actually tends toward the visible." McKenna strings his thoughts together into a breathless oral continuum. "The small mouth-noise way of communicating is highly provisional; we may be moving toward an environment of language that is beheld rather than heard."

Still, the assembled admirers hang on McKenna's every word, as if each syllable were leaving a hallucinatory aftervision on the adrenal cortex. They too dream of a Cyberia around the corner, and virtual reality is the closest simulation of what a world free of time, location, or even a personal identity might look like. Psychedelics and VR are both ways of creating a new, nonlinear reality, where self-expression is a community event.

"You mean like ESP?"

Terence never corrects anyone—he only interpolates their responses. "This would be like a kind of telepathy, but it would be much more than that: A world of visible language is a world where the individual doesn't really exist in the same way that the print-created world sanctions what we call 'point of view.' That's really what an ego is: it's a consistently defined point of view within a context of narrative. Well, if you replace the idea that life is a narrative with the idea that life is a vision, then you displace the linear progression of events. I think this is technically within reach."

To Terence, the invention of virtual reality, like the resurgence of psychoactive drugs, serves as a kind of technological philosopher's stone, bringing an inkling of the future reality into the present. It's both a hint from our hyperdimensional future and an active, creative effort by cyberians to reach that future.

"I like the concept of the philosopher's stone. The next messiah might be a machine rather than a person. The philosopher's stone is a living stone. It is being made. We are making it. We are like tunnelers drilling toward something. The overmind is drilling toward us, and we are drilling toward it. And when we meet, there will be an enormous revelation of the true nature of being. I think every person who takes five or six grams of psilocybin mushrooms in silent darkness is probably on a par with Christ and Buddha, at least in terms of the input."

So, according to McKenna, the psychedelic vision provides a glimpse of the truth cyberians are yearning for. But have psychedelics and virtual reality really come to us as a philosopher's stone, or is it simply that our philosopher's stoned?

## Morphogenetic Fields Forever

Cyberians share a psychedelic common ground. To them, drugs are not simply a recreational escape but a conscious and sometimes daring foray into new possible realities. Psychedelics give them access to what McKenna is calling the overmind and what we call

Cyberia. However stoned they might be when they get there, psychedelic explorers are convinced that they are experiencing something real, and bringing back something useful for themselves and the rest of us.

Psychedelic exploration, however personal, is thought to benefit more than the sole explorer. Each tripper believes he is opening the door between humanity and hyperspace a little wider. The few cyberians who haven't taken psychedelics still feel they have personally experienced and integrated the psychedelic vision through the trips of others, and value the role of these chemicals in the overall development of Cyberia. It is as if each psychedelic journey completes another piece of a universal puzzle.

But, even though they have a vast computer net and communications infrastructure at their disposal, psychedelic cyberians need not communicate their findings so directly. Rather, they believe they are each sharing and benefiting from a collective experience. As we'll see, one of the most common realizations of the psychedelic trip is that "all is one." At the euphoric peak of a trip, all people, particles, personalities, and planets are seen as part of one great entity or reality—one big fractal.

It may have been that realization that led Cambridge biologist Rupert Sheldrake to develop his theory of morphogenetic fields, now common knowledge to most cyberians. From *morph,* meaning "forms," and *genesis,* meaning "birth," these fields are a kind of cumulative record of the past behaviors of species, groups, and even molecules, so that one member of a set can learn from the experience of all the others.

A failed animal-behavior test is still one of the best proofs of Sheldrake's idea. Scientists were attempting to determine if learned skills could be passed on from parents to children genetically. They taught adult mice how to go through a certain maze, then taught their offspring, and their offspring, and so on for twenty years and fifty generations of mice. Indeed, the descendants of the taught mice knew how to get through the maze very quickly without instruction, but so did the descendants of the control group, who had never seen the maze at all! Later, a scientist decided to repeat this experiment on a different continent with the same mouse species, but they already knew how to go through the maze, too! As explained by morphic resonance, the traits need not have been passed on genetically. The information leak was due not to bad experimental procedure but to the morphogenetic field, which stored the experience of the earlier mice from which all subsequent mice could benefit.

Similarly, if scientists are developing a new crystalline structure, it may take years to "coax" atoms to form the specific crystal. But once the crystal is developed in one laboratory, it can be created instantly in any other laboratory in the world. According to Sheldrake, this is because, like the mice, the atoms are all "connected" to one another through morphogenetic fields, and they "learn" from the experiences of other atoms.

Sheldrake's picture of reality is a vast fractal of resonating fields. Everything, no matter how small, is constantly affecting everything else. If the tiniest detail in a fractal pattern echoes the overall design of the entire fractal, then a change to (or the experience of) this remote piece changes the overall picture (through the principles of feedback and iteration). Echoing the realizations of his best friends, Ralph Abraham and Terence McKenna, Sheldrake is the third member of the famous "Trialogues" at Esalen, where the three elder statesmen (by cyberian standards) discuss onstage the ongoing unfolding of reality before captivated audiences of cyberians. These men are, quite consciously, putting into practice the idea of morphogenetic fields. Even if these Trialogues were held in private (as they were for years), Cyberia as a whole would benefit from the intellectual developments. By pioneering the new "headspace," the three men leave their own legacy through morphic resonance, if not direct communication through their publishing, lectures, or media events.

Likewise, each cyberian psychedelic explorer feels that by tripping he is leaving his own legacy for others to follow, while himself benefiting from the past psychedelic experiences of explorers before him. For precisely this reason, McKenna advises using only organic psychedelics, which have well-developed morphogenetic fields: "I always say there are three tests for a drug. It should occur in nature. That gives it a morphogenetic field of resonance to the life of the planet. It should have a history of shamanic usage [which gives it a morphogenetic field of resonance to the consciousness of other human beings]. And it should be similar to or related to neurotransmitters in the brain. What's interesting about that series of filters, is that it leaves you with the most powerful hallucinogens there are: psilocybin, DMT, ayahuasca, and, to some degree, LSD."

These are the substances that stock the arsenal of the drug-using cyberian. Psychedelics use among cyberians has developed directly out of the drug culture of the1960s. The first tripsters—the people associated with Leary on the East Coast, and Ken Kesey on the West Coast—came to startling moral and philosophical conclusions that reshaped our culture. For today's users, drugs are part of the continuing evolution of the human species toward greater intelligence, empathy, and awareness.

From the principle of morphogenesis, cyberians infer that psychedelic substances have the ability to reshape the experience of reality and thus—if observer and observed are one—the reality itself. It's hardly disputed that, even in a tangible, cultural sense, the introduction of psychedelics into our society in the 1960s altered the sensibilities of users and nonusers alike. The trickle-down effect through the arts, media, and even big business created what can be called a postpsychedelic climate, in which everything from women's rights, civil rights, and peace activism to spirituality and the computer revolution found suitable conditions for growth.

As these psychoactive plants and chemicals once again see the light of day, an even more self-consciously creative community is finding out about designer reality. While drugs in the 1960s worked to overcome social, moral, and intellectual rigidity, drugs now enhance the privileges of the already free. Cyberians using drugs do not need to learn that reality is arbitrary and manipulable, or that the landscape of consciousness is broader than normal waking-state awareness suggests. They have already learned this through the experiences of men like Leary and Kesey. Instead, they take chemicals for the express purpose of manipulating that reality and exploring the uncharted regions of consciousness.

## Integrating the Bell Curve

LSD was the first synthesized chemical to induce basically the same effect as the organic psychedelics used by shamans in ancient cultures. Psychedelics break down one's basic assumptions about life, presenting them instead as arbitrary choices on the part of the individual and his society. The tripper feels liberated into a free-form reality, where his mind and point of view can alter his external circumstances. Psychedelics provide a way to look at life unencumbered by the filters and models one normally uses to process reality. (Whether psychedelics impose a new set of their own filters is irrelevant here. At least the subjective experience of the trip is that the organizing framework of reality has been obliterated.)

Nina Graboi, the author of *One Foot in the Future,* a novel about her own spiritual journey, was among the first pioneers of LSD in the 1960s. Born in 1918 and trained as an actress, she soon became part of New York's bohemian subculture, and kept company with everyone from Tim Leary to Alan Watts. She now works as an assistant to mathematician Ralph Abraham, and occasionally hosts large conferences on psychedelics. She spoke to me at her Santa Cruz beach apartment, over tea and cookies. She believes from what she has seen over the past seven decades that what psychedelics do to an individual, LSD did to society, breaking us free of cause-and-effect logic and into an optimistic creativity.

"Materialism really was at its densest and darkest before the sixties and it did not allow us to see that anything else existed. Then acid came along just at the right time—I really think so. It was very important for some people to reach states of mind that allowed them to see that there is more, that we are more than just these physical bodies. I can't help feeling that there were forces at work that went beyond anything that I can imagine. After the whole LSD craze, all of a sudden, the skies opened up and books came pouring down and wisdom came. And something started happening. I think by now there are enough of us to have created a morphogenetic field of awareness, that are open to more than the materialists believe."

But Graboi believes that the LSD vision needs to be integrated into the experience of America at large. It's not enough to tune in, turn on, and drop out. The impulse now is to recreate reality consciously—and that happens both through a morphogenetic resonance as well as good old-fashioned work.

"I don't think we have a thing to learn from the past, now. We really have to start creating new forms, and seeing real ways of being. This was almost like the mammalian state coming to a somewhat higher octave in the sixties, which was like a quantum leap forward in consciousness. It was a gas. The end of a stage and the beginning of a new one. So right now there are still these two elements very much alive: the old society wanting to pull backward and keep us where we were, and the new one saying, 'Hey, there are new frontiers to conquer and they are in our minds and our hearts.'"

Nina does not consider herself a cyberian, but she does admit she's part of the same effort, and desperately hopes our society can reach this "higher octave." As with all psychedelics, "coming down" is the hardest part. Most would prefer simply to "bring up" everything else . . . to make the rest of the world conform to the trip.

The acid experience follows what can be called a bell curve: the user takes the drug, goes up in about an hour, stays up for a couple of hours, then comes down over a period of three or four hours. It is during the coming-down time—which makes up the majority of the experience—that the clarity of vision or particular insight must be integrated into the normal waking-state consciousness. Like the Greek hero who has visited the gods, the tripper must figure out how the peak of his Aristotelian journey makes sense. The integration of LSD into the sixties' culture was an analogous process. The tripping community had to integrate the truth of their vision into a society that could not grasp such concepts. The bell curve of the sixties touched ground in the form of political activism, sexual liberation, the new age movement, and new scientific and mathematical models.

Cyberians today consider the LSD trip a traditional experience. Even though there are new psychedelics that more exactly match the cyberian checklist for ease of use, length of trip, and overall intensity, LSD provides a uniquely epic journey for the tripper, where the majority of time and energy in the odyssey is spent bringing it all back home. While cyberians usually surf the waves of consciousness for no reason but fun, they take acid because there's work to be done.

When Jaida and Cindy, two twenty-year-old women from Santa Cruz, reunited after being away from each other for almost a year, they chose LSD because they wanted to go through an intense experience of reconnection. Besides, it was the only drug they could obtain on short notice. They began by smoking some pot and hitchhiking to a nearby beachtown. By the time they got there, the girls were stoned and the beach was pitch black. They spent the rest of the night talking and sleeping on what they guessed was a sand dune, and decided to "drop" at dawn. As the sun rose, the acid took effect.

When the girls stood up, Jaida accidentally stepped on a crab claw that was sticking out of the sand. Blood flowed out of her foot. As she describes it now:

"The pain was just so . . . incredible. I could feel the movement of the pain all the way up to my brain, going up the tendrils, yet it was very enjoyable. And blood was coming out, but it was incredibly beautiful. At the same time, there was still the part of me that said 'you have to deal with this,' which I was very grateful for."

Once Jaida's foot was bandaged, the girls began to walk together. As they walked and talked, they slipped into a commonly experienced acid phenomenon: shared consciousness. "It's the only time I've ever been psychic with Cindy. It's like one of those things that you can't believe . . . there's no evidence or anything. Whatever I was thinking, she would be thinking. We were making a lot of commentary about the people we were looking at, and there'd be these long stretches of silence and I would just be sort of thinking along, and then she would say word for word what I was thinking. Like that. And then I would say something and it would be exactly what she was thinking. And we just did that for about four or five hours. She's a very different physical type from me, but it reached the point where I could feel how she felt in her body. I had the very deep sensation of being inside her body, hearing her think, and being able to say everything that she was thinking. We were in a reality together, and we shared the same space. Our bodies didn't separate us from each other. We were one thing."

But then came the downside of the bell curve. The girls slowly became more "disjointed." They began to disagree about tiny things—which way to walk, whether to eat. "There was this feeling of losing it. I could feel we were moving away from it with every step. There was a terrible disappointment that set in. We couldn't hold on to that perfect attunement."

By the time the girls got back to their campsite on the sand dune, their disillusionment was complete. The sand dune was actually the local trash dump. As they climbed the stinking mound of garbage to gather their sleeping bags, they found the "crab claw" on which Jaida had stepped. It was really a used tampon and a broken bottle. And now Jaida's foot was beginning to smart.

Jaida's reintegration was twofold: She could no more bring back her empathic ability than she could the belief that she had stepped on a crab claw. What Jaida retained from the experience, though, came during the painful crash landing. She was able to see how it was only her interpretation that made her experience pain as bad, or the tampon and glass as less natural than a crab claw. As in the experience of a Buddha, the garbage dump was as beautiful as a sand dune . . . until they decided it was otherwise. Losing her telepathic union with her friend symbolized and recapitulated the distance that had grown between them over the past year. They had lost touch, and the trip had heightened both their friendship and their separation.

Most acid trippers try to prolong that moment on the peak of the bell curve, but to do so is futile. Coming down is almost inevitably disillusioning to some degree. Again, though, like in a Greek tragedy, it is during the reintegration that insight occurs, and progress is made—however slight—toward a more all-encompassing or cyberian outlook. In order to come down with a minimum of despair and maximum of progess, the tripper must guide his own transition back to normal consciousness and real life while maintaining the integrity of whatever truths he may have gleaned at the apogee of his journey. The LSD state itself is not an end in itself. While it may offer a brief exposure to post-paradigm thinking or even hyperdimensional abilities, the real value of the LSD trip is the *change* in consciousness, and the development of skills in the user to cope with that change. Just as when a person takes a vacation, it is not that the place visited is any better than where he started. It's just different. The traveler returns home changed.

Eugene Schoenfeld, M.D., is the Global Village Town Physician. A practicing psychologist, he wrote the famous "Dr. Hip" advice column in the sixties; he now treats recovering drug addicts. It's easy to see why he has become such a trusted friend and counselor to Cyberia's many chemical casualties. His rich eyes seem to absorb the anxiety of whoever stares into them. One gentle nod of his large, shiny head shows he understands. This man has been there. This man groks. The doctor believes that the desire to alter consciousness, specifically psychedelically, is a healthy urge.

"I think what happens is that it allows people to sense things in a way that they don't ordinarily sense them because we couldn't live that way. If our brains were always the way that they are under the influence of LSD, we couldn't function. Perhaps it is that when babies are born—that's the way they perceive things. Gradually they integrate their experience because we cannot function if we *see music,* for example. We can't live that way.

"Part of the reason why people take drugs is to change their sense of reality, change their sensation, change from the ordinary mind state. And if they had *that* state all the time, they would seek to change *it.* It seems that humans need to change their minds in some way. There's a reason why people start talking about 'tripping.' It's related to trips people take when they physically change their environment. I'm convinced that if there were a way to trip all the time on LSD, they would want to change their reality to something else. That is part of the need."

The sense of being on a voyage, of "tripping," is the essence of a classic psychedelic experience. The user is a traveler, and an acid or mushroom trip is a heroic journey or visionquest through unexplored regions, followed by a reentry into mundane reality. Entry to the psychedelic realm almost always involves an abandonment of the structures by which one organizes reality, and a subsequent shedding of one's ego—usually defined by those same organizational structures. On the way back, the tripper realizes that reality itself has been arbitrarily arranged. The voyager sees that there may be such a thing as an objective world, but whatever it is we're experiencing as reality on a mass scale sure isn't it. With the help of a psychedelic journey, one can come back and consciously choose a different reality from the one that's been agreed upon by the incumbent society. This can be manifest on a personal, theoretical, political, technological, or even spiritual level.

As Dr. Schoenfeld, who once served as Tim Leary's family physician and now shares his expertise with cyberians as co-host of the DRUGS conference on the WELL, explains, "that quality—that nonjudgmental quality could be carried over without the effects of the drug. After all, one hopes to learn something from a drug experience that he can use afterward. (All this interest in meditation and yoga, all these various disciplines, it all began with people taking these drugs and wanting to recreate these states without drugs.) So, to the extent that they can, that is a useful quality. And this nonjudgmental quality is something I think that can be carried over from a drug experience."

## Over There

So, the use of psychedelics can be seen as a means toward experiencing free-flowing designer reality: the goal, and the fun, is to manipulate intentionally one's objectivity in order to reaffirm the arbitrary nature of all the mind's constructs, revealing, perhaps, something truer beneath the surface, material reality. You take a trip on which you go nowhere, but everything has changed anyway.

To some, though, it is not just the change of consciousness that makes psychedelics so appealing, but the qualitative difference in the states of awareness they offer. The place people "go" on a trip—the psychedelic corridors of Cyberia—may even be a real space. According to Terence McKenna's frontline correspondence from that place, it is quite different from normal waking-state consciousness:

The voyager journeys "into an invisible realm in which the causality of the ordinary world is replaced with the rationale of natural magic. In this realm, language, ideas, and meaning have greater power than cause and effect. Sympathies, resonances, intentions, and personal will are linguistically magnified through poetic rhetoric. The imagination is invoked and sometimes its forms are beheld visibly. Within the magical mind-set of the shaman, the ordinary connections of the world and what we call natural laws are deemphasized or ignored."[1]

As McKenna describes it, this is not just a mindspace but more of a netherworld, where the common laws of nature are no longer enforced. It is a place where cause-and-effect logic no longer holds, where events and objects function more as icons or symbols, where thoughts are beheld rather than verbalized, and where phenomena like morphic resonance and the fractal reality become consciously experienced. This is the description of Cyberia.

As such, this psychedelic world is not something experienced personally or privately, but, like the rest of Cyberia, as a great group project. The psychedelic world each tripper visits is the same world, so that changes made by one are felt by the others. Regions explored by any traveler become part of the overall map. This is a hyperdimensional terrain on which the traditional solo visionquest becomes a sacred community event.

This feeling of being part of a morphogenetic unfolding is more tangible on psilocybin mushrooms than on LSD. McKenna voices Cyberia's enchantment with the ancient organic brain food: "I think that people should grow mushrooms. They are the real connector back into the archaic, even more so than LSD, which was largely psychoanalytical. It didn't connect you up to the greeny engines of creation. Psilocybin is perfect."

Like LSD, mushrooms provide an eight-hour, bell-curve trip, but it is characterized by more physical and visual "hallucinations" and a much less intellectual edge. Users don't overanalyze their experiences, opting instead to revel in them more fully. Mushrooms are thought to have their own morphogenetic field, which has developed over centuries of their own evolution and their use by ancient cultures. The mushroom trip is much more predictable, cyberians argue, because its morphogenetic field is so much better established than that of acid, which has only been used for a couple of decades, and mostly by inexperienced Western travelers.

As a result, mushroom experiences are, in many ways, less intensely disorienting than LSD trips; the "place" one goes on mushrooms is more natural and user-friendly than the place accessed on acid or other more synthetic psychedelics. Likewise, 'shroomers feel more tangibly a part of the timeless, locationless community of other users, or even animals, fairies, or the "greeny engines" of the spirit of Nature herself.

For this feeling of morphic community and interconnection with nature to become more tangible, groups of 'shroomers often choose to create visionquest hot spots. Students at U.C. Santa Cruz have developed a secret section of woods dedicated to mushroom tripping called Elf Land (the place just behind Ralph Abraham's office). Some students believe that fairies prepared and maintain the multidimensional area of the woods for 'shroomers. Others even claim to have found psilocybin mushrooms—which these fairies are said to leave behind them—growing in Elf Land. Most of all, Elf Land serves as a real-world reference plane for the otherworldly, dimensionless mushroom plane. And, like the morphogenetic mushroom field, Elf Land is shared and modified by everyone who trips there, making the location a kind of cumulative record of a series of mushroom trips.

Mariah is tripping in Elf Land for the first time. A sophomore at U.C. Santa Cruz, the English major had heard of Elf Land since she began taking mushrooms last year, but never really believed in it as a real, physical place. She eats the mushrooms in her dorm with her friends Mark and Rita, then the trio head out to the woods. It's still afternoon, so the paths are easy to follow, but Rita—a much more plugged-in, pop-cultural, fashion-conscious communications major than one would expect to find tripping in the woods of Santa Cruz—suddenly veers off into a patch of poison oak.

Mark, a senior mathematics major and Rita's boyfriend, grabs Rita by the arm, afraid that she's stoned and losing her way.

"It's a pathless path, Mariah," Rita assures the younger girl, without even looking at Mark. Rita knows that Mariah's fears are the most pressing, and that Mark's concerns will be answered by these indirect means. Rita has made it clear that this trip is for Mariah.

"It's the perfect place to trip." Rita puts her arm around Mariah. "People continually put things there. Some of it's very subtle, too. Every time you go there, there's different stuff there. And it's all hidden in the trees up past the fire trails, up in the deep woods there." She points a little farther up the hill.

Then Mariah sees something—a little rock on the ground with an arrow painted on it. "Lookee here!" She stops, picks it up, and turns it over. Painted on the back are the words "This way to Elf Land."

"Someone left this for me?" Mariah asks, the mushrooms taking full effect now, and the fluorescent words on the gray rock beginning to vibrate.

"Just for you, Mariah," Rita whispers, "and for everyone. Come on."

"Here's another one!" Mark is at an opening to the deeper woods, standing next to another sign, this one carved into the side of a tree: "Welcome to Elf Land."

As the three pass through the opening, they walk into another world. It's a shared state of consciousness, not just among the three trippers but among them and everyone else who has ever tripped in Elf Land or anywhere else.

Mariah is thinking about her name; how she got it, how it's shaped her, how it's like the name Mary from the Bible, but changed somehow, too. Updated. At the same moment as these thoughts, she comes upon a small shrine that has been set up in a patch of ferns between two tall trees. The two-foot statue is of the Virgin Mary, but she has been decorated—updated—with a Day-Glo costume.

"How'd that get there?" Mariah wonders out loud.

Meanwhile, Mark has wandered off by himself. He's been disturbed about his relationship with Rita. She seems so addicted to popular culture—not the die-hard Deadhead he remembers from their freshman year. Should they stay together after graduation? Get married, even?

He stands against a tree and leans his head against its trunk, looking up into the branches. He looks at the way each larger branch splits in two. Each smaller branch then splits in two, and so and so on until the branches become leaves. Each leaf, then, begins with a single vein, then splits, by two, into smaller and smaller veins. Mark is reminded of chaos math theory, in which ordered systems, like a river flowing smoothly, become chaotic through a process called bifurcation, or dividing by twos. A river splits in two if there's a rock in its path, the two separate sections preserving—between the two of them—the order and magnitude of the original. A species can bifurcate into two different mutations if conditions require it. And a relationship can break up if . . .

As Mark stares at the bifurcated pairs of branches and leaves, he realizes that bifurcation is the nature of decision making. He's caught in the duality of a painful choice, and the tree is echoing the nature of decision-making itself.

"Making a decision?" Mariah asks innocently. She has read the small sign nailed into the side of the tree: "Tree of Decision."

"I wonder who left that there?" Mark wonders aloud.

"Doesn't matter," answers Rita, emerging from nowhere. "Someone last week, last year. A tripper, an elf . . . whoever."

As if on a visionquest, Mark and Mariah were presented with a set of symbols in material form that they could analyze and integrate into a pattern. They were "beholding" their thoughts in physical form. The reality of their trip was confirmed not just by their fantasies but by the totems and signs left for them by other trippers experiencing the same things at different times.

Mushrooms very often give users the feeling of being connected with the past and the future. Whether the 'shroomers know about morphogenetic fields, they do feel connected with the spirit of the woods, and everyone who has traveled before in the same space. Going up is the voyage to that space, peaking is the un-self-conscious experience of the new world, and coming down is the reintegration during which the essence of the peak experience is translated into a language or set of images a person can refer to later, at baseline reality.

chapter six

## Making Connections

### Distribution and Manufacture

For some cyberians, making sense of the events in their lives and feeling the connections with other trippers is not enough. They use psychedelics to forge new connections between cultures, people, or even individual atoms. It is important to them that the real world, and not just the psychedelic space, consciously reflect the interconnectivity that underlies reality. Just as a fractal exhibits self-similarity, the psychedelic subculture should reflect the quality of a single trip.

LSD distributors, in particular, believe that acid functions as a twentieth-century psychic grease, allowing modern people to move their mental machinery through the ever-increasing demands of an information-based society. (Acid, unlike mushrooms, can be mass-produced, too.) Leo is an LSD dealer from the Bay Area who believes that his distribution of psychedelics is a social service. One of his favorite distribution points is the parking lot at Grateful Dead shows, where thousands of people mill about, looking for "doses."

Tonight's concert has already begun, but most of the crowd of young merchants who follow the Dead don't have tickets for the show. Instead, they wander about the lot, smoke pot with one another, and prepare for the concertgoers who will exit the arena in two or three hours.

Leo is well into his own acid trip of the evening (he says he's been tripping every day for several months) and sits in a makeshift tent, explaining his philosophy to a young couple who make falafel and beaded bracelets. While his rationale is the result of a few years in the military and a few others with skinheads, he does express the psychedelic concept of interconnectivity and networking from a modern cyberian standpoint. The Deadheads (who many cyberians feel are still caught in the sixties) are deep into a conversation about how they can feel their "third eye" while tripping, and how it makes them feel connected to everything in the world. Leo expands their premise.

"The sixth sense of society as a whole also lies in its connectivity and its ability to intercommunicate. When society becomes enlightened, its third eye happens to be that connectivity. That's the evolutionary factor."

Leo tries in vain to get them to understand the concepts of feedback and iteration, and how they relate to human society connecting through telephones and the media. The bong gets passed around again, and Leo tries a different tack.

"I'm attempting to work this on a subversive level by distributing a large amount of LSD throughout the U.S. and trying to reach other countries, too." One of the Deadheads laughs, just liking the sound of breaking the law. Leo rolls his eyes and stresses the global significance of his subversion.

"LSD's definitely an interconnectivity catalyst for the countercultures and subcultures that we're tuned in to. We're able now, with our information-age technologies, to know about groups and countercultures who are communicating together and sharing common resources and information—like all you Deadheads living in this parking lot. As these groups develop their own identities, they gain a certain amount of awareness about themselves as a collective conscious. That offers a channel for catalytic tools like LSD to be exchanged, putting all these groups on the same wavelength."

The falafel merchant shrugs, too stoned or too straight to understand Leo's point. "I don't get it. Is LSD making this happen, or is it happening so people can get more LSD?"

"LSD is part of and a result of this interconnectedness. It's mind expansive and group-mind expansive. And what it does is act as a catalyst for culture and individuals. Now that we've left the industrial age and come into the information age, the rate information exchanges is increasing exponentially. It's very fast; you can look at it in binary terms. Two, four, eight, sixteen, thirty-two—that's how fast the information multiplies. What's going on is, the way people learn, is they cause an imprint in their subconscious, and then they're able to build a type of structure on their imprint which represents their knowledge. And how they see their own knowledge is their own wisdom . . . it's their knowledge of their knowledge."

Both Deadheads are lost now. The girl has started mindlessly unbeading a bracelet and the boy is reloading the bong. But Leo doesn't care that he can't make an impact on these people. He just continues to reel out his run-on sentences into the datapool in the hope that they get picked up morphogenetically.

"LSD primes the mind for subconscious imprintation—makes it more susceptible to it. We're able to learn more information at a faster rate because we're able to imprint ourselves at the same rate as the information is being developed, because in the LSD state you're able to conceive such a vast quantity of anything. When I'm on LSD sometimes I can think in broad terms and sometimes I even gain vocabulary that I've never used before and I'm able to retain that in the future."

"If you gave us another hit of your LSD, Leo," the bead girl smiles, "maybe we'd know what you're talking about, too."

This is where traditional, sixties-style tripsters differ from their cyberian offspring. The sixth sense, or "group-mind oversoul," to which Leo has dedicated himself (but which these old-fashioned-type Deadheads can't understand) is the locus of awareness that most cyberian psychedelic explorers seek. Whether it be Mariah in Elf Land or Leo in the LSD distribution net, the cyberian difference is that psychedelic activity now becomes part of an overall fractal pattern, experienced, in one way or another, by everyone.

While Leo draws the lines of interconnectivity between users and groups of users, other reality designers at remote sublevels of the psychedelic fractal network are more concerned with the lines of interconnectivity between the very atoms of the substances they take. Becker, Leo's LSD source, is a twenty-eight-year-old chemistry grad student with a strong background in illicit psychopharmacology. His experience of psychedelics is on a different fractal order from that of classical personal tripsters or even Leo and other cultural catalysts. Becker knows about drugs from the inside out, so his answer to any drug's problems lies in its chemistry. If a drug is illegal, alter its chemistry to make it legal again. If a drug is too short-acting, figure out a way to stunt the user's ability to metabolize it.

Becker lives in a suburban Bay Area commune, inhabited mostly by local college students. He has appropriated the entire attic for his psychopharmacology lab. Test tubes, beakers, and Bunsen burners are everywhere. When Leo knocks on the tiny attic door, Becker automatically shuts off a gas valve and turns down the stereo. He is not at ease. Once he learns his guest is not an unwelcome intruder but Leo, he relaxes visibly. As he walks to the door and disengages its triple locks, he also frees his long blonde hair from its ponytail. Leo stomps in with his army boots and collapses onto a box of styrofoam "peanuts."

Leo complains about the Deadheads he met the night before. He's wondering if Becker can whip something up with better transformational properties than those of LSD.

Becker has just the answer. He takes off his tiny spectacles and explains how he spent all of last night creating his first batch of 2CB (in chemist's lingo, 4-Bromo-2,5-dimethoxyphenethylamine). "It's called Venus, and it's a synthetic version of mescaline, with a few designer improvements."

Becker's problem with mescaline, another organic psychedelic, is that it is metabolized by the body very quickly. By the time the user begins to trip heavily, he's already on the way down. To figure out how to modify the substance, Becker took a large dose, then went on an internal visionquest into the chemical structure of the active mescaline molecule.

"The native mescaline molecule is a ring. I saw how the methoxy group which hangs on that ring could be pried off easily by the metabolism, rendering the molecule impotent in an hour or so. By replacing that methoxy group with bromine, which can hang on much tighter, the drug becomes ten times stronger. The body can't break it down, and it goes much much further because it can stay planted in the brain's receptor site that much longer."

"But how much do you have to take? And how do you know it's not toxic?" Leo asks, fingering the white powder in its petri dish.

"It's *less* toxic, Leo, don't you see? Plus it's much more effective, so you don't have to take as much. That way you don't get any side effects either. I'm on it right now!"

Leo had dropped a tab of acid about two hours ago but it wasn't doing anything. He licks his finger, dabs it in the mound of powder, and puts it on his tongue.

"That's a pretty big hit," Becker warns. "Probably about eight doses."

Leo just shrugs and swallows. He can handle it. "How fast can you make this stuff?"

"That's the joy. It's really simple to make. Just think of it as stir, filter, wash, and dry. That's all there is to it."

As Becker goes over an ingredients checklist for a mass-production schedule, Leo collapses into a hammock and waits for the new drug to take effect. Both believe that they are on to something new and important.

By designing new chemicals, psychopharmacologists like Becker design reality from the inside out. They decide what they'd like reality to be like, then—in a submolecular shamanic visionquest—compose a chemical that will alter their observations about reality in a specific way. Then, Leo, by distributing the new chemical to others who will have the same experience, literally spreads the new designer reality. The world changes because it is observed differently.

The other reason to make new drugs is to create unknown and, hence, legal psychedelics before the FDA has a chance to classify them as illegal. A relatively new law, however, has made that difficult. The Analog Substance Act classifies yet-to-be-designed chemicals illegal if they are intended to serve the same function as ones that are already illegal. This law was passed shortly after the "Ecstasy craze" in Texas, where the new, mild psychedelic got so popular that it was available for purchase by credit card at bars. As a result, according to Becker, "Lloyd Bentsen put a bee in the bonnet of the Drug Enforcement Agency, and it was stamped illegal fast."

But rather than simply stamping out Ecstasy use, its illegality prompted chemists like Becker to develop new substances. Like computer hackers who understand the technology better than its adult users, the kids making drugs know more about the chemistry than the regulatory agencies. The young chemists began creating new drugs just like Ecstasy, with just one or two atoms in different places. In Becker's language, "Thus, Ecstasy began to stand for MDMA, MDM, Adam, X, M-Ethyl, M methyl 3-4-methyline dioxy, also N-ethyl, which was sometimes called Eve, which had one more carbon, or actually $CH_2$, added on." This flurry of psychopharmacological innovation prompted the Analog Act, and now almost everything with psychedelic intent is illegal or Schedule 1 (most controlled).

Despite its illegality, Ecstasy, even more than LSD and mush-rooms, has remained on the top of the cyberian designer-substance hit parade. LSD, mushrooms, and mescaline—all powerful, relatively long-acting psychedelics—bifurcated, so to speak, into two shorter-acting substances, the mild, user-friendly Ecstasy, and the earth-shatteringly powerful and short-acting DMT. Both drugs can be found in many carefully manipulated chemical variations, and epit-omize the psychedelic-substance priorities in Cyberia.

## The E Conspiracy

The circuits of the brain which mediate alarm, fear, flight, fight, lust, and territo-rial paranoia are temporarily disconnected. You see everything with total clarity, undistorted by animalistic urges. You have reached a state which the ancients have called nirvana, all seeing bliss.[2]

—Thomas Pynchon on MDMA

Cyberians consider Ecstasy, or E as it's called by its wide-grinning users, one of the most universally pleasant drugs yet invented. While negative experiences on Ecstasy are not unheard of, they are certainly few and far between. Everyone knows somebody who's had a bad acid trip. Ecstasy does not carry the same stigma, which may be part of the reason why people don't "freak out" on it.

As Dr. Schoenfeld explains, another part of the reason may be that some of the substances sold as "Ecstasy" aren't yet illegal, so users don't have the same negative associations and paranoia. In addition, according to the doctor, the Ecstasy drugs are nonaddictive and shorter-acting.

"As you know, there are drugs being used that the DEA [Drug Enforcement Agency] isn't aware of. Once they get aware of them, they'll try to make them illegal; but people who take substances are becoming aware of these new drugs, which are nonaddictive, and which don't last as long as the other drugs used to last. They don't have the same adverse effects. For example, there are a few reports of people having bad experiences with MDMA or occasional freak-outs, but it's highly unusual. And even with LSD it wasn't that common to have freak-outs. You'd hear about the cases where people tried to fly or stop trains or things like that, but compared with the amount of use there was, that was uncommon. With a drug like MDMA, it's still less common for people to have bad experiences."

But E is not just a kinder, gentler acid. The quality of the E-xperience is very different. Bruce Eisner wrote the book *Ecstasy: The MDMA Story,* still the most authoritative and enlightening text on the drug's history and use. His scholarly and personal research on the chemical is vast, and he describes the essence of the E-xperience well:

"You discover a secret doorway into a room in your house that you did not previously know existed. It is a room in which both your inner experience and your relations with others seem magically transformed. You feel really good about yourself and your life. At the same time, everyone who comes into this room seems more lovable. You find your thoughts flowing, turning into words that previously were blocked by fear and inhibition.

"After several hours, you return to your familiar abode, feeling tired but different, more open. And your memory of your mystical passage may help you in the days and weeks ahead to make all the other rooms of your house more enjoyable."[3]

The main advantage of E is that it allows you to "take your ego with you." Acid or even mushrooms can have the unrelenting abrasiveness of a belt sander against the ego. E, on the other hand, does not disrupt "ego integrity" or create what psychologists call "depersonalization." Instead, the user feels as open and loving and connected as he might feel on a stronger psychedelic but without the vulnerability of losing his "self" in the process. If anything, E strengthens one's sense of self, so that the issues that arise in the course of a trip seem less threatening and infinitely more manageable. E creates a loving ego resiliency in which no personal problem seems too big or scary. This is why it has become popular in the younger gay and other alternative-lifestyles communities, where identity crises are commonplace.

## E-volution

"You touch the darkness—the feminine, the gross, whatever you *see* as dark," Jody Radzik explains to Diana as they hand out flyers in the street for a new house club. "When you're on Ecstasy, the drug forces you to become who you really are. You don't get any positive experience from a drug like cocaine; it's a lie. But with Ecstasy, it can have a positive effect on the *rest of your life!*"

Jody and Diana are on their way to a club called Osmosis, a house event which occurs every Thursday night at DV8, a downtown San Francisco venue, for which Radzik serves as promotional director. Promoting house, though, is almost like promoting Ecstasy. The drug and subculture have defined and fostered each other. Osmosis is proud of the fact that it mixes gay, straight, "glam," and house culture, and Radzik—a gamine, extremely young thirty-year-old with a modified Hamlet haircut and a mile-a-minute mouth—credits E with their success.

"There's a sexual element to house. E is an aphrodisiac and promiscuity is big. In everyday life men usually repress their 'anima.' Ecstasy forces you to experience what's really going on inside." Diana (who runs her own house club down the block) is amused by Jody's inclination to talk about taboo subjects. Jody goes on proudly, exuberantly, and loud enough for everyone else on the street to hear. Being publicly outrageous is a valued personality trait in E culture adapted from Kesey's Merry Pranksters.

"E has a threshold. It puts you in that *aahh* experience, and you stay there. It might get more intense with the number of hits you take, but it's not like acid, which, with the more hits you take, the farther you're walking from consensus culture. With E, your ability to operate within the confines of culture remain. You can take a lot of E and still know that that's a red light, or that there's a cop here and you don't want to fuck up too much. On acid, you can be completely out of your head, and walking in a completely different reality."

E is not simply watered-down LSD. While acid was a "test," Ecstasy is a "becoming." Acid involved a heroic journey, while E is an extended moment. The traditional bell curve of the acid trip and its sometimes brutal examination and stripping of ego is replaced with a similar vision but without the paranoia and catharsis. By presenting insight as a moment of timelessness, E allows for a much more cyberian set of conclusions than the more traditional, vision-quest psychedelics.

Rather than squashing personal taste and creating legions of Birkenstock clones, E tends to stimulate the user's own inner nature. Hidden aspects of one's personality—be it homosexuality, transvestitism, or just love and creativity—demand free expression.

All this is allowed to happen, right away, in the E-nvironment of the house club. Reintegration on E is unnecessary because the E-xperience itself has an immediately social context. If anything, the E trip is more socially integrated than baseline reality. E turns a room of normal, paranoid nightclubbers into a teeming mass of ecstatic Global Villagers. To Radzik, the club lights, music, and Ecstasy are inseparable elements of a designer ritual, just like the campfire, drumbeats, and peace pipe of a Native American tribal dance.

Arriving at the club in time for the sound check, Jody and Diana dance a while under the work lights. Jody's diatribe continues as he demonstrates the new hip-hop steps he picked up in Los Angeles last week.

"The Ecstasy comes *through* the house music. The different polyrhythmic elements and the bass . . . this is current North American shamanism. It's technoshamanism. E has a lot to do with it. It really does. I get a little nervous but I've got to tell the truth about things. But the system is probably going to react against the E element."

Diana cuts in: "And then they'll just shut you down like they closed our party last week." She takes a cigarette from behind her ear and lights it.

Jody still dances while Diana stands and smokes. Neither he nor the E culture will be taken down that easily. "E is an enzyme that's splicing the system. E is like a cultural neurotransmitter that's creating synaptic connections between different people. We're all cells in the organism. E is helping us to link up and form more dendrites. And our culture is finally starting to acknowledge the ability of an individual to create his own reality. What you end up with, what we all have in common, is common human sense."

Jody's E-inspired philosophy borrows heavily from the scientific and mathematics theories of the past couple of decades. House kids talk about fractals, chaos, and morphogenetic fields in the same sentence as Deee-Lite's latest CD. Jody's "cultural neurotransmitter" image refers back to James Lovelock's Gaia hypothesis, which is the now well-supported notion that planet Earth is itself a giant, biological organism. The planet is thought to maintain conditions for sustaining life through a complex series of feedbacks and iterations. A population of ocean microorganisms, for example, may regulate the weather by controlling how much moisture is released into the atmosphere. The more feedback loops Gaia has (in the form of living plants and animals), the more precisely "she" can maintain the ecosystem.

Evolution is seen more as a groping toward than a random series of natural selections. Gaia is becoming conscious. Radzik and others have inferred that human beings serve as Gaia's brain cells. Each human being is an individual neuron, but unaware of his connection to the global organism as a whole. Evolution, then, depends on humanity's ability to link up to one another and become a global consciousness.

These revelations all occur to house kids like Jody under the influence of E. This is why they call the drug a "cultural enzyme." The Ecstasy helps them see how they're all connected. They accept themselves and one another at face value, delighted to make their acquaintance. Everyone exposed to E instantly links up to the Gaian neural net. As more people become connected, more feedback and iteration can occur, and the Gaian mind can become more fully conscious.

Jody and Diana both believe that house culture and the Gaian mindset literally "infect" newcomers to the club like a virus. As Osmosis opens, Jody watches a crowd of uninitiated clubbers step out onto the dance floor, who, despite their extremely "straight" dress, are having a pretty Ex-uberant time.

"This looks like a group of people that might be experimenting with Ecstasy for the first time. They're going to remember this night for the rest of their lives. This is going to change them. They are going to be better people now. They're infected. It's like an information virus. They take it with them into their lives. Look at them. They're dancing with each other as a group. Not so much with their own partners. They're all smiling. They are going to change as a result of their participation in house. Their worldview is going to change."

Indeed, the growing crowd does seem uncharacteristically gleeful for a Thursday-night dance club. Gone are the pickup lines, drunken businessmen, speedheads, and cokewhores. The purposeful social machinations—getting laid, scoring drugs, or gaining status—seem to be overrun by the sheer drive toward bliss. Boys don't need to dance with their dates because there's no need for possessiveness or control. Everyone feels secure—even secure enough to dance without a partner in a group of strangers.

Whether that carries into their daily life is another story. Certainly, a number of new cyberian "converts" are made each evening. But the conversions are made passively, as the name of the club implies, through Osmosis. Unlike acid, which forces users to find ways to integrate their vision into working society, E leads them to believe that integration occurs in the same moment as the bliss. The transformation is a natural byproduct—a side effect of the cultural virus.

As club regulars arrive, they wink knowingly at one another. Jody winks and nods at a few, who gesture back coyly. The only information communicated, really, is "I am, are you?" The winkers are not so much the "in" crowd as the fraternity of the converted. They're all part of what one T-shirt calls "The E Conspiracy." These are the carriers of the cultural virus. No need to say anything at all. The E and the music will take care of everything (wink, wink).

"The sixties went awry because they wanted a sweeping cultural change to go on overtly," explains Radzik, nodding to two girls he's sure he has seen before. They wink back. "And that didn't happen. What's different about house is that no one's trying to 'spread the message.' It's more like, we're into it because we love it, but we're not out to convert people. 'Groove is in the heart' [a Deee-Lite lyric]. We just want to expose people to it. People decide that they're into it because they respond to it on a heart level. I think the bullshit's going to come apart of its own accord."

So is this a dance floor filled with socially aware, fully realized designer beings? Certainly not. It's a dance floor filled with smart kids, sexy kids, not-so smart kids, and not-so sexy kids, but they do seem to share an understanding, in the body, of the timeless quality of bliss and how to achieve it through a combination of dance and E. Even the music, playing at precisely 120 beats per minute, the rate of the fetal heartbeat, draws one into a sense of timeless connection to the greater womb—Gaia. The lyrics all emphasize the sound "eee." "Evereeebodeee's freee," drones one vocal, in pleeesing gleeeful breeezes, winding their way onto the extreeemely wide smiles of dancing boys and girls. It's just the E! Likewise, the way in which E infiltrates society is much less time-based and confrontational than was the case with acid. There is no need for a heroic journey and reintegration. E overwhelms its obstacles through the experience of bliss, so there's nothing to say or do about it. The "meta" agenda here is to create a society with no agenda.

As Jody screams over the din of the house music, "Fuck the agendas. We just have to manifest our culture. You have to trust your heart. That's what Jesus really said. And that's what E does. It shows people they have their own common sense. They realize, I don't need this!"

Bruce Eisner shows up at about midnight, exploring the house scene and its relationship to Ecstasy for the second edition of his book *Ecstasy: The MDMA Story.* A veteran of the sixties and just a bit too old to fit in with this crowd, he almost sighs as he explains to E-nthusiastic clubbers how E's preservation of social skills and ego make it a much better social transformer than the psychedelics of his day.

"In the sixties, we were sure we were going to have this revolution that would change everything overnight. And it never came. We got the seventies instead."

A few girls laugh. They were born in the seventies. Bruce smiles slowly. He's got a dozen stoned kids hanging on his every word, but all he really wants is to understand *them.*

"With E," says Eisner, "you don't get so far out, like on acid, where you lose touch with the physical world. It allows you an easier time to bring the insights back in. Huxley talked a lot about the importance of integrating the mystical experience with the worldly experience. He had that one trip where he decided, 'The clear light is an ice cube. What's important is love and work in the world.' And love and work in the world is what Ecstasy shows you. It's a model for enlightenment, and the challenge is bringing that into the real world."

So maybe revolution has become E-volution as house culture awakens us to the fact that there may be method behind Gaia's madness. Life naturally evolves toward greater self-awareness; we don't need to push it anywhere. And as quantum theory teaches, just becoming aware of something changes it. We redesign reality and ourselves effortlessly through the expansion of our awareness.

And we expand our awareness simply by becoming more blissful. The universe, then, is not a cold sea of indifference and natural selection but the warm, living waters of an oversoul composed of waves of love—Gaia's morphogenetic fields.

The mock self-assuredness of the "me" generation gives way to the inner wink-wink-say-no-more knowing of the E generation, as the sixties bell curve finally touches down, and ego fully reintegrates into a postpsychedelic culture.

# chapter seven

## The Blast Furnace of Disillusion

For those still intent on smashing the ego into oblivion and discovering the very edge of what it means to be sentient, DMT (dimethyltryptamine, and its cousin, 5-hydroxytryptamine) is the only answer. It is a naturally occurring hallucinogen that is usually smoked, although shamans snort it and some aggressive Western users inject it. Its effect is immediate—definitely within a minute, usually within seconds—and all-encompassing. It cannot even be described in terms of magnitude (one user says, "It's like taking every LSD experience you've ever had and putting them on the head of a pin"), but makes more sense when thought of as a true, hyperdimensional shift. As Terence McKenna describes it:

"The experience that engulfs one's entire being as one slips beneath the surface of the DMT-ecstasy feels like the penetration of a membrane. The mind and the self literally unfold before one's eyes. There is a sense that one is made new, yet unchanged, as if one were made of gold and had just been recast in the furnace of one's birth. Breathing is normal, heartbeat steady, the mind clear and observing. But what of the world? What of incoming sensory data?

"Under the influence of DMT, the world becomes an Arabian labyrinth, a palace, a more than possible Martian jewel, vast with motifs that flood the gaping mind with complex and wordless awe. Color and the sense of a reality-unlocking secret nearby pervade the experience. There is a sense of other times, and of one's own infancy, and of wonder, wonder, and more wonder. It is an audience with the alien nuncio. In the midst of this experience, apparently at the end of human history, guarding gates that seem surely to open on the howling maelstrom of the unspeakable emptiness between the stars, is the Aeon.

"The Aeon, as Heraclitus presciently observed, is a child at play with colored balls. Many diminutive beings are present there—the tykes, the self-transforming machine elves of hyperspace. Are they the children destined to be father to the man? One has the impression of entering into an ecology of souls that lies beyond the portals of what we naively call death. I do not know. Are they the synesthetic embodiment of ourselves as the Other, or of the Other as ourselves? Are they the elves lost to us since the fading of the magic light of childhood? Here is a tremendum barely to be told, an epiphany beyond our wildest dreams. Here is the realm of that which is stranger than we *can* suppose. Here is the mystery, alive, unscathed, still as new for us as when our ancestors lived it fifteen thousand summers ago. The tryptamine entities offer the gift of new language; they sing in pearly voices that rain down as colored petals and flow through the air like hot metal to become toys and such gifts as gods would give their children. The sense of emotional connection is terrifying and intense. The Mysteries revealed are real and if ever fully told will leave no stone upon another in the small world we have gone so ill in.

"This is not the mecurial world of the UFO, to be invoked from lonely hilltops; this is not the siren song of lost Atlantis wailing through the trailer courts of crack-crazed America. DMT is not one of our irrational illusions. I believe that what we experience in the presence of DMT is real news. It is a nearby dimension—frightening, transformative, and beyond our powers to imagine, and yet to be explored in the usual way. We must send the fearless experts, whatever they may come to mean, to explore and to report on what they find."[4]

DMT is the most hard-core cyberian drug experience for several reasons. The user "penetrates" another dimension, experiences timelessness, and then enjoys nonverbal and nonlinear communication and connectedness. Even "mind" and "self" unfold, freeing the user to roam about this dimension unencumbered by physical, emotional, and mental barriers. This is a psychopharmacological virtual reality.

DMT is metabolized almost as soon as it enters the system, a fact that, McKenna argues, indicates a long history of human co-evolution with its molecular structure and a well-developed morphogenetic field. He sees DMT and human beings as companions in the journey toward a hyperdimensional reality. Still, the intensity and severity of the DMT experience make any user aware that he has taken something foreign into his system, and that he may never be the same. Nearly everyone who smokes DMT reports hearing a high-pitched tone corresponding to what they believe is a "carrier wave" of reality at that moment. The visual world begins to vibrate at the same frequency until everything breaks up into geometric patterns and crystalline twinkles. This is when the "machine elves" show up, if they're going to. They look like little elves, and sometimes hold wands or crystals and seem to be dancing or operating some kind of light-and-glass machinery. The elves appear to be enjoying themselves intensely. But usually by the time the human voyager realizes that the elves are inviting him to join in the dance, they vanish and a different set of images parades by.

Terence and his brother Dennis McKenna's experiences on DMT shape many of the cyberian conclusions about reality. They believe that DMT works by latching on to the DNA in a user's own cells. Modern science has concluded that the DNA molecule is the carrier of genetic information in living things. Biologists have determined that its double helix (two spirals) shape allows it to split up and replicate. The McKenna brothers—on hearing that high-pitched tone during their DMT trips—became convinced that they were listening to the sound of their own DNA. They proposed that the two strands of DNA work like tuning forks, literally "singing," or resonating instructions to the cell and organism in which they reside. They believe that an ingested DMT molecule will attach itself to the user's DNA, causing the two strands of the double helix to vibrate against each other more intensely. This is why the user hears a tone and also experiences such a radically different reality. The DNA sings new instructions.

Terence and Dennis went to the Amazon to conduct experiments on themselves and test these theories using the state-of-the-art organic tryptamines of the Jivaro Indian medicine men. Dennis heard the most tones, so he became the main subject, while Terence observed and speculated. The two young men succeeded in putting Dennis into a completely psychotic state for several weeks. But as Dennis freaked out, Terence sat on the other side of their tent making notes and having insights. What he realized in a sudden flash was that the structure of DNA resembles that of the ancient Chinese I Ching sequence. Further, their functions are the same.

As a gene carrier, DNA is what links any being to the ancestors in his evolutionary past and the offspring in his evolutionary future. The double-helix structure of the molecule can be seen as a pair of metaphorical spiral staircases: one going down into history, the other up into the future. Its purpose is to compress linear time into these two active springs. (As Sheldrake would also later conclude, the DNA is what "sings" morphogenetic fields over time and space.) The I Ching is thought to work the same way, and uses a sixty-four-part structure almost identical to that of DNA to help people predict future events and understand their personal roles in the overall continuum of time and space. Finally, back in the United States, Terence and Dennis used computers to compute the I Ching as a huge fractal equation for all of human history. According to their fractal, called "Time Wave Zero," history and time as we know it will end in the year 2012. This date has also been linked with the Mayan Tzolkin calendar, which many believe also calls 2012 the end of linear time. It makes the notion of a simple, global renaissance pale by comparison.

Many cyberians agree with Terence that the end of history is fast approaching. When history is over, human experience will feel like, you guessed it: a DMT trip. Experimentation with tryptamines, then, is preparation for the coming hyperdimensional shift into a timeless, nonpersonalized reality. It helps cyberians discriminate between what is linear, temporary, and arbitrary, and what is truly hyper-dimensional. This isn't an easy task.

## Downloading Infinity

Just as the most earth-shattering information off the computer net is useless without a computer capable of downloading it into a form that a user can understand, the DMT experience provides nothing to a user who can't similarly download some essence of timeless hyperspace into a form he can understand in linear reality. However amazing and blissful the DMT euphoria may be, coming down is much trickier than with any other hallucinogen. It's no wonder, though. DMT brings one into a new dimension—a dimension where the restrictions of time and self don't exist—so stepping back into frictional, cause-and-effect reality must be a letdown.

Most cyberian users do their DMT in pairs or small groups, so that they may help one another come down safely and document as much of every experience as possible. The intensity of these shared experiences has led to the formation of what could be called DMT cults.

In the woody hills behind Oakland, about a dozen small trailers and tents surround such a household called Horizon. The plywood structure of the main house looks more like a storage shed than a home, but compared to the amenities offered by the tents, this "main house" is luxurious. On passing through the crudely attached plexiglass back door (there is no "front" door), I realize I've walked into something more foreign to modern society than a simple sub-culture. Two girls sit at the kitchen table scraping the skin off a cactus with the meticulous care of brain surgeons, in the first step of a refinement process that they hope will yield several doses of a potent psychoactive. My entrance does not deter them from their task. I wait in the kitchen for the DMT participants to show up and begin their scheduled ritual.

Dan finally arrives, a stack of psychology journals overburdening his tattered Swiss Army shoulder bag. About thirty, Dan is the head of the household and its group activities—his doctoral thesis on shared states of consciousness probably qualifying him for the position. Or maybe it's his bright blues eyes and silky, Jesus-length hair. He leads the evening drug rituals, decides on doses, and judges whether to intervene when someone is in great physical discomfort or freaking out too heavily. Tonight, thanks to a connection made to Becker's lab by one of the residents over a computer bulletin board, a new batch of "5 MAO" DMT has arrived, a close relative of DMT but with even more powerfully mind-bending effects. Dan is aware that he'll have to watch extra carefully for disasters tonight—his well-traveled math professor has warned him, "On 5 MAO, you begin to see the words 'brain damage' literally printed out in front of your eyes."

Upon Dan's arrival, other members of Horizon emerge from corners of the house I didn't even notice before. Dan is a charismatic and articulate man, but a soft-spoken and low-profiled leader. His presence serves as a personified conscience or monitor. As long as Dan is around, the others feel safe venturing out as far as they can. Dan is watching to make sure nothing goes wrong. Or at least nothing *too* wrong. As if by rote, the group forms a circle in the main room of the house. Then, one by one, each member smokes

the sacred orange powder from a glass pipe and experiences a five-
to ten-minute DMT trip. They don't all do this together, but one at
a time.

The first two adventurers log fairly typical experiences. One girl
curls up into a ball, but emerges understanding how the nature of
reality is holographic. "Each particle of reality reflects, in a dim way,
the whole picture. It doesn't matter who you are or where you are.
Everything that ever happened or ever will happen is available to
everyone and everything right now."

The next voyager, a short, dark-haired boy named Armand, has
just come home from a three-month visionquest in South America.
Instead of returning to classes at school, he has been taking acid
every day this week in preparation for tonight's ceremony. He
remarks—using brief but enthusiastic sentence fragments—how
this circle ceremony is exactly the same way he took ayahuasca
and ibogaine (organic psychedelics) with a shaman in the Amazon.
Then he lights his pipe and almost immediately falls back onto a
pile of pillows. He writhes around for several minutes with his eyes
rolled back, then rises, announcing that he's been gone for three
days. He met an entire race of forest creatures, and they needed his
help. As he describes the place where he's been, what the people
look like, how he's eaten with them and even made love with one
of them, another girl in the circle (one of the cactus scrapers) suddenly perks up.

"Hey! That's the story I've been writing!"

Dan establishes that the boy hasn't read the girl's story; then,
with techniques he has developed in shared-states psychology, he
helps the two relate their stories to each other. Armand has, indeed, been living in Sabrina's fantasy story. He decides to go back
to help his new interdimensional friends.

Still stoned, Armand rolls back his eyes and he's gone. He spends
about ten more minutes moving around on his back. When he rises
again, he explains that in the five minutes he was absent from the
other dimension, several weeks went by and the crisis was averted
without him. Armand can't bring himself to feel happy about this.
He worries that his need to come back and tell his experience to the
rest of the circle deprived him of his chance to save the forest creatures.

"But they were saved anyway," Dan reminds him. "It's only your ego getting in the way now."

Armand shrugs. Dan doesn't want to let him reenter like this, because the boy might be depressed for weeks.

"Think of it this way," he says, putting a comforting hand on Armand's shoulder, "maybe what you and Sabrina did out here, recounting the story and verifying the reality of the forest people, is what actually saved them."

But before Dan is through, someone else suddenly lights the pipe. It is a scruffy young man named Jonathan (whose main interest, he later tells me, is making music for other people to listen to while they're on acid) who has broken the decorum. He had a bad day in the recording studio and wants to make up for it with a good DMT trip. Now.

As soon as he inhales the DMT smoke, his expression changes to one of fear—like the look on a young kid after the safety bar slams down on a roller coaster. He's stuck on this ride. Bizarre visions that Jonathan knows he won't remember whiz by. He can see the other people in the room, but he can also see past them, through them, around them. He can see their experiences in the lines of their faces, then the lines become his whole reality. They point everywhere. The walls of the room are gone. "This is cool," he thinks. "I can take it." Then he gasps in terror, "*Who* thinks it's cool?"

The flip side of Jonathan's euphoria is that he doesn't know who he is.

"Oh fuck! Oh fuck!" the boy who used to call himself Jonathan screams.

Sabrina moves to touch him, but Dan holds her back. "Let him go," the leader warns, "he's got to get through it."

Just then Andy, a musician who lives downstairs, barges in. "Fuck! This new sampler just erased my entire drum machine's memory! That's all my samples! All my patterns! Weeks . . . months of work!" Dan quickly gets Andy out, but the synchronicity is not lost on the members of the circle.

"Jonathan, are you okay?" Dan asks gently. The tripper stares up at him from the floor. "Jonathan?"

Jonathan suddenly sits up. "I'm your creation, aren't I?"

"What do you mean?"

"You made me, didn't you? I'm only here when you're on DMT. Otherwise I don't exist, do I?" Jonathan stares cynically at his creator. "And you gave me this drug now, because it was time for me to know, right?"

Sabrina is worried. She's been attracted to the boy for some time and would hate to lose him now. "Jonathan?" she says, putting her hand on his back.

Jonathan lurches forward as if he's been stabbed. He breathes heavily, holding his head in his hands, crying intensely and then suddenly stopping.

Hours later, after everyone else has their chance to try the new drug, Jonathan explains what happened to him when Sabrina touched his back. "I had forgotten who I was. I had no identity other than being Dan's creation. Then, all of a sudden I heard my name—Jonathan. And I remembered my last name, and my mom, and I went, 'Wait a minute.' It was as if all the fragments of my life had been blown apart and I was sticking them back in my body. I was eagerly grabbing the information; I wanted this illusion of my life. I was eagerly pasting it back on me. I was willingly accepting this illusion."

Sabrina feeds Jonathan chocolate chip cookies in the kitchen as life at Horizon hums back to normal. Dan watches Jonathan out of the corner of his eye.

"There's still this conversation going on in my head saying— 'We're sorry you had to find out this way,'" Jonathan says.

"You still think you're a DMT creation of Dan's?" Sabrina asks.

"No. Jonathan is just a role I'm playing! It's as if the whole search of life is not to obtain some kind of knowledge, but trying to remember what you lost at birth. 'We're sorry you had to find out this way. Such a shock to you. But now you know . . . you're not Jonathan.'"

Sabrina frowns. She was hoping that the cyberian truth wouldn't be so depressing.

Jonathan reads her instantly and takes her hand. "It was a good experience, Sabrina, don't you see? Whatever God is, we're all one thing. We're all part of the same thing. We've got no identity of our own. 5 MAO DMT is like when you die. Life is like this dream, and when you die you go, 'Oh wow! It was so real!' And then discovering that higher level—it's not like 'Oh my god I'm *that* higher self?'

It's more like discovering 'I'm not *that* back there. I thought I was Jonathan—how silly!'"

Dan smiles and quietly moves out of the room. The download has been successful.

## Straight and Stoned

It's hard to know whether these people are touching the next reality or simply frying their brains. Transformation, no doubt, is occurring in either case. But no matter how much permanent damage may be taking place, there is substantial evidence that these voyagers are experiencing something at least as revelatory as in any other mystical tradition. The growing numbers of normal-seeming Americans who are enjoying DMT on a regular basis attests, at least, to the fact that even the most extremely disorienting DMT adventures need not hamper one's ability to lead a "productive" life.

World sharing and discovery of parallel realities fills the DMT afternoons of "Gracie and Zarkov," she a published anthropologist, he an established and successful investment analyst. Sex swingers in the 1970s, they became psychedelic voyagers in the 1980s and self-published their findings in *Notes from Underground: A Gracie and Zarkov Reader* out of their East Bay home.

A cross between an opium den and a sex chamber, their bedroom takes up at least half of their house. While most people's parties end up in the kitchen, Gracie and Zarkov's end up here in the bedroom, which is equipped with an elaborate lighting system hidden behind translucent sheets on the walls and in the ceiling panels, a remote control sound system, and several cabinets filled with straps, studs, and belly-dancing gear.

Their writings on psychedelics are a detailed and well-thought-out cross between the *Physician's Desk Reference* and a wine-tasting guide; in describing the drug 2CB they point out details such as "there is a long, low-level tail to the trip."[5] They've become regular *Mondo 2000* contributors, avid heavy-metal fans, and frequent DMT travelers. They spend their free hours experimenting with new types of psychedelics and new combinations of old ones. Gracie occasionally manifests the spirit of a female goddess, most often Kali, and the two indulge in hyperhedonism on an order unimaginable by others in their professional fields—hence the pseudonyms. But Zarkov's practical, rationalist Wall Street sensibilities shine through his story-telling about psychedelics. To Zarkov, it's all a question of hardware and software.

"Tryptamines are a real phenomenon. If you take a high dose of tryptamines you see certain things. I am a believer that you are not a blank slate when you're born. You're a long complicated product of genetic engineering by the Goddess, under all sorts of selection criteria. And there's a hell of a lot of hardware and wetware, so that DMT's not going to change everybody, or everybody positively. That has to do with how you're wired up, and how you're raised. Now, my experiences have been extremely positive, but several of my closest friends are dead as a result of psychedelic drugs. If you're not up to handling heavy equipment, DMT is a very dangerous, very powerful hallucinogen. It's *extremely* strong."

Gracie and Zarkov can be considered designer beings. They use their DMT experiences to consciously recreate their identities in their professional worlds.

"Gracie and I have developed the ability to write some software to become significantly different people. That is a big advantage in terms of being able to run our lives." They sometimes like to think of themselves as anthropologists from another dimension, merely observing the interactions and concerns of human beings.

Zarkov makes practical use out of the sublime DMT state to re-design the personality he uses in real life. He enjoys his DMT experience, then downloads it in order to devise new business strategies or even new sexual techniques—but he does not take any of it too seriously. Zarkov remains convinced that our reality is not making a wholesale leap out of history. His views sharply contrast those of his good friend Terence McKenna.

"I don't buy Terence's whole package. I just say that right out. On the other hand, Terence is on to a lot of very important things. Does that mean that the world's going to come to an end in 2012? Does that mean that there's going to be a major bifurcation? I don't see it that way. A drug is a tool, like a microscope, a telescope, or a radio. Is it some godlike metaphysical entity? Where I part company with Terence is where he talks about the drug as a metaphysical entity which looks, smells, tastes, and acts like God. I don't believe in God."

Terence attributes Zarkov's obstinacy to an inability to translate the experience of the infinite, egoless reality into a model that can jive with his experience of daily, straight life. Zarkov is great at downloading useful information, but, still attached to his personality, he is not equipped to deal with the most crushing nonpersonal cyberian conclusions. It's a question of his ability to download threatening material.

"Zarkov is terrified of psilocybin, and a fairly ego-bound person. He is forceful, opinionated, and it never enters his mind that he might not be entirely 100 percent correct. The couple of times that he's tried to take mushrooms it's just been too rough for him, because of the dissolving of the ego and surrender. This is the issue for most males and most dominator types—is how can you fling yourself into the blast furnace of disillusion?"

The point here is not to pit Zarkov and McKenna against each other, but to distinguish the specific qualities of the cyberian psychedelic experience from other sorts of psychedelic experiences. What makes a vision qualify for the renaissance is that it is an experience of greater mystical dimensionality, which can then be translated down, at least in part, to the three-dimensional realm. One must retain an inkling of the infinite—an intimation of immortality. As Terence argues:

"You have to download it [the DMT experience] into some kind of model, and I don't know why I'm so able to do that. It may be because of a bad upbringing. Because really there is nothing new about this. This is what lurks behind Kabbalism and Catholic hermeneutics. If you talk to the village priest, that's bullshit; but if you talk to the theologians of the Jesuit order, they will tell you God will enter history. History is the shock wave of eschatology—the fall of all these dimensional models. This is the secret that lies behind religion, but religion has been subverted for millenia as a tool of social control through the notion of morality. Morality has nothing to do with it. It isn't good people who go to heaven. It's *smart* people who go to heaven."

## chapter eight

Earth Girl—a beautiful if slightly otherworldly twenty-year-old from Los Angeles—is at Mr. Floppy's Firm and Floppy house party in Oakland, explaining the effects of Psuper Cybertonic to several young girls who have traveled from the suburbs to get a taste of the house scene. Adorning her Smart Bar (a Peter Max version of Lucy's psychiatrist's booth) are several posters of mushrooms, spaceships, and loose quotes from *The Starseed Transmissions:*

99

"As this new awareness increasingly filters into everyday levels of human function, and as more and more individual human cells become aware of what is taking place, the change will accelerate exponentially. Eventually, the psychic pressure exerted by a critical mass of humanity will reach levels that are sufficient to tip the scales. At that moment, the rest of humanity will experience the instantaneous transformation of a proportion you cannot now conceive."

Earth Girl and her traveling Smart Bar offer two brain nutrient mixtures: the Cybertonic and a stimulant drink called Energy Elicksure, made from ephedra (an herb related to the active ingredient in Sudafed, the cold medicine that keeps one from getting drowsy) and a few amino acid uppers. Her advice to the high-schoolers is heartfelt but somewhat underinformed. She relies heavily on the fact that these herbs are "100 percent safe, used for centuries by ancient cultures, and make you feel really good." The girls all buy the Cybertonic for $3 a glass and chug it down. "Light up and live," Earth Girl calls after the kids as they return to the dance floor.

A punkish boy stumbles up to the bar at about 4:00 A.M. His girlfriend wants to dance till dawn but the LSD he took at three that afternoon has sucked about as much in adrenaline as it offered in insight. Earth Girl sells him a large cup of tangy Energy Elicksure, and soon he's back under the strobe lights, pulsing with new life.

It is the kind of scene that would horrify parents. What the hell's going on?

Earth Girl isn't really selling drugs; she's selling nutrients. Drugs are patented medications that enhance brain function; nutrients are nonpatented substances that the body uses more like food to do the same thing, usually less invasively but also a bit less effectively. They include substances like the amino acid L-pryoglutamate, the herb Gingko biloba, niacin, lecithin, and certain vitamins. Earth Girl's brews are slightly altered versions of prepackaged nutrient mixes available at health food stores or through multilevel marketers. These mixes bear the names of Durk Pearson and Sandy Shaw, whose book *Life Extension* first publicized the existence of smart chemicals and the notion of nutrient-enhanced "designer beings" back in the 1970s.

Smart drugs (with names like vasopressin—a snorted spray— hydergine and piracetum) are generally unavailable in this country. Depending on the legal weather, these drugs can be purchased through the mail from pharmaceutical companies overseas because of a loophole demanded by AIDS patients who wanted access to drugs not approved for use in the United States. (For more information, see Dean and Morgenthaler, *Smart Drugs and Nutrients*.) Smart drugs fall between the cracks of America's ability to comprehend the uses of medication, which is why we have such a cloudy understanding of their abilities and their categorization.

Most cyberians understand the science by now. Acetylcholine is one of the chemicals that allow for transmission of information at the nerve synapses. As we get older, our supply of acetylcholine decreases. While we can't just eat acetylcholine to increase the supply in the brain, we can take its precursors, such as choline, as well as chemicals that tend to increase our own production of acetylcholine by the cholinergic system. Some of these chemicals are now called "nootropics" (*noos,* "mind" + *tropein,* "to turn"—that is, "acting on the mind"), the new class of drugs that provide cognitive enhancement with no toxicity.

The most widely used, over-the-counter smart nutrients are mixtures of several forms of choline along with a few of the enzymes and co-enzymes that turn them into acetylcholine. Earth Girl's Cybertonic is a combination of choline, acetylcholine precursors, and co-factors. Their effect is noticeable over time but not very dramatic. The sudden increase in popularity and marketing visibility of these nutrients is due to the fact that other, much more potent smart substances have arrived in Cyberia. It is a case of fame by association.

The pyrrolidone derivatives are the smart substances deserving the most attention. In an unknown way, they improve the functioning of the cholinergic system. They increase memory, boost intelligence, and enhance certain kinds of learning. They were originally used for diseases of old age such as Alzheimer's and senility. The most widely distributed one in Europe is a geriatric medication called piracetam, which is unavailable in the United States. (Users here purchase it directly from European distributors through the mail.) It is a fast-acting, easy-to-notice cognitive enhancer. Walter Kirn, a novelist and smart drugs user (whom we'll meet later), describes piracetam's effect as "going through life wearing a miner's lamp with a beam of intelligence." Nearly everyone who takes it experiences greater ability to conceptualize complex problems and to retain information.

Users' reactions to the drugs differ, and all have their preferred combinations and dosages. It's quite common to see a bottle of vasopressin on a computer terminal, next to a bar of chocolate or a pack of cigarettes. A particularly dense passage of text to understand or a complex series of steps to write into a program? A blast of vasopressin and everything gets clear in less than a minute. Going to have a difficult day filled with interviews? Probably better off with piracetam or pyroglutamate in a few doses spread out over the course of the day—that added articulateness and recall will come in handy. And, of course, don't forget the daily dose of hydergine until the end of the semester. Jet lag still a problem? Maybe some L-tyrosine (an amino acid) to wake up this morning instead of coffee—it works as well, without the jitters or the stress to the adrenal system. Smart drugs even help psychedelics users come down off difficult trips.

Smart drugs don't get cyberians high or stoned, but they do seem to help them cope with complex computer problems, ego-bending philosophical or spiritual inquiry, odd hours, a highly pressurized work environment, or a creativity lapse. The most common perception among users is that they have gained the ability to deal with more than one or two parameters of a problem at the same time. A computer programmer, for example, gains the ability to track three or four different interdependent functions through a series of program commands rather than only one. Smart drugs give some writers the ability to keep half-a-dozen plot points in mind at once. Psychedelics users report the ability to download more of the information and realizations of a trip when they augment the coming-down period with smart drugs.

A typical smart drug user receives his supplies from laboratories in Europe, then creates his own regimen based on self-experimentation. "Personal neurochemical adjustment," as users call it, is designer consciousness.

Earth Girl's distributor, Lila Mellow-Whipkit, a large, bald, hedonistic smart drugs enthusiast, loves explaining how this neurochemical self-modulation fits in to the new paradigm. Lila is a transvestite—but I never figured out which way he or she was cross-dressing. Lila, most probably, is a man dressing as a woman, but the few times I came into contact with "him" in men's clothes, I was sure she must be a woman in drag. This is precisely Lila's message: designer identity to the point where even one's sex is negotiable. No matter how variable her wardrobe, she (let's call Lila a woman, for now) is probably one of Cyberia's leading authorities on self-modulated intelligence. She can often be found at a rave, sitting behind Earth Girl's Smart Bar and sharing her wealth of data and insight with newcomers. Here's a sample, culled from literally hours of non-stop downloading by Lila to a rotating crowd of enthusiasts:

"Personal neurochemical adjustment—the equivalent is personal paradigm and belief adjustment. It's based on a basic presupposition stolen from cybernetics that's used in NLP [neurolinguistic programming]: the organism with the most requisite behavior—the broadest variety of requisite behavior—will always control any situation."

To Lila, smart drugs, NLP, and cybernetics are all basically the same thing: programming.

"In other words, if two people interact and they're trying to get something done, the one who has the most variety in behavior is the one who will be in charge and decide where it's gonna go. It's an excellent operating presupposition. It works most of the time, because that person's more able to compromise and come up with ideas, they're less stuck. Think about children who are getting a good Christian education right now. Where are those people gonna be in the future? They're gonna be what Hunter S. Thompson called 'the doomed.' They are the doomed. They have one belief system; they have one basic operating strategy, which is the avoidance of pleasure. That's about it in Christianity as far as your real life. You get to kneel and pray to this dead guy."

What Lila argues is twofold. First, smart drugs and nutrients open up new neural pathways, allow for new thoughts and more flexibility in conceptualizing. Those who take smart drugs can understand more patterns and survive better. Second, and more important, the implicit argument she makes is that the idea of smart drugs and the willingness to experiment with them are themselves heralds of the new paradigm. Not only is a smart drugs user more equipped to deal with the increasingly complex reality matrix; a person willing to take smart drugs is already coping better. He has taken the first step toward becoming a designer being.

## The Readiness Is All

Downloading the massive information wave emanating from the end of time is no easy task. Sure, a stockbroker can use smart drugs to help himself draw broader conclusions about certain market data, but cyberians have always known that the real destiny of these chemicals is to foster the processing of the inconceivable.

Mark Heley had just graduated Cambridge when he first found smart drugs. An experienced psychedelic explorer, Heley already believed that the earth is heading toward a great bifurcation point. As a would-be usher of the final paradigm, he knew what was required of him: a hierarchical leap in his mind's ability to identify, process, store, and articulate the complexities of eschatological acceleration. Mark was already smart—very smart—but he'd need to be even smarter to face the challenges ahead. He knew that smart drugs were going to play a major role in the formation of Cyberia, and he knew he was going to be a part of it.

At that time Earth Girl, who hadn't yet abandoned her given name, Neysa, was visiting England. Her mother was a New Age extremist, and Neysa, age eighteen, had left the West Coast to get away from what she saw as trivial and fake spirituality. She wasn't going back until she knew she had something to fill the vacuum.

As a writer for England's *ID,* Heley exploited his Cambridge philosophy education to become an articulate launcher of cultural viruses. In articles and lectures on topics ranging from permaculture farming techniques to technoshamanism, Heley defined the ways and memes of cyberian culture in London. He was DJing for a house club and running a "brain gym" (brain machine rental store), and in the process he gathered a wide following for a twenty-four-year-old. Neysa, for the time being, was just hanging out. When they met, they knew it would be forever.

In many ways, Heley and Neysa are opposites. He's an intellectual who grounds every psychedelic revelation into a plan. He's all business, and even his most far-reaching DMT experiences mean nothing to him if he can't process them into concrete realizations about the nature of reality. If those realizations are to be worth anything, he must also quickly determine how to communicate them to others through articles, chemicals, club events, or cultural viruses. Heley is a mind. So much so, that his body, often neglected through aggressive chemical use and lack of sleep, revolts in the form of Chronic Fatigue Syndrome, which incapacitates him completely for weeks or even months at a time.

Neysa lives through her body almost exclusively. She can feel what she calls spiritual "weather," evaluate people at a glance, and predict events in the weeks ahead entirely through her body. She is incapable of articulating her experience through words, but has developed her own "language of heart," which takes the form of a smile, a touch, an embrace, or even sex. Wherever she goes, a cluster of admirers forms around her looking for the security that her carefree yet self-assured manner offers them. With the help of Heley and his cyberian epiphanies, Neysa was able to embrace the New Age ideas of her mother in a new, cyberian context. Then she was complete: Earth Girl was born.

Where Heley valued smart drugs for their mental effects, Earth Girl saw them as a physical preparation for the coming age. They both knew that smart drugs and the cyberian designer mindset that the chemicals fostered needed to be broadcast to a wider audience. America was ripe and ready. A few books on the substances had come out in the United States, but popular, club culture had no idea what was going on. Together, then, they decided to put smart drugs and cyber culture on the map.

After severing ties with his partners at the Mind Gym in London, Mark Heley came back to the Bay Area with Neysa and a new idea: Smart Bars. They could distribute the drugs as healthy fruit drinks over the counter right next to the dance floor. Mark's media savvy and pharmaceutical experience could develop the idea into a workable concept. Neysa's personality and flair made her the perfect barperson and iconic representation of new, designer being. Their mission was clear.

In San Francisco, Heley was introduced to Diana, a Berkeley dropout who, with her friend Preston, was running Toon Town, an underground roving house event for kids fed up with haughty dance hall atmospheres. Heley's multidimensional language and strong ideas soon earned him Diana as his new girlfriend, as well as a position as one of the coordinators of Toon Town. Heley's presence quickly manifested as an infusion of cyber-culture viruses. Rooms were set aside for brain machines, virtual reality demonstrations, sales of books and tapes, and the infamous Smart Bar. While Preston would later resist Heley's metabrainstorm, for the time being it made Toon Town the highest profile house gathering in town. That, coupled with Diana's gentle pleading and positive attitude, kept competition between the two men in check.

Heley, who by now had inherited and updated Ken Kesey's role as charismatic visionary of the San Francisco psychedelic underground, invited the press and public to sample the Smart Bar and other attractions at the "cyber disco" party. While he tells only the facts to the press, "Smart drugs enhance neurofunctioning legally and safely," he shares the real secret of his success with anyone who thinks to ask.

"My theory is that all that's happening is really the same thing. There are cultural viruses which are actually no more than elaborate placebos to draw people in. They're not the actual things that are happening. For example, smart drugs and virtual reality, these are two of my favorite cultural viruses because they really hit wide and hard. Virtual reality comes from the heart of a society which is really wired in to technology; it's a powerful cultural virus for people to interface with a computer in a harmonious way. And yet, if you try to experience it, you're sadly disappointed. Or you take a smart drug and even after designing an intelligent program, you realize that you've had all this inside you in the first place. People think they're going to get evolved using smart drugs, when actually you've got to be evolved to want to use them in the first place."

But Earth Girl shares a different story. Her enthusiasm for smart drugs and her newfound fame are irresistible. She puts her hair up in a Bardot-meets-Diller dredlocked beehive, and wears Day-Glo silk robes. She offers her take on the smart drug virus to the crowds who have gathered.

"For me they're really good 'cause I do enjoy getting high, as everyone does. I love altered states—they're fun. But I can't do the 'body degeneration trip' anymore, especially the mental one. Pot turns me into a moron. And a lot of these other kids are doing so many drugs in one night that they're depleting themselves of vitamins and minerals that these drinks put back. Will they feel more love and communication ability from the Psuper Cybertonic? Probably not. But at least they're going to be maintaining a balance. They're tripping forever. They don't eat for days. So I say, 'Okay, here, have some of this, this is all of the daily whatever you need. It's cheap, and it's actually, really, really, really, really good for you so just like get into it.'"

Mark gets pretty annoyed as Earth Girl babbles on to the press. He knows her words are heartfelt, but they're also mindless and dangerous. Soon, Earth Girl is more of a phenomenon than the smart drinks themselves. She's gathered a posse of young, sexually nondescript hangers-on whom she calls the Foxy Seven. To anyone uninvolved in the scene, Earth Girl begins to look more and more like a space cadet—or, in even the best light, a new version of the stereotypical San Francisco "fag hag." The control she exhibits over her seven assistant bartenders is absolute. She is their mother and spiritual guide. She holds out the promise of glory and adventure, and it's all in the form of an elaborate theater/comic book/cosmic fantasy.

Earth Girl shares her new vision of the Smart Bar mission with her squadron as they set up her portable booth.

"We're doing this because what we really are is, writers and performers. This is the perfect way to get in. We're going to make our own comic book. We can keep launching all of our stuff. That's why we all have to dress up. We're the Foxy Seven—Earth Girl, Galactic Greg, Dynama, Greenfire. We get to play. Play and serve "

Earth Girl takes on the tone of a restaurant manager briefing her new waiters, but in the language of a *Course in Miracles* instructor on local cable access. "When people are talking to you and asking questions, they're looking at you like you're an authority, so you conceive thought. And the stuff that we put up—the pictures of mushrooms, quotes from *The Starseed Transmissions*—it will help you keep on suggesting all this stuff hypnotically and subliminally. I mean, everyone needs a little awareness kick, as far as I'm concerned."

Heley begins to feel it is Earth Girl who needs the awareness kick. First, she has started bringing the Smart Bar, which Toon Town paid for, to other clubs. Heley has been working a carefully controlled culturo-viral experiment—now it is "out." Second, the kind of indiscriminate, overflowing enthusiasm she exhibits clouds many of the issues that Heley is attempting to clarify. She's even been on national television news saying, "Smart drugs are really really really really really really really really really really good!"

But things get even worse when *Rolling Stone* shows up to do a piece on smart drugs. Of course, Earth Girl is the center of the interview: "Alcohol, cigarettes, coffee—work culture is drug culture," she explains to their reporter. "With smart drugs, there's no hangover, you're not depressed, you have a better memory. Instead of getting fucked up and making a fool of yourself, you're more in touch."[6]

Heley is incensed by her blanket statements, which counteract months of his machinations. He broods in a back room with the contempt of a spurned lover. "Alcohol is out there. Its dangers are well known. It's promoted by a massive machine. She's running up against something which she can never ever hope to defeat. What are they going to do? Stop selling alcohol? No fucking way. It just has to be played out. What you've got to do is move the ground. You don't attack the monster. You infect him, like a virus. Neysa's attitude is almost like a sixties' 'left' thing; it's like, 'attack the monster.' But if you do that, you become the monster. You're playing to spectacle. What we should do is simply infect the monster and let it destroy itself. By activating a media virus. And a media virus isn't a media attack, it's something which exposes things internally."

This conflict made for a tense week in Cyberia, as Earth Girl explains: "Honestly, the best way to tell on a reflection level is the weather, as I'm sure you know. And if you just check the weather out for the past three days it's just like . . . it's still . . . we're coming out, we're trying to come out of it."

It seemed to be a week in which cyberians were learning that somewhere else, someone else was doing exactly the same thing they were. Someone else was writing a book about cyber culture. Someone else was mixing a new house tune. Someone else was creating a club. Someone else was doing a Smart Bar. In addition, it had been raining for four days, and nearly everyone was fighting the same cold. No one was fully sick, but everyone felt under the weather.

Sitting with Earth Girl in a Thai restaurant on Haight Street, I take some of the herbal formulas that Lila Mellow-Whipkit has given me for my sniffles. Earth Girl explains to me how everything fits together. In spite of her generalizations, Earth Girl is a sensitive, "spiritually mature" young woman. It would be a mistake to let her cosmic jargon obscure her quite perceptive observations on human nature in the trenches of Cyberia:

"The weirdness of this weekend is that everyone's discovering all these parallel things that are going on and everyone's reeling from the fear of 'do it first.' But this is just the realization of a universal mind! Of course everyone's doing it all at the same time. It's all part of the same thing! Everyone's fighting a cold, and feels like they've got a cold, but . . . it's not breaking through . . . it's a slightly physical thing, but it's much more psychological because in this time all the fear can get in and all these negative thoughts and all this stuff can get in, and it *is* getting in. It did get in . . . but now I feel today we're coming out of it. We've still got a lot of shit we've got to work out personally, like, group-wise."

To Earth Girl and her followers, the current friction is really morphogenetic stress. Many people are having the same ideas at the same times because they are all connected morphogenetically. The sickness and fear results from the inability to break the fiction of individuality. But in the cyber culture world, the denizens must realize that they are all connected. Their commitment to the metatransformation of humanity has put them all into the same "weather system." They must be content with never "owning" an idea. There is no room for pride or credit.

But Earth Girl also seems to realize that her final allegiance is to herself and the Foxy Seven. Survival and ambition—however rationalized—still take precedence. By the time the *Rolling Stone* piece goes to press, Earth Girl has gone off to Big Heart City, another club in town, which gives her their entire basement (which was the location of Tim Leary's reception last month) to create a smart drugs lounge. There, she will be queen bee, and will never again have to put up with Heley or his mild-mannered political arrogance. Her Smart Lounge will just "light up and live."

Heley, meanwhile, partners with Chris, an electrical engineering student and smart nutrients chemist whose knowledge of neurochemistry is as vast as Earth Girl's knowledge of spiritual weather.

It stops raining Friday afternoon, and Chris, Heley, Preston, and Diana convene at 650 Howard Street (a club that has become the temporary home of Toon Town) to eat the free hors' d'oeuvres that the daytime bar gives out during happy hour. Having reviewed the *Rolling Stone* article, they now discuss strategies to keep their new and improved Smart Bar sans Earth Girl, called the Nutrient Cafe, on the cutting edge of neuro-enhancement. Mark gets on one of his articulate impassioned riffs about the smart drugs virus, as the others drink beer and nod. Not that they haven't heard all this before, but nodding generally keeps Mark from getting too worked up and pissed off. Heley's main regret is that the Smart Bar, which was supposed to be an outlet for true information about good drugs and bad drug laws, turned into a media joke.

"It's a war on information. If you're not capable of fighting the wrong information then you're not capable of fighting the machine. The point is, that if we manage to combine the subtlety of good information with the bludgeon of its media impact, we'd have had a tool against the war on drugs. What do we have at the moment? Petty hype for a bunch of multilevel marketing people who want to scam a few fucking dollars out of something that doesn't do what they say it does.

"What could have happened is that we could have gotten to a level where we could have argued the case for the complete restructuring of the drug patenting laws just on their own internal logic. Piracetam is not available in the U.S., not because of any toxicity, or any side effects, but because it's not patented. Because the company that invented it didn't patent it. At the time, it just wasn't thought of as commercially viable. The psychotropic effects of piracetam were discovered years later. Also, there's no FDA approval procedure for a nootropic drug. It has to be for Alzheimer's, or it has to be for treating strokes."

Heley's disgust is well founded. Today, most smart drugs are not available in the United States even to victims of geriatric disease. In order for a drug to get FDA approval, a pharmaceutical company must spend millions of dollars on tests. It's worth it to these companies to do the tests only if they know they will have a patent on the medication; with piracetam, the companies know they cannot get a patent. So, instead, they race to develop substances similar to piracetam and then patent those. Meanwhile, only the underground knows of piracetam's existence, and it's in the pharmaceutical companies' best interests to keep it that way. The FDA obliges, and most doctors who know of the drug do not buck the system or risk liability by ordering unapproved substances from overseas.

In even more ludicrous cases, chemicals and nutrients like DHEA (not legal in the United States) and L-pyroglutamate (which is available at any good health store) have been studied by pharmaceutical companies and proven to enhance cognitive skills in humans. But the companies intentionally conceal these studies and instead attempt to develop variants of these chemicals that can be patented and sold more profitably. Some of these substances have even been shown to be effective in treating AIDS, but, again, since the drugs are not patentable, the studies done on them are suppressed. In one case, a scientist has been issued a court order not to reveal the results of his discoveries about DHEA.[7] Heley believes that smart drugs, as a cultural virus, will expose how the American health-care business may be our nation's most serious health threat:

"Smart drugs is a good way of burrowing in there. The argumentation that surrounds smart drugs, the web of the cultural virus, is just a worm designed to eat into those regulatory bodies and explode them by turning the mirror back on themselves. If we can create a cogent argument we can show up their structural inadequacies. The war on drugs, for example, being this blanket war on drugs. You can advertise cigarettes and alcohol and there are all these horrible over-the-counter drugs that you can buy; painkillers in this country are pretty fucking dubious to say the least. But the thing that can't be said in American culture, because of that massive media attack, is that some drugs are *good for you* in some ways.

"What I object to is the smart drug argument being completely obscured. Now the FDA has a counteraction. Their counterattack has been to close the loophole which allows the importation of smart drugs. And that is the only rational piece of legislation in the entire cannon of American drug laws. And that wasn't a loophole established by the smart drugs movement; it was established by Act Up, and by AIDS activist organizations over a long period of time with sustained political pressure of an absolutely enormous magnitude. All the FDA is waiting for is one public excuse for closing this, and it's gone."

Diana rises to get more food. Heley realizes he's bandstanding a bit, and justifies himself. "I admit that we made a mistake with this thing. It got out of hand. What we're doing now is we're actually trying to put this right. Doing this Nutrient Cafe: really straight-forward. We're not hyping, we're not going to do a media virus about it, but we'll provide a really good product within a certain milieu, and lots of information about it. And if we completely stay within the laws as they exist at the moment, it'll just do the fucking job without all of the bollocks."

Diana returns with some chicken wings and joins in the conversation. "That bar never even evolved. When we started it the whole idea was that Mark and Neysa [Earth Girl] would create these products. They knew that Durk and Sandy products were shit anyway. That's never happened. . . . "

Mark defends: "Well, it's not just that they're shit; they're old. It's told and tired."

"The only thing that's evolved down in that basement [Earth Girl's new Smart Lounge]," Diana continues with candor, "is that there are more decorations. And there's more flash and there's more superstars. And that's not the point. There's no books down there, there's no information, there's no pamphlets, there's no nothing, and the people that designed it didn't know shit about it. Not that I do, but I'm not selling the stuff."

Mark interrupts: "I'm certainly not washing my hands of it, because we're all partly responsible; we instituted a lot of the processes that led to this thing. But I find myself radically disagreeing with the way she's doing it. It's not her, it's not even the way that she's approaching it. It's the way that she's allowing it to go. It's a group thing. It's not Neysa, the owners of Big Heart City, *Rolling Stone,* or Lila Mellow-Whipkit. It's basically what all of them want out of it. This is a propagation of an immediate product over something which is an informational thing. How many people have ever fucking taken smart drugs since we started this? That's a measure of its failure. The people that fucking do the Smart Bar don't even use them."

He stares off into space. He knows his ego is probably as responsible for his upset as the political vulnerability of Earth Girl's glamour image.

"It's a matter of fine balance. I really believe that if it had gone other ways, that FDA loophole wouldn't even be in question. I think we'll still manage to keep it open, maybe we have to do some repair work. It should never ever have been this way. It's just my stupidity to allow it to happen."

Maybe he should have taken more smart drugs.

# 3

# Technoshamanism: The Transition Team

## chapter nine

Much more than arenas for drug activism, Toon Town and other "house" events are Cyberia's spiritual conventions. House is more than a dance craze or cultural sensation. House is cyberian religion. But the priests and priestesses who hope to usher in the age of Cyberia have problems of their own.

115

We're at an early Toon Town—the night *Rolling Stone* came to write about Earth Girl and the Smart Bar. It's their first party since one fateful night three weeks ago when their giant, outdoor, illegal rave got crashed by the cops and they lost thousands of dollars. Preston is still a little pissed at Heley over that mishap. The English newcomer got too ambitious, and now Preston and Diana's baby, Toon Town, is in serious debt. They may never recover, and all Heley can think about are his damn cultural viruses. This used to be a dance club!

Heley's in no mood for arguments now. It's 11:00 P.M. Earth Girl hasn't shown up with her bar—correction: with Toon Town's bar. She isn't picking up her phone. The laser is malfunctioning. It's still early, but it's already clear that either the owners of this venue or the hired doorpeople are stealing money. The *Rolling Stone* reporter is on his way to write about the Smart Bar, which is nowhere to be found. R.U. Sirius and Jas Morgan, the editors of *Mondo 2000* magazine, arrive with about forty friends whom they'd like added to the guest list. Tonight, Heley thinks, is supposed to be a party for the new issue, but, on entering the club, R.U. Sirius announces that the real release party will happen in a few weeks at Toon Town's competitor Big Heart City. Tonight is "just a party" that *Mondo* is co-sponsoring. News to Heley. News to Preston. News to Diana. (Had Toon Town maintained a working telephone, I later learn from R.U. Sirius, they may have, indeed, been chosen to host the event. At least they would have learned that it had been cancelled weeks ago. This simple communications lapse developed into a long-standing grudge.)

Bryan Hughes, the virtual reality guide, is setting up a VR demo on a balcony above the dance floor. Along with his gear he's brought a guest list of several hundred names. Cap'n Crunch, notorious reformed hacker and the original phone phreaque, and his assistant are trying to hook up his Video Toaster, but the projector isn't working. The place is buzzing, but Heley is not. Perched on a balcony overlooking the dance floor, he turns away from the confusion, takes off his glasses, and pinches the bridge of his nose. He's angry. Chris—the future nutrient king—mixes Heley a special concoction of pyroglutamate to take the edge off the apparent conflux of crises.

Diana and Preston are running around with wires and paperwork, arguing about the limits of the building's voltage. They perform much more actual physical business than Heley does, but they know, even begrudgingly, that he's engaged in an equally important preparation, so they give him all the space he needs. Heley is the technoshaman. He is the high priest for this cyber mass, and he must make an accurate forecast of the spiritual weather before it begins. He is guiding the entire movement through a dangerous storm. But instead of using the stars for navigation, he must read the events of the week, the status of key cultural viruses, the psychological states of his crewmembers, and the tone and texture of his own psychedelic visionquests. Tonight, most of Heley's calculations and intuitions indicate doom. He brought cyber house to San Francisco and was willing to man the helm, but now it's getting out of control.

"I brought the house thing to *Mondo,* I did their article, and I introduced them to it." What Heley perceives as their disloyalty has undermined his efforts to bring real, hard-core, spiritual, consciousness-raising cyber-influenced house to America. "Sometimes I just feel like there's only fifteen of us really doing this. There's Fraser Clark in England, who does *Evolution* magazine, there's me, there's Nick from Anarchic Adjustment, Jody Radzik, Deee-Lite. I don't mean that we're creating it, but we are painting the signs. We're indicating the direction." Heley looks down at the confusion of people, machinery, and wires on the dance floor and sighs. "God knows what direction this is pointing in."

It was about three weeks ago that things began to get messy. Heley, Preston, and Diana had arranged a huge "rave"—a party where thousands take E and dance to house, usually outside, overnight, and illegally—at an abandoned warehouse and yard. A club competing for the same business on Saturday night found their map point (a small hand-out circulated through the underground community indicating where the party was to be held) and notified the police, who were more than willing to shut it down. Heley recounts the bust with the conviction of a modern-day Joan of Arc.

"They arrived and they only saw people having a good time. People having a party. There's no rational argument they can make against us. They smell it. They smell it and they understand."

Heley swigs down the rest of his pyroglutamate and soon appears to have gained a new clarity and, along with it, a new reason to fight on. "This is not a countermovement. It is the shape of the thing that will replace them. But it will be painless for them. It's not a thing to be frightened of. If you're frightened of acceptance, yes, be afraid because this thing is a reintegration. The trouble is that it just dissolves the old lies—all the things you just know are untrue. We're not living that life anymore. You can only live the old lies when the rest of the paraphernalia is in place. Really, house just destroys that. It's not a reactionary thing."

Let's leave Toon Town for a moment to get a look at the history of this thing called "house." Most Americans say it began in Chicago, where DJs at smaller, private parties and membership-only clubs (particularly one called The Warehouse) began aggressively mixing records, adding their own electronic percussion and sampling tracks, making music that—like the home-made vinaigrette at an Italian restaurant—was called "house." The fast disco and hip-hop-influenced recordings would sample pieces of music that were called "bites" (others spell it "bytes," to indicate that these are digital samples that can be measured in terms of RAM size). Especially evocative bites were called "acid bites." Thus, music of the house, made up of these acid bites, became known as "acid house."

When this sound got to England, it was reinterpreted, along with its name. Folklore has it that industrial (hard, fast, high-tech, and psychedelic) music superstar Genesis P. Orridge was in a record store when he saw a bin of disks labeled "acid," which he figured was psychedelic music—tunes to play while on LSD. He and his co-horts added their own hallucinogenic flavor to the beats and samples, and British acid house was born.

"When I heard acid house music would be playing, I figured for sure they meant it was a psychedelic dance club—music to take acid to," explains Lyle, an ex-punker from Brixton who has followed the house scene since its beginnings in the suburbs of London. "It began on an island, Ibetha, off the coast of Spain. Everyone goes there on holiday, does Ecstasy, and stays up all night. We got back to England and decided we didn't want to give it up and started raving on the weekends."

Lyle's explanation is as good as any for how raves got started. These Woodstock-like fests begin on a Friday evening and carry on through Sunday afternoon. Dancing is nonstop. They became most popular in the late 1980s, when thousands of cars could be seen on any weekend heading toward whichever suburb—Stratford, Brighton—was hosting the party. Police began cracking down on them in 1990 or so, but then they went legit by renting out permitted club space. News of raves eventually rebounded to the United States, where the original house clubs began to incorporate the British hallucinogenic style and substances. San Francisco, where psychedelics are still the most popular, was most receptive to the new movement, which is why Heley and other English ravers wound up there.

As Heley suggests, there's more to raves and house than meets the eye. Coming to an understanding of the house phenomenon requires a working knowledge of the new technology, science, and drugs that shape Cyberia, as well as an awareness of the new spiritual dimension (or perhaps archaic spiritual revival) arising out them. Just as the new, quantum sciences and chaos mathematics developed out of the inability of materialist models to effectively map our reality, house is meant as a final reaction to the failings of a work ethic–based, overindustrialized culture.

The ravers see themselves and the creation of their subculture as part of the overall fractal equation for the postmodern experience. One of the principles of chaos math, for example, is phase-locking, which is what allows the various cells of an organism to work harmoniously or causes a group of women living together to synchronize their menstrual cycles. Phase-locking brings the participants—be they atoms, cells, or human beings—into linked cycles that promote the creation of a single, interdependent organism where feedback and iteration can take place immediately and effectively. A phase-locked group begins to take on the look of a fractal equation, where each tiny part reflects the nature and shape of the larger ones.

Members of rave culture phase-locked by changing their circadian rhythms. They self-consciously changed their basic relationship to the planet's movements by sleeping during the day and partying all night. As Heley says in defiance: "It's in the face of the network that tells you seven to eight-thirty is prime time. You sleep during prime time. You share the same place physically as that society, but you're actually moving into a different dimension by shifting through the hours. It's an opportunity to break out from all the dualistic things."

Of course, sleeping days and partying nights is just as dualistic as working days and sleeping nights, but the point here is that the "dualistic things" considered important by mainstream culture are not hard realities, and they are certainly not the "best" realities. Ravers were able to create a subculture different from the work-a-day society in which they had felt so helpless. They used to be the victims of a top-down hierarchy. As the poor workers to a mean boss or the powerless kids to a domineering father or even the working class to a rigid monarchy, they were just numbers in an old-style linear math equation. Now, phase-locked as part of a living, breathing fractal equation, they feel more directly involved in the creation of reality.

"When you move away from a massive guilt trip in which there is a direct hierarchy," says Heley, "you suddenly find that it doesn't matter a fuck what your boss or the authorities think of you. You're creating yourself moment by moment in an environment that is created by people who are like-minded. It's a liberation, and it's completely in the face of twentieth-century society."

The ultimate phase-locking occurs in the dance itself, where thousands of these "like-minded" young people play out house culture's tribal ceremony. The dance links everyone together in a synchronous moment. They're on the same drugs, in the same circadian rhythm, dancing to the same 120-beat-per-minute soundtrack. They are fully synchronized. It's at these moments that the new reality is spontaneously developed.

"The dance empowers you. It reintegrates you. And then you can start again. It's an ancient, spiritual thing. It's where we have always communicated to each other on the fullest level. Instead of being in this extremely cerebral, narrow-bandwidth-television society, people learn instead to communicate with their bodies. They don't need to say anything. There is just a bond with everyone around them. A love, an openness. If you look at a society as repressed as England, you see how much impact that can have."

The various forms of social repression in England, along with its own deeply rooted pagan history, made it the most fertile soil in which house could grow. As Heley shares: "I felt it was slipping out of history. That this was an alternative history."

House became massive in England. News of raves was always spread precariously by word of mouth or tiny fliers, but somehow everyone who needed to know what was happening and where, found out. Either one knew what was happening or one didn't. It was as simple as that. By the end of the 1980s, house was everywhere in the United Kingdom, but it had never seen the light of day. Tens of thousands of kids were partying every weekend. Mainstream culture was not even aware of their existence. By the time the tabloids caught on and published their headlines proclaiming the arrival of house, the ravers had realized they'd gone off the map altogether.

## Off the Map and into the Counterculture

Today, the English house scene still defines the pulse for other house-infected cities. Whether through the brain-drain of emigrés like Heley or the exportation of London-mixed dance tracks, Great Britain still holds the most coherently articulated expression of the house ethic. Although there's less technology, fewer gays, and fewer smart chemicals at London clubs, there's a much clearer sense of house's role as a countercultural agent.

Some argue that this is because London's morphogenetic field of counterculture is more developed than America's. London's pagan cultures have endured centuries of repression and distillation. Their phase-locking was probably achieved somewhere in the twelfth century. Symbols and even personalities from ancient pagan times still live in London house.

One such pagan hero is Fraser Clark, a self-proclaimed psyche-delic warrior from the 1960s who began *Encyclopaedia Psychedelica* magazine, which has since mutated into London house culture's 'zine *Evolution*. At his London flat, which he shares with two or three students half his age, the long-haired Welshman rolls some sort of cigarette and explains to me what's happening. From the British perspective, this is a historical battle for religious freedom.

"A kid grows up in a Christian culture and thinks he's probably the only one questioning these ideas. When he comes to house," the English are fond of using the word alone like that, as if it's a religion, "he suddenly realizes he's got a whole alternative history. He might get into UFOs or whatever there is—drugs, witches, it's all in there."

And all quite accessible. To participate in this experience of reso-nance, each participant must feel like part of the source of the event. Where a traditional Christian ritual is dominated by a priest who dictates the ceremony to a crowd of followers, pagan rituals are free-for-alls created by a group of equals. For house events to provide the same kinds of experiences, they had to abandon even traditional rock and roll concert ethos, which pedestals a particular artist and falls into the duality of audience and performer, observer and object. The house scene liberates the dancers into total partici-pation. Fraser, whose new club UFO opens tonight, explains the ad-vantages of a no-star system:

"Nobody is that much better than the next guy that he needs a whole stage and twenty thousand people fillin' up a stadium to see him. Nobody's that much better than the audience. We don't need that and people don't want it anymore. A lot of the music you'll hear tonight is never gonna be on a record. Kids just mix it the week before and play it that one night."

So the house movement is determined to have no stars. It is "in the face" of a recording industry that needs egos and idolatry in order to survive. It depends, instead, on a community in resonance. The fractal equation must be kept in balance. If one star were to rise above the crowd, the spontaneous feedback creating the fractal would be obliterated. The kids don't want to dance even facing their partners, much less a stage. Everyone in the room must become "one." This means no performers, no audience, no leaders, no egos. For the fractal rule of self-similarity to hold, this also means that every house club must share in the cooperative spirit of all clubs. Even a club must resist the temptation to become a "star." Every club and every rave must establish itself as part of one community, or what Fraser calls "the posse."

"It looks sort of like a tribe, but a tribe is somehow geographically separate from the main culture." Fraser finishes his cigarette and feeds his dog some leftover Indian food from dinner. "A posse is very definitely an urban thing. It's just a group of people, sharing technology, sharing all the raves and music as an organization. We even call them 'posses putting on raves.' I really don't think there's such a thing as personal illumination anymore. Either everybody gets it or nobody gets it. I really think that's the truth."

UFO, a collective effort of Fraser's posse, opens in an abandoned set of train tunnels at Camden Lock market. This English party is not at all like a San Francisco or even a New York club. It is an indoor version of the old-style massive outdoor raves. The clothing is reminiscent of a Dead show, but maybe slightly less grungy. Batik drawstring pants, jerseys with fractal patches, love beads, dredlocks, yin-yang T-shirts, and colorful ski caps abound. In the first tunnel, kids sit in small clusters on the dirt floor, smoking hash out of Turkish metal pipes, sharing freshly squeezed orange juice, and shouting above the din of the house music. In one corner, sharply contrasting the medieval attire, ancient stone, and general filth, are sets of brain machines for rent. In the second tunnel, dozens of kids dance to the throbbing house beat. Even though we're in a dungeon, there's nothing "down" about the dancing. With every one of the 120 beats per minute, the dancers articulate another optimistic pulse. Up up up up. The hands explode upward again and again and again. No one dances sexy or cool. They just pulse with the rhythm, smile, and make eye contact with their friends. No need for partners or even groups. This is a free-for-all.

A cluster of young men are hovering near the turntables with the nervous head-nodding and note-taking of streetcorner bookies. They are the DJs, who are each scheduled to spin records for several hours until the party breaks up at dawn. Tonight's music will be mostly hard-core, techno-acid-style house, but there are many house genres to choose from. There's "bleep," which samples from the sounds of the earliest Pong games to extremely high-tech telephone connection and modem signals. New York house, or "garage" sound, is more bluesy and the most soulful; it uses many piano samples and depends on mostly black female singers. There's also "headstrong" house, for the hardest of headbangers; "techno," from Detroit; "dub," coined from Gibson's Neuromancer for Reggae-influenced house; and "new beat," from Northern Europe. Less intense versions of house include "deep" house, with more space on the top layers and a generally airier sound, and the least throbbing kind, "ambient" house, which has no real rhythm at all but simply fills the space with breathy textures of sound. Of course, any or all of these styles may be combined into a single song or mix, along with samples of anything else: Native American "whoops," tribal chanting, evangelists shouting, or even a state trooper calling a mother to inform her "your son is dead."

The DJs consider themselves the technoshamans of the evening. Their object is to bring the participants into a technoshamanic trance, much in the way ancient shamans brought members of their tribes into similar states of consciousness. A DJ named Marcus speaks for the group:

"There's a sequence. You build people up, you take 'em back down. It can be brilliant. Some DJs will get people tweaking into a real animal thing, and others might get into this smooth flow where everyone gets into an equilibrium with each other. But the goal is to hit that magical experience that everyone will talk about afterwards. Between 120 beats a minute and these sounds that the human ear has never heard before, you put them to music and it appeals to some primal level of consciousness."

If it didn't, house would never had made it across the Atlantic to America, where it could manifest not only on a primal level but a marketing one.

chapter ten

## Making the Golden Rule Trendy

Building on the foundations of shamanism in the English house
scene, Americans in San Francisco focus on the techno side. While

the English rave has a quality of medievalism, tribal energy, and Old
World paganism, the American cyber disco is the most modern mutation of bliss induction, and uses whatever means necessary to
bring people into the fractal pattern.

As Jody Radzik explains: "In a really good house experience, you
want to create something like the Electric Kool-Aid Acid Test. You're
trying to create an environment where people can get outside of
themselves. There gets to be a certain point in the night where
people just cut loose. The party just reaches a kind of critical mass.
A synergy of shared consciousness occurs and *boom*. You'll know it.
It'll have a certain sparkle to it." Rising above the muted grit and
gristle of the British pagans, American technojunkies sparkle and
buzz to the same throbbing beat.

Rather than abandoning the television aesthetic and discouraging
the urge to be "hip," club promoters use hipness as bait. Jody
Radzik, who designs house clothing when he's not promoting the
club Osmosis, believes that as house gets on MTV, "a whole new
culture will be created. This will be a result of it being trendy. At the
bottom line, that's what makes things run: narcissism. Trendiness.
I'm always trying to be the trendiest I can be. It's my job. I do design. People get into this because it's a hip new thing. Then maybe
they have an opening and get exposed to new ideas. But the fuel
that's going to generate the growth of this culture is going to be
trendiness and hipness. We're using the cultural marketing thing
against itself. They consume the culture, and get transformed.
House makes the Golden Rule trendy. That's why I'm trying to
create the trendiest sportswear company in the world."

For Radzik, marketing is the perfect transformational tool. He
refuses to discard the system that has dominated until now. Instead,

using marketing, he allows the system to destroy itself. The machinery of the industrial culture—be it technology, economics, or even the more subtle underlying psychological principles and social mechanisms—is turned against itself for its own good. Just as the earth uses its own systems of feedback and iteration to maintain a viable biosphere, house culture exploits the positive feedback loops of marketing and data sharing to further human consciousness. Radzik explains his take on the Gaia hypothesis and McKenna's prediction about the year 2012:

"This bifurcation we're coming up to, this shift, will be the awakening of the planet's awareness. That's the shared belief of the raver camp in the scene. House is the vehicle for disseminating that culture to the rest of the planet."

And how does house conduct this dissemination? By imparting a direct experience of the infinite. In the dance is the eternal bliss moment. The social, audio, and visual sampling of innumerable cultures and times compresses the history and future of civilization into a single moment, when anything seems possible. The discontinuous musical and visual sampling trains the dancers to cope with a discontinuous reality. This is a lesson in coping with nonlinear experience—a test run in Cyberia. A tour of Radzik's clothing studio makes this amply clear. His design arsenal is made up of the illustrations from an eclectic set of texts: *Decorative Art of India,* with pictures of Indian rugs woven into patterns reminiscent of fractals; *Molecular Cell Biology,* with atomic diagrams and electron microscopy of cells and organic molecules; *The Turbulent Mirror: An Illustrated Guide to Chaos Theory and the Science of Wholeness,* with fractals and mathematical diagrams; and *Yantra: The Tantric Symbol of Cosmic Unity,* a collection of hieroglyphics and graffiti-like ancient scribblings. Radzik composes his designs by computer scanning images from books like these and then recombining them. With a keen eye for the similarities of these images, Radzik creates visually what house does musically: the discontinuous sampling of the symbology of bliss over time. The images' similarities give a feeling of comfort and metacontinuity.

Radzik leafs through the pages of his books, scanning images for his next promotional flier. "The arcane and future groove in the now. It's like this fantastic coincidence. House culture is a meeting point for all these different things. Music, finally, is the universal language of love. The nightclub people are the ones who help manifest it into popular culture. What I do is creative anthropology. I observe what's happening in the house culture, and market it back at those people."

It's important to realize that this seemingly mercenary attitude is not inconsistent with house philosophy—in fact, it's not considered mercenary at all. Marketing is merely one of the feedback loops that can promote the house philosophy back into itself, and amplify the experience. It does not suck from the system, it adds to it. Everything relates to house in a self-conscious or "meta" way. House music is not just music, but samples of music recombined into a kind of meta-music.

House is merely a construction—a framework—like language or any other shell. Once something is "in the house," it has been incorporated into the fractal pattern of metaconsciousness, and is a subject of and contributor to the greater schematic. It has become a part of the self-similar universe—one with the galactic dance. That's why the mechanisms for change in house might be "in your face," but they are almost never confrontational. With no dualities, there's nothing to confront. "House, like punk, is an anarchic, rebellious movement," admits Radzik "but it isn't a violent or negative one. If the planet's a living organism, then it doesn't make sense to fuck with each other."

Nick Phillip, twenty-two, a recent emigré from Britain and now the designer for Anarchic Adjustment clothing, is one of Radzik's best friends and conspirators. He agrees wholeheartedly that participants in house are within a construct that allows for global change.

"The kids now are not going to turn on, tune in, drop out. They're going to drop *in*. They're going to infiltrate society and change things from within. They're going to use business, music, or whatever they can to change people. What we're doing speaks for itself. People who are involved in the scene are creating this stuff for themselves."

## Finally Going Mental

Nick has arrived at Toon Town tonight with a supply of his most popular jerseys to be sold at the club's small shop, and he senses that the crowd needs an infusion of life. Heley has moved down from the balcony and is making suggestions to Buck, the rookie DJ who will play until 2:00 A.M. when Jëno, the technoshaman extra-ordinaire, takes over. Nick makes his way to the dance floor like a prizefighter taking the ring, and his pugilistic fury is more reminiscent of punk slamdancing than blissful house explosions. It's called "going mental" and it looks pretty intense, but his enthusiasm is contagious and others are either encouraged enough to join in or frightened off the dance floor altogether. Apparently, part of the reason for the evening's discontinuity is that the venue's previous event, a birthday party for a yuppie named Norman, had not been let out before Toon Town began. Diana and Preston have urged Buck to play the most brutal house music he can find in the hopes of scaring these people away.

Many house regulars have retreated to a "brain machine lounge," where they smoke and chat like members of a bridge club. The room has been set aside for David, a distributor of the "light and sound" devices, to demonstrate the new technology to house kids and maybe make a few sales. The machines consist of a set of goggles and headphones.

"No, it's not virtual reality," David says, probably for the hundredth time, to a newcomer to the room. "It's for relaxation and it can get you high." The goggles flash lights and the headphones beep sounds at exact frequencies, coaxing the brain into particular wave patterns. Ultimately, the brain machines can put the user into the brain state of an advanced meditator.

While the kids play with the machines, David uses his knowledge of new science to flirt with an attractive young woman who is waiting to sample a headset. He is working on an article, he explains, about the physics of David Bohm.

"It's all about discontinuity. Things that look separate in our reality, the explicate order, are all linked together in what Bohm says is the implicate order."

David grabs a pen and draws a picture on the back of his hand to make his point. "If two positrons shoot out of an atom at the same time, and you shove one, the other will move, too."

"How does it know to move? ESP?" asks the girl.

"No. It happens at the same exact time."

A couple of other kids perk up to hear the explanation. "That's because on the implicate order, the positrons are still linked together."

David is interrupted by a fourteen-year-old boy who seems to have a better handle on the idea. "Bohm used the analogy of a goldfish and two TVs. If you put two cameras on a single goldfish, and connected them to two TVs, you might think these were pictures of two different fish. But when one fish moves, the other will move at exactly the same time. It's not because they're connected. It's because they're the same fish!"

"Right," David chimes in, eager to get credit for his knowledge before the girl disappears under the goggles. "The real goldfish in the bowl is the implicate order. The monitors—the way we see and experience it—is the explicate order."

The young boy rolls his eyes. Clearly, David doesn't understand the implications of all this. "Kind of, only, man. The implicate order is timeless truth. It's the way things are. The explicate order is the way they manifest for us in time and three dimensions."

David surrenders to the child's brilliance. "Do you take smart drugs, or what?"

In another private room, actually a kind of DJ lounge, Jody Radzik, a DJ named Pete, and a more flamboyant crowd who call themselves "personal friends of the DJs" smoke pot and talk about similar issues. This is all very heady for a dance club. The center of attention is a state-of-the-art transvestite calling "her"self Gregory, who is trying to understand the merits of trendiness in house culture.

Radzik takes a stab at a simple response: "House makes the Golden Rule trendy. It makes spirituality trendy."

"But is trendiness good?" Gregory asks, her eyes shifting in that tweaking-on-psychedelics-paranoid way.

"The culture is just pushing a pseudopod into a new direction and that's a trend." Radzik says, using the biological metaphor to reassure her. "The ideas have a life of their own. They have an existence outside the human beings. The human beings receive the ideas, and that manifests them."

"That's the implicate order being downloaded into the explicate order!" The girl from the brain machine room has a near religious experience in relating the two conversations. "We were talking about the same thing in there!" She beams. "Two conversations. Distinct on the explicate order, linked on the implicate order. I get it now!"

Pete, the DJ, seems a little uncomfortable when the conversation gets too far into science. Sounding as brainy as he can, he tries to ground everything back to music. "The ecstasy comes through the music. The different polyrhythmic elements and the bass. It's technoshamanism."

Gregory kisses Pete's hands as if she's recognized the messiah. "You're our spiritual leader, aren't you!"

"Well, spiritual leader entails a lot of responsibility and I don't think I want to take that on."

"Nobody does," Radzik says, once again trying to bring it all together. It's the unspoken rule here that if everyone's point of view can be integrated into the same picture, it will all be okay. "Nobody wants to be a spiritual leader. 'Cause everyone's got the access to the E-xperience. Everyone can create their own situation in the social context. House lets all those different experiences get on and synergize."

Gregory's eyes widen. She slowly rises, her arms outstretched, her head falling back. "With E, at 120 cycles a second through our heart, we're dancing. We must dance!"

Radzik's been overpowered. "Well, the E's not responsible, but . . ."

Gregory might be on the verge of a bad trip. She whips her head to face Radzik directly. "It'll literally bust our spines, won't it?"

Radzik tries to regain control of the previously quiet gathering. "That's a lie! Propaganda."

But Gregory doesn't seem to mind her suspicions about permanent neurological damage. She clenches her fists together as if to hold back an orgasm. "The peak threshold is bliss, is E, is now. We've condensed it down. It's powerpacked. It's now. We all, man and woman, we come together and dance. All our technology. We've heard of the side effects. E diminishes a vital chemical in our bodies every time we take it. The chemical is the essence of life. This is a gift which cannot be replaced. We're taking this fluid and spending it. The E is undermining our very existence. I feel a little bit of my life force being spent each time. It's bliss. You're dancing it. E gathers all your life's bliss at one time. If the world were supposed to end, we'd come together, take E, and dance!"

Gregory's allusion to a recent study linking MDMA to spinal fluid reduction in mammals, coupled with her oversimplified E-xuberance for the dance, gets everyone a little uncomfortable. Is this the transformed being we've been working to create? Luckily, the moment is interrupted by a young visual artist and video wizard who just happens to be distributing an MAO inhibitor called Syrian Rue. Radzik introduces me as, "Don't worry, he's cool," which garners me four of the capsules. I put them in my pocket and thank the boy, but he's already busy rigging a projector to show a film loop on a wall near the dance floor. It's a ten-second cycle of two boys fighting over a microscope. I ask Radzik about the pills I've been given.

"It's called Syrian Rue. Mark Heley will be able to tell you a lot more about it. It has to be taken with other psychedelics. It has a synergistic effect. It's made from a bark." Not enough information to merit sampling. I leave it in my pocket and work my way back out into the club. I search for the periphery so that I may observe but not participate . . . fully. Leaning against a noncommittal wall near the edge of the club is Bob, an Asian computer programmer from Oakland whom I met last week at Mr. Floppy's, where he operated the camera for some television interviews and got bitten by the house bug. He continues a conversation we had been having there, as if there were no break in continuity:

"Thought is a distraction of the moment. Whenever we're in a space we're processing information. In our reality, we're bombarded with information. So in Reichian terms, we put this armor on. You know the song, 'I Wanna Be Sedated'? I think a lot of people are anesthetized by their surroundings. It takes some really piercing hard information to break that. Like piercing your cheeks. If you get Zen, you've got to let go, and let it all come in. But if you let it all in, you go crazy. But if you let it come in without processing it, without calling it good or bad . . . people who label things bad have got a lot of heaviness. Go Zen about it. There is no black or white, then you can let everything in."

I give him one of my capsules of Syrian Rue and move on.

## Engineering the Synchronization Beam

Our evening at Toon Town is getting into full swing. Most of Norman's birthday partiers are gone, and several hundred hard-core house people have crowded onto the dance floor. Buck, the novice

DJ, is spinning well, and steering the energy toward deeper, techno-acid house. Nick, the rave pugilist, is on a small stage pumping his fists into the air, and the laser is finally functioning.

Meanwhile, on a balcony, Bryan Hughes, the cyberspace guide, leads a young man through his first virtual reality experience. Cap'n'Crunch uses one of his cameras to capture an image of the boy in his VR goggles. Another of Crunch's video leads comes straight from the virtual reality machine. He uses his Video Toaster to combine the two images and then projects a composite video picture onto a giant screen above the dance floor. The resulting image is one of the boy actually appearing to move through the virtual reality space he is unfolding in the computer. Superimposed on that picture are further video images of people on the dance floor watching the giant projection. Gregory notices me staring at the self-referential computer-video infinity. "Works kind of like a fractal, doesn't it?" I have to agree.

But Bruce Eisner, MDMA expert, who stares at the same video depiction of virtual reality, shakes his head. He is amused but un-convinced. "Maybe one day the mystical vision will be realized in some kind of neurological link-up or a virtual reality. Technology does have a great promise. It could become seamless, so that what we think of today as magic will eventually be done by technology, and eventually we won't even see the technology. A neo-Garden of Eden made possible by technology. But the main rub is human nature. That's where I have a problem with the virtual reality people. I was at the Whole Life Expo, and Timothy [Leary] was there with John Barlow and Ken Goffman [R.U. Sirius] and they were doing a panel on virtual reality and I sat there for an hour and a half and lis-tened to them talk about virtual reality the way they talked about LSD in the sixties—it was this thing that was intrinsically liberating. You hook yourself up to this thing and automatically you're bet-ter—you got it. And so I asked him a question. I said, 'It seems to me that technology can be used for good or for bad. In the sixties, Leary told us he was looking for the cure for human nature. How is a new media intrinsically good?'

"Leary looked at me and said, 'Bruce, I'm going to talk to you as I would to a ten-year-old child.' And then he went on to ex-plain how when we have virtual reality, no one will have to fly anymore. No one will have to go to Japan to make a deal. You can do it in Hawaii on the beach. Fine. But why is that intrinsically liberating?"

Eisner seems almost sad. He's not in tune with the same harmonic as these kids but can, deep down, remember the sixties and his own acid experiences. He refuses to be lulled into that false optimism again. He stares out, losing himself in thought.

Meanwhile, the pulse on the dance floor deepens. I can feel the bass passing through my body like the subsonic frequencies of an as-yet-uninvented kidney therapy. The frenzy of the crowd iterates back to the DJ, and in turn to Mark at the laser. The walls are covered with projected images of fractals, tribes dancing, the fight over the microscope, a cartoon smiley shoots at evil, attacking letters. Another monitor displays the virtual reality bombardments of attacker pilots in the Gulf War, intercut with tribal dancing and the wild computer holographics of a tape called "Video Drug." The strobe flashes like a brain machine.

"Do you know where I can get some Syrian Rue?" asks a young house girl named Mimi, pulling me out of my trance and into another. I recognize her from other house events; this makes her part of our posse. Her face is soft and young—almost supernaturally so. It's as if she isn't a regular human being but an extremely human being. Her eyes are large and clear, almost like a Disney character's. . . . Then it hits me! She's a *toon!* She's a soft and squishy new evolved being! The iterations have created a new human. I produce the coveted capsule from my shirt pocket and hand it to her. She pops it in her mouth and washes it down with a choline drink, then hops back out onto the dance floor. It's not as if I could have asked her to dance. One doesn't dance with someone. One just dances. No purpose. No agenda.

A smell like flowers. From where? Lavender water. Who? Earth Girl! She's arrived with her Smart Bar and has already set up. At her side is Galactic Greg, one of her brightly clad bartenders. Earth Girl embraces me as if recognizing me from lifetimes before this one, and pours me a complimentary Cybertonic. It nicely washes down the L-pyroglutamate I had earlier. I offer her one of my two remaining Syrian Rue capsules, but Lila Mellow-Whipkit stops her from accepting: "You've got to be careful with MAO inhibitors."

Meanwhile, Galactic Greg begins explaining his own and Earth Girl's mission:

"Earth Girl, Galactic Greg, Psychic Sarah, Disco Denise, Audrey Latina, Computer Guy, and his assistant Dynama. We all make up the Foxy Seven, and we are environmental crime fighters. And performers. Our performances are rituals to augment our psychic powers, and then in return we use our psychic powers to help change the world. We are building the infrastructure right now. Everything's all happening so rapidly and really naturally. All these people in the infrastructure are coming together like a big family reunion—all the star-seeded children."

I'm not sure how seriously to take Galactic Greg, for whom metaphor and reality seem to have merged. I wonder if he realizes that this will be the Foxy Seven's last night at Toon Town. Earth Girl has already made her deal with Big Heart City, and Mark Heley has already signed contracts with Chris for the new and improved Nutrient Cafe.

But right now none of that seems to matter. Toon Town is in absolutely full swing, and not even the apocalypse could break the spell of the technoshamanic trance. I work my way up to the laser controls, where I find Mark Heley and one of his assistants dancing as they furiously pound the consoles. They are one with the technology. Just at the moment that Jëno, who is now the DJ, shifts from a hard, agro, techno sound to a broad, airy, feminine, ambient one, the laser transforms from a sharp-edged flurry into a large hollow tunnel cut through the fog in the room. All hands on the dance floor are raised. Another sixteen bars of techno layered with tribal rhythms begins the 120-beat-per-minute drone once again, drawing in anyone who hasn't already reached the dance floor. Screams and whoops. Whistles blowing. Chanting. We're at the peak. Whatever it is that goes on at a house party that everyone talks about later is happening now.

Mark has the uncanny ability to articulate the event as it occurs, but the din requires that he shout, and his Oxbridge elocution gives way to a more urban, East End accent.

"It's a transposition of the fractal/harmonic. Every Toon Town is a psychedelic event. We're the transition team. It's like a Mayan temple, and acts as a relay station. An antenna. It's a harmonic thing—

beaming out something. It's a landing beacon for starships. We are trying to attract something down. Through time, toward us."

Hands continue to reach into the air, and dancers look up at the ceiling . . . or past the ceiling. Are they looking for the UFOs? Do they somehow hear what Mark is saying? The music shifts back and forth between a familiar "garage" house sound to an amazingly dense assemblage of electronic orchestral thrusts.

"Every new piece of house music is another clue. A new strand of the DNA pattern. A new piece of information. We need to create a synchronization wave for the planet. House is synchronic engineering."

Mark is referring to a recently revived Mayan idea that the planet, in the year 2012, will have passed through the galactic time wave of history. Time itself will end as the planet moves up to a new plane of reality.

The weird orchestral sound gives way to a more ambient passage. A few dancers leave the floor and head to the Smart Bar. Others browse the clothing boutique and bookshop that Diana has set up.

"Media viruses work at the same level," Mark continues. "Smart drugs, life extension, house, acid, and VR most importantly exist in people's imaginations. This is a clue. Mayan mathematics just came into existence and disappeared. We're in the endgame. This is postapocalyptic. We're living under the mushroom cloud. Being busted at precisely 11:30 last week. It was a group sacrifice—just like the Mayans."

Mark's assistant nudges him to play with the laser a little more. The crowd is getting hyped again, and Jëno, accordingly, is playing more "agro" beats.

"I consider myself to be more of a technoshaman now than when I was DJing. You don't need to be the one controlling the decks. There's a feedback energy loop going on between the people there—it's just a mind thing. The DJs that we work with are just tuned in to these frequencies. You can influence the fractal pattern at a different vortex, a different corner."

We look down at the sea of bodies. The pattern their bright clothes makes on the floor looks something like one of the fractals being projected onto the wall. Look closer and the pattern repeats itself in the movements of individual dancer's bodies, then again in the patterns printed on their T-shirts. The boy in the VR television loop discovers the torus in Bryan's demo tour. The whole screen turns to cosmic stars. The dancers respond. The DJ responds. The lasers respond. The pattern iterates, feeds back, absorbs, adjusts, and feeds back again. Heley translates:

"At a house event, the dance floor is really a very complex fractal pattern, consisting of the entirety of all the people there, and their second-to-second interactions, and everyone is influencing everyone else in a really interesting way. A really nonverbal way. You can just be yourself, but you can redefine yourself, moment to moment. That's the essence of the dance."

Jëno takes off his headphones for a moment and stares at the crowd. Rather than look for another record or adjust the control of the mix, he closes his eyes and begins to dance, flailing his arms in the air.

"Jëno just tunes in to the frequency that's already there and reiterates it. He is anticipating the energy changes before they happen, not because he's tuned in to the records, but because he's tuned in to a sort of psychic template which exists above the people that are there and unifies them. It's the transpersonal essence of what's going on."

Mark has described the house version of Bohm's laws of the implicate and explicate order. The dance floor is the explicate order, and the DJ is the link from the dancers to their implicate whole. They only think they are separate goldfish because they experience life in old-fashioned space-time. Through the iterated and reiterated samples of music, they regain access to the experience of total unification. It is religious bliss. All is one. And, of course, this realization occurs simultaneously on many levels of consciousness.

"Everything is important," Mark continues. "The Ecstasy, the lights, even the configuration of the planets. The dance is a holistic experience. You're there in your totality, so duality is irrelevant. It's where your body is mind. It's a question of reintegration. You dance yourself back into your body. It's got a lot to do with self-acceptance. There's no level of separation as there is in words, when there's always a linguistic separation between subject and objects. The song *is* the meaning. It lets you avoid a lot of the semantic loops that tie people in to things like career, and other fictional ghosts that are generated by our society for the purpose of mass control. It's a different frequency that you tune in to when you dance than the one that's generally broadcast by TV shows, the media, politics."

This new frequency, finally, is the frequency of the apocalypse. Terence McKenna's 2012, the Mayan calendar, and the great, last rave of all time are all part of one giant concrescence. Over the loudspeakers, samples of Terence McKenna's meandering voice now mix with the rest of the soundtrack. He's on a house record, his own words helping the dancers to tunnel toward the overmind, as the overmind lovingly drills backward through time toward them.

"If we imagine ourselves in four-dimensional space-time," Heley explains, "in that very dubious construct of Einsteinian space-time—we're sort of swimming towards the object from which the frequency emanates. It's like these are fragments of DNA information that are squeezed into a certain specific time frame. It's a constant exploration and discovery of how those resonate with our own DNA information in that particular moment of time. Basically it's that fact—and the rich sampling of all the moments placed within that context—that gives you this amazingly flexible framework for reintegrating yourself into your body and also communicating as a group. You're moving to a certain time-space and you're in a group state of consciousness. You're at one with it and you become the moment."

I realize that Mark's perception and retelling is LSD-enhanced; he's just beginning to feel the full effect of a hit he took about an hour ago. Still, he's concerned that it's not strong enough to take him to any kind of "edge." I offer him my two remaining Syrian Rue capsules. He pops them down immediately, explaining that they enhance the effect of other psychedelics and are related to ayahuasca, one of the main ingredients (along with DMT) used by shamans to make the most potent brews. I surmise that it puts a new twist on things the way one might turbocharge a car with NO2, add salt to spaghetti water to raise its boiling point, or throw a starship into warp drive. In an ominous synchronicity, down on the dance floor Diana helps a disoriented girl to a chair at the side of the room.

Mark goes on, the new chemical accelerating his speech toward the climax of his cosmic drama: "The human body has not been fully danced. We don't dance our full dance yet. Time is accelerating towards this point in the year 2012 when the story of the human race will have been unfolded. We're reaching a bifurcation point. There's so much instability in our current paradigm that it's just shaking apart. A lot of people I know feel we're reaching an endgame. There's that feeling in the air. I feel myself being dragged through different time zones and it's intense. When you surrender to it, it becomes even stronger. Exponentially so. It's amazing."

But what about the people who haven't been exposed to house? All those people Diana so desperately hopes to bring into the scene before it's all over? If they aren't dancing when the spaceships or the galactic beam comes, won't they be left out? How are people to guide themselves toward Cyberia? As Mark tries to reassure me, I become conscious that my questioning may be starting to affect his trip.

"Well, bliss is the most rigorous master you could imagine," he says. "It's not even the morphogenetic field of humanity." Then suddenly his face registers a new thought. "If your antenna is finely tuned, you'll find it. In a way, everyone is tuned in. One point in humanity rises, all of humanity rises." He adds, as if he's never thought this before: "But I imagine that there are some towns in the Midwest where a house record has never even been played."

These kinds of conceptual uncertainties grow into physically realized landmines for the shamanic warrior. Mark senses his own doubts, as the Syrian Rue drives his trip down a frictionless psychic tunnel. Instinctively, he hands the laser controls to an assistant. He stares at me intently. "There's only so much energy. My only tack is to just keep my head down and push ahead. Diana may bring in more people someday. But until then, I've got to do what I can with what I've got. We'll struggle and struggle until we give up. Then it will break through."

He works his way to the dance floor. The bodies are writhing, peaking. It is in the middle of this swirl that Mark reaches the highest part of his trip. He realizes that the fractal pattern that surrounds him is of his own making. The synesthetic congruities between movement, sound, and light bring a feeling of certainty and wholeness. His body and mind are united, as he literally steps under the looking glass that he created. Both God and Adam at once, his very existence literally dissolves the fiction of creator and created, beginning and end. He has constructed his own womb and stepped inside. In his self-conception is the essence of timelessness. The beginning is the end.

But timelessness is only temporary. How long can this last? In that very wondering is the initial descent. The perfection of the fractal pattern has begun to decay. Reentry into time is imminent. Has he become the UFO?

Damage can occur on the way back. Downloading the cogent information requires every shamanic skill he can muster. The Syrian Rue has caused a kind of time phasing. Mark searches for a way to bring himself back into crystalline alignment, even if at a different frequency from before. He doesn't care how he comes back, as long as he can find the way home. His body is gone, dispersed throughout the room.

He tries to recreate his body by finding his point of view. A point of reference can serve as the seed. But his field of vision is compressing and expanding . . . expanding as far out as the sun and even the galactic core. He is riding through the precarious Mayan Tzolkin calendar. He closes his eyes and fixes on the galactic core— on that time a year or so ago, tripping in a field, in the sun. He was like a dolphin under water, swimming under the surface yet still warmed by the sun. It was beautiful. And as he lay there, a new Gaia program came down from the sun to the earth, and needed his head to do it. The light used him to download the precious information. His own body. Strange ganglia sprouted from the back of his head straight into the soil beneath him. Beautiful.

But no. That's not what's going on here. Everything is phase shifted. It's out of control. No panic or all is lost. He could spin out and be gone forever. Mark must get down carefully. He doesn't care what he brings back anymore, as long as he gets back. He realizes that somehow he's gotten himself onto a flight of steps. Real steps, somewhere in the club. Perfect image. It's where he is. Stuck on the stairway. It's life or death now. Bliss is merciless. The rigorous master. The music continues to pound and eventually draws him back into the vortex. Everything spins. This is dangerously disorienting. He's completely losing polarity. He's on the steps, but which way is he facing? Is he going up or down? The back and the front are the same!

But wait! This isn't so bad. There's complete knowledge of what's on both sides! He can see in front and behind at the same time! There's no duality—but, alas, no orientation, either. There's no up the stairs or down. No before the trip or after. No higher than the peak or lower. Suddenly everything is static. Paralyzed. Stillness.

It is in this brief fulcrum of stability that the transmission occurs. Like an electrical earthquake, an alien thing passes up through Heley's muscles, bringing his whole being up into a faster, shamanic shape-shifting frequency. This is the state of being, Heley realizes, in which master shamans turn into pumas or eagles or visit the dead.

Suddenly, then, it's all clear. The duality is not within life as judgments or ideas. Life itself is one side of it. It's life itself that is rooted in dimension. That's one side of the whole thing. The explicate order. That's the place where will is necessary. ("I'll just keep my head down and press on.")

The *will*. Mark summons his will, knowing that this navigation through the iron gate of the moment back down into dimensional space-time requires it. He *must* summon his will. He senses movement.

He passes through the I Ching sequence as if it were a cloud formation—the effortless binary expression of the universe. Ahh, he realizes, the creation of time and history were necessary. Without them, we'd never have created will. We need the will in order to move toward something. But what? Toward 2012. Toward the overmind. The galactic event. But now he must continue his descent.

He passes over a shamanic conference. Eight old men sitting in a spotlight. He is offered an apprenticeship by these dead warriors, but refuses. He's made the right choice, he thinks, and begins to travel faster. He's gained either power or stupidity.

He just needs to remember that everything is fractal; he just needs to find the fractal pattern on any level and the rest will fall into place. But stretch out too far and the pattern breaks. The illusion of personal reality is gone, and so goes the person with it.

Diana, Preston, and Nick come to the rescue, finding Heley stuck on the stairs, trembling. He can't even speak to them, but just their focus is helping. As they stare at Heley and call to him, he becomes anchored in the present. Then all the Heleys on each of the fractal levels are able to redefine into shape. He finally finds himself back on the stairs, leaning against the wall. Preston looks at him and asks simply, "Are you going up or down?"

"If I only knew," Mark says, grinning.

"Mark had a really, really bad trip," Nick Phillip announces at his design studio the next day. "He took some Syrian Rue and LSD. He got a weird side effect and he was cog-wheeling. It took us two hours to get him into the car. He wouldn't let us touch him!" Nick dials Heley's number angrily. Mark picks up the phone after about ten rings.

"You should fucking reevaluate what you're doing!" Nick scolds him.

"It was brilliant, Nick. Just brilliant!"

"So brilliant!? You shouldn't do those bloody MAO inhibitors! You could die, you know!"

Mark hides his extreme weariness by speaking in clipped sentences.

"I experienced some polarities, that's all"

Nick covers the mouthpiece and talks to the room and to the air: "That's *sooo* Mark Heley!"

"There were just not enough people to absorb the beam," Mark explains logically, "and I had to do it alone."

The responsibilities of the technoshaman never end. Like the shamans of ancient cultures, they must translate the wave forms of other dimensions down into the explicate reality for the purposes of forecasting the future and charting a safe path through it. And as Heley's adventure indicates, it's networking the potential of this beam that defines success in spiritual Cyberia.

## chapter eleven

There is a growing spiritual subculture dedicated to channeling the beam, and it is characterized by pagan ethics, reliance on technology, and interconnectivity through vast networks. The neopagan revival incorporates ancient and modern skills in free-for-all sampling of whatever works, making no distinction between occult magic and high technology. In the words of one neopagan, "The magic of today is the technology of tomorrow. It's all magic. It's all technology."

Again, it's easiest to get a fix on the neopagan revival back in England, where the stones still resonate from the murders of over 50 million pagans throughout the Dark Ages. Fraser Clark, pater of the Zippy movement ("zen-inspired pagan professionals"), sees the current surge of pagan spirit in the cyberian subculture as the most recent advance in an ancient religious struggle. Youth culture is the only answer.

As Fraser prepares to head to work (it's about one in the afternoon) he invites me to read what he's just typed onto his computer screen:

```
EVER SINCE THEY MANAGED TO BLACKBALL THE HIPPY
TO DEATH, THE CORRECT MODE OF YOUTH (AS HOPE
AND CONSCIENCE OF THE CULTURE) HAS BEEN
SYSTEMATICALLY SCHIZOPHRENED FROM ITS HISTORICAL
ROOTS. AND WE'RE TALKING ABOUT ROOTS THAT GO
BACK THROUGH THE PUNKS, HIPPIES, REBELS, BEATS,
BOHEMIANS, SOCIALISTS, ROMANTICS, ALCHEMISTS, THE
SHAKERS AND THE QUAKERS, WITCHES, HERETICS AND,
RIGHT BACK IN THE ROOTS, PAGANS. YET THE HUMAN
SPIRIT STILL REVITALIZED ITSELF! WE PAGANI (LATIN
FOR NONMILITARY PERSONNEL, BY THE WAY) HAVE BEEN
COOPERATING AND BREEDING UNSTOPPABLY, TOGETHER
WITH OUR PERSONAL GODS AND SUCCUBI LIKE PERSONAL
COMPUTERS! UNTIL NOW, JUST WHEN THE ROMAN
```

CHRISTIAN MONOTHEISTIC MIND STATE REACHES OUT TO
GRASP THE WHOLE PLANET BY THE SHORT HAIRS, THE
ALTERNATIVE CULTURE BIRTHS ITSELF.[1]

Fraser has dedicated his life to the spread of pagan consciousness, specifically through the youth culture, which he sees as our last hope for planetary survival. "The system cannot be allowed to go on for another ten years or it really will destroy us all, it's as simple as that," Fraser tells me as we walk with his hairless dog from his house in Hampstead to Camden Lock Market. His tone is always conspiratorial, reverberating a personal paranoia left over from the sixties, and an inherited paranoia passed down through pagan history. "If we had this conversation in the thirteenth or fourteenth century, we'd be burned at the stake for it. We'd never even be able to imagine things being as good as they are now . . . or as bad as they are now." Fraser brings a broad perspective to the archaic revival, helping would-be pagans to see their role in the historical struggle against the forces of monotheistic tyranny.

"The actual witch-hunts came in like waves of hysteria just like drug stories in the press do now. You know, every so often along comes a story about witches in their midst so let's burn a few. So it came in waves. Another thing that came in waves is the plague. The black death." I can tell that Fraser wants me to draw the parallel myself. Deep down, this man is a teacher. His theory (which has been espoused elsewhere in pagan literature) is that the sudden rises in black death can always be traced to a surge in witch killing and cat killing. The church would reward people who killed cats because they were associated with witches. The rat population would be free to increase, and more plague would spread. As he puts it, "Hysteria caused the plague." Meanwhile, our current and potential plagues—AIDS, pollution, nuclear war—are seen to be caused by similar repression of the pagan spirit, which he seeks to revitalize in the youth culture of England, in any way possible.

To this end, Fraser has become a spokesman and advocate for the modern, urban neopagans. Like both their own ancestors and the most current mathematicians and physicists, they have abandoned organized rules of logic in favor of reality hacking—riding the waves, watching for trends, keeping an open mind, and staying connected to the flow. It's not important whether the natural system is a forest, an interdimensional plane, a subway, or a computer network. For the neopagan, exploration itself is a kind of understanding, and the process of exploring is the meaning of life.

## Interdimensional Scrolling

One urban neopagan, Green Fire, is a witch who works for Earth Girl at the Smart Drugs Lounge under Big Heart City and as a psychic for a 900-number phone service called Ultraviolet Visions. The house scene is like a self-similar hypertext adventure. Each new person is like a new screen, with its own menus and links to other screens. But they're all somehow united in purpose and direction. Although each member of the global neopagan network goes on his own visionquests, they are all on a collective pilgrimage toward that great chaos attractor at the end of time.

Today, Earth Girl and other members of her Foxy Seven are busy remodeling the new basement home of the Smart Bar. Toys and trinkets are everywhere. In one corner sits a six-foot geodesic dome lined with pink fur and foam, dubbed the Space Pussy. The soft being inside, who believes he's a direct descendant of the magical "Shee" beings, is Green Fire, an impish and androgynous twenty-something-year-old whose Peter Pan gestures belie the gravity with which he approaches his mission: to save the planet by bringing back the Shee, the ancient fairie race that originally inhabited Ireland before the planet was overrun with the "Naziish alien energy" that has been directing human activity for the past few millennia.

Green Fire believes we are fast approaching a kind of spiritual dawn. "There is more light now than ever before. Even Joe Blow now is starting to experience a little bit of magic through technology." Green Fire seamlessly blends the magic of the ancients with the technology of the future. "High technology and high magic are the same thing. They both use tools from inner resources and outer resources. Magic from the ancient past and technology from the future are really both one. That is how we are creating the present; we're speeding up things, we are quickening our energies; time and space are not as rigid as they used to be; the belief system isn't there. Those who did control it have left the plane; they have been forced out because it no longer is their time. Those of us who know how to work through time and space are using our abilities to *bend* time and space into a reality that will benefit people the most."

So, like house music and its ability to "condense" time through juxtaposition of historical "bytes," Green Fire's witchery gives him an active role in the creation of the moment. The ancients call forward in time to the present, giving Green Fire the techniques of sorcery, while the wave form of the future calls back in time through computer technology.

Earth Girl joins us in the Space Pussy to make sure Green Fire is presenting himself in the best possible light. Diana, from Toon Town, follows her in. Diana has come to the Smart Lounge as an emissary of peace. The subtext never reaches the surface, but Diana's presence is threefold: first, to understand exactly why Earth Girl left Toon Town for Big Heart City; second, to gather as many facts as possible about Heley's competition; and third, and most apparently, to make sure everyone stays friends. No matter how stiff the competition and how hot the tempers, everyone is in this thing together. There's only one galactic beam.

Giving the gift of vulnerability as a peace offering, Diana mentions Heley's "bad" trip last night at Toon Town.

"He doesn't have the tools to be traveling that far out," Earth Girl responds in a genuinely caring tone.

No one says anything for a while. The Space Pussy, too, is silent, itself an emblem of Earth Girl's betrayal of Toon Town and her ex-boyfriend, Heley. Diana shifts uncomfortably: Why would he leave her for me? Earth Girl, knowing she's being stared at, fingers the lace on her flowing satin dress—a striking contrast to Diana's tomboyish overalls and baseball cap.

Diana lights a cigarette and laughs. They all pretend the moment of silence was spent contemplating Mark's weird Syrian Rue adventure. "He doesn't feel bad today. He even thinks he may have touched the ability to shape-shift."

"We humans are all shape-shifters," Green Fire comments, getting the conversation back on track. "We just need to learn to access our DNA codes. It's very computer-oriented. We are computers; our minds are computers; our little cells are computers. We are bio-organic computers. We are crystals. We are made out of crystals. I even put powdered crystals into the smart drinks."

Green Fire's words seem a little hollow given the emotional reality of Diana and Earth Girl's conflict, so the two girls leave. But despite its inability to tackle everyday, real-world strife, Green Fire's cyber pagan cosmology beautifully demonstrates the particular eclecticism of the new spirituality. It is not an everything-plus-the-kitchen-sink grab bag of religious generalizations, but a synthesis of old and new ideas whose organization is based on a postquantum notion of time. The juxtaposition of magic and computers, shape-shifting and DNA, crystals and pharmaceuticals, is itself indicative of a time compression preceding the great leap into hyperspace, or timelessness.

But until that leap, the realities of romance and business still shape the experiences of cyberians. Diana and Earth Girl must still cope with the fact that they're in the same business and have shared the same boyfriend. Green Fire must cope with the fact that his goddess, Earth Girl, will eventually realize the futility of her comicbook-style leadership, dissolve the Foxy Seven, and go into business for herself.

But in the Space Pussy, for the time being, all is quite well. In the safety of his cocooned emotional playground, Green Fire is free to take daring leaps into interdimensional zones that a parent, professional, or reality-based adult would not. Instead of using Heley's psychedelics and house music, or a hacker's home computer and modem, he practices his magic using techniques from the Celtic shamanic traditions. (Unless, of course, he just happens upon a fairie ring of mushrooms in the forest.)

He'll begin with a purification ritual and an herbal bath, then some breathing techniques and chanting for an hour or so, which brings him into a psychedelic clarity.

"Everything mundane leaves so I know I'm in the trance. I'll cast the circle and invoke the elements. Sometimes I'll have to do a dance to help tap in to some of the Celtic energies. Then I will begin the journey down. Now, that's just like—that's something close to mushrooms, LSD, or DMT."

Green Fire's fairie realm is also very close to the computer experience. His description of this world, his iconic presence, the way he moves about, as well as the hypertext quality of his experiences, make it sound like a cyberspace fantasy game.

"They'll take me inside. Sometimes I feel like I'm falling or flying. Sometimes I just *whoosh,* and I'm there. Depends on what kind of passage it is. Then I'm there, and it's a real place. Usually once I get there my body is still in this dimension. I've gone through my cells, my DNA, and I've opened a doorway and I've gone to that other dimension. So I will need to have an archetype there. It's a dream-like state, but it's also very physical. This is the strange part. I can feel stuff there through that body. I can smell, I can taste, I can touch, and I can hear. My guides will be there, my totems—and they usually guide me to certain cities I need to go to."

Just as I was guided through virtual reality by gentle Bryan Hughes, Green Fire is guided by his fairies through Celtic Cyberia. This is a virtual world! Each doorway is another screen. Each totem allows him to "load" more "worlds." Through an archetypal virtual suit, he can see and feel his hyperdimensional reality. And, like Mark Heley in the shamanic fractal, or me in the Intel virtual reality demo program, he must prove he is a worthy interdimensional traveler. As McKenna would say, thoughts are "beheld." As Heley would say, "bliss is a rigorous master."

"Whatever I think becomes real. Just to even get there I have to be very clear. My emotions and my thoughts steer me. Really, in-stead of me moving, the place moves. I think something, and then I'm kind of like, there. So if I start feeling dark and weird, I find my-self in the dark places of that land. And there are dark places."

Things get eerie. Green Fire describes how realities "scroll" by as on a computer screen, and it's as if he's describing the thickest places in the "ice" in William Gibson's *Neuromancer,* where a hacker/cowboy can lose his soul. Green Fire moves through the fairie matrix like a hacker through the network, from system to system, always leaving a back door open. But Green Fire is making his systems breaches without the protection of David Troup's Body-guard program. Instead, he must depend on his mental discipline. He's in the ultimate designer reality, where his thoughts become what's real, whether he likes it or not.

"It's a discipline to keep my emotions in check—to keep certain archetypal images in my mind. I have to keep them because they're doorways, and if I don't have those doorways positioned correctly, they could lead me to a place that I wouldn't want to be. It's like a puzzle or a maze and I could get lost. Magic is a dangerous thing. There's a new age belief that you can never get hurt; that's not true. You can get hurt very bad. Not everybody should do magic. Even those of us who are made to do it, we fuck up quite a bit. I fuck up quite a bit."

While a computer hacker who ventures into the wrong system might find the Secret Service knocking at his door, a witch who ventures into the wrong dimension risks psychological or spiritual damage. But just as the most aggressive cyberian hackers make sacramental use of psychedelics to augment their computer skills, adventurous witches make use of the computer net to keep informed of pagan technologies. The communications and computer networks are a self-similar extension of the pagan need for a map to hyperspace.

Green Fire's journeys through the multidimensional "net" are also reflected in the way he conducts business through the communications net on earth. Most of his income is generated through a national psychic phone service, Ultraviolet Visions, which offers psychic readings, astrology, tarot card analysis and other psychic services through a 900 number. The office in which the psychics operate is decorated in what Earth Girl likes to call "New Delphic Revival"—twenty-two stations around a big glass table with pillars, each station corresponding to one of the twenty-two cards of the tarot's major arcana. Of course, the billing is handled by computer through the phone company.

# chapter twelve

## Gardeners Ov Thee Abyss

The strength of any magic in Cyberia is directly proportional to that magic's ability to permeate the network. Like cultural viruses, the techniques of magic are thought to gain strength as they gain acceptance by larger groups of people. Computer technology fits in to cyberian spirituality in two ways: as a way to spread magic, and as a magic itself.

Thee Temple Ov Psychick Youth is a nett-work for the dissemination of majick (their spellings) through the culture for the purpose of human emancipation. TOPY (rhymes with soapy) began as a fan club and ideological forum for Genesis P. Orridge, founder of industrial band Throbbing Gristle and its house spin-off Psychic TV, but soon developed into a massive cultish web of majick practitioners and datasphere enthusiasts. They are the most severe example of techno-paganism, consciously stretching backward through medievalism to ancient pagan spirituality and up through computer technology to the creation of a global, informational being. They predate and maybe even spawned house culture, but have remained pretty separate from the lovey-dovey, soft and squishy Ecstasy crowd.

All male initiates to TOPY take the name Coyote, and all women Kali. The name is followed by a number so that members can identify one another. Kali is the name of a female sex goddess known as "the destroyer"; the coyote is found in many mythologies, usually symbolizing wisdom and an adventurous nature.

The nett-work consists of access points, or stations, which are post office boxes, fax machines, computer modems, or 800 phone numbers. Each access point gathers information from places off the web, then distributes it throughout the network, and in turn takes information from the web and makes it available to local members. As one initiate explains: "The main memory can be accessed from the stations, then downloaded via correspondents through Xeroxes." Or, in English, someone reads his mail or plays his message machine, then types it up and gives copies to his friends. "The main memory" refers to the TOPY idea that all its members compose a single, informational being.

The information passed about consists of "majickal techniques" from drugs and incantations to computer hardware and engineering tricks, as well as general TOPY philosophy. In some ways, the entire TOPY network is really just an elaborate metaphor for the postmodern Gaian brain. The information they pass around is much less important than the way in which it is passed. TOPY documents are immediately recognizable because they spell words in obsolete or newly made-up ways. This is seen as a way of retaking control of language, which has been used and abused for so long by the illegitimate power mongers of Western culture, who are directing the planet toward certain doom.

However well TOPY has permeated the net, its members rarely peep up out of the underground into the light of day and consensus reality. For all their 800-number accessibility, very few cyberians regularly socialize with flesh-and-blood TOPY members. It's almost as if their presence as human beings is less important than their presence as a cultural virus or informational entity.

## All on the Same Side

Today, Diana is on Haight Street, distributing fliers for the next Toon Town. Unlike most promoters, who target "likely" clubgoers—kids with house-style clothes, computer-hippies, college cliques—Diana is dedicated to spreading the house phenomenon to the uninitiated. A freespirited club girl with a slight Mother Teresa complex, Diana is the female, emotional, caring counter to Toon Town's otherwise heady patriarchy, especially now that Earth Girl works at Big Heart City. Each human to whom she hands a flier is a potential link to dozens more. The more people brought in to the scene, she reasons, the more it grows, the more they grow, the further enlightened and loving the world is. This is the philosophy that got Diana to leave protective campus life at Berkeley and move into the city to promote Toon Town full-time.

When Diana approaches an unlikely cluster of young men clad in leather and army fatigues and smoking a joint in front of a record store, she unwittingly hits the networking jackpot. Her Toon Town promotional bill is snarfed up by the trio, who exchange it for a leaflet of their own, "The Wheel of Torture," a poem by Coyote 107:

# EYE WAS ON THEE WHEEL OV TORTURE

ON THAT TABLE, I WAS SPUN LIKE AZ A VORTICE. IN AN ACT OV ATTRACTING VIOLENCE TO MY BEING. THEE VIOLENCE WAS EXPRESSED THROUGH TORTURE, WHICH BECAME AN ACT OV ALCHEMICAL PROCESS. MY SENSES WERE BEING PULVERIZED. THROWN INTO SHOCK. PULVERIZATION WAS BEING SHOVED DOWN MY THROAT. EVERY OUNCE OV MY EMOTION WAS NULLIFIED. STEPPED ON AND SPIT ON. TOTAL APPLICATION OV NEGATION. TOTAL ACT OV NON SERVITUDE. REJECTING MY OWN PERSONALITY. NOT LETTING MY EGO TAKE KONTROL. VIOLATING MY OWN EGO IZ AN ACT OV KONTROL OVER IT. A REBELLION AND A REJECTION. HOPING FOR COMPLETE REVOLUTION WITHIN MYSELF AND NOT WAITING FOR THEE GENERATIONZ TO CATCH UP. (FUCK THE EVOLUTIONARY PROCESS! WHEN THINGS NEED TO CHANGE THEY WILL; THROUGH WILL.) THIS TYPE OV NULLIFICATION IZ THEE PROCESS OV PURIFICATION THROUGH PULVERIZATION. AN INITIATION INTO THE SELF. THE TRUE SELF. NOT THEE ILLUZION OUR EGO FEEDZ US. LOSS OV EGO IZ PART OV THEE AWAKENING PROCCESS. THEE LIBERATION PROCESS. TO LIBERATE YOURSELF IZ TO NEGATE AND NULLIFY THAT WHICH RESTRICTS YOU. WHAT RESTRICTS YOU FROM EXPRESSION AND EXPLORATION. EXPLORE YOURSELF AND BE READY. BE ABLE AND CAPABLE. TRANZFORM AND COMMUNICATE. TRUE COMMUNICATION ONLY HAPPENZ BETWEEN EQUALS. YOU MUST MUTATE TO COMMUNICATE. YOU MUST SHARE VIBRATIONAL FREQUENCY, WHICH IZ WHAT YOU ARE. ALL LIFE IZ VIBRATION AND MOVEMENT. NOTHING IZ IN A FIXED POSITION. FIXED POSITIONS ARE ONLY TEMPORARY. TRUE STATES ARE TEMPORAL BECAUSE CHANGE IZ INEVITABLE. CHANGE MAKES BALANCE. CHANGE IZ MOVEMENT. MOVEMENT IZ UNIVERSAL YET DEPENDENT AND DEFINABLE. MOVEMENT HAS VELOCITY AND DIRECTION. MOVEMENT IZ MAJICK. MAJICK IS SETTING FORTH THEE WILL INTO MOTION TOWARDS A GOAL. ALLEGORY IZ THEE VEHICAL. LEARN TO KONTROL THEE VEHICAL. GET BEHIND THE WHEEL. STEER YOUR LIFE IN THEE DIRECTION YOU CHOOSE. YOU DON'T HAVE TO MAKE PIT-STOPS FOR YOUR EGO.

PULVERIZE & PURITY.

The majick, kontrol, and steering happen in two ways. First, the techniques and ideas spread throughout the United States and England empower individual pagans to develop their own personal strategies for moving through life. Second, and more important, the dissemination of the information itself creates a sub- or even countercultural infrastructure. In a "meta" way, the new lines of communication create the global, informational being, in this case based on majick and pagan technology. Unlike Green Fire, though, whose gentle androgyny is quite Disney in its softness, TOPY members are medieval-styled skinheads. Pierced lips and noses, tattoos, army clothes, spikes, leather, bizarre beards, crew cuts, shaved heads and mohawks for the men; the women dress either in sixties naturale or psychedelic party clothes beneath heavy army coats and leather jackets.

"Magick. Cool. We're into that, too," Diana says, looking up from the small document. Unlike most with whom the TOPYs come in contact, Diana knows that they're not punk rockers. "We have a Nutrient Cafe, a virtual reality booth, brain machines. Plus a lot of good information about all those things." Diana's attempt at cross-culturalization opens a Pandora's box.

"We're trying to achieve total control over information." Kurt, the leader of the group, speaks with a forced eloquence, ironically counterpointing his belligerent styling. "That allows us to decontrol the imprints that are implanted within the information itself. Everyone has the right to exchange information. What flows through TOPY is occult-lit, computer-tech, shamanistic information and majick—majick as actually a technology, as a tool, or a sort of correlative technology based on intuitive will. It's an intuitive correlative technology that is used by the individual who's realized that he or she has his or her own will which they have the freedom to exercise the way they want. That's kind of how I see majick."

To TOPYs, magic is just the realization and redirection of the will toward conscious ends. To do this, people must disconnect from all sources of information that attempt to program them into unconscious submission, and replace them with information that opens them to their own magical and technological abilities.

While Kurt is more "in your face" and confrontational about his majickal designs on culture than is Green Fire or Earth Girl,

Diana is confident that they all share in the basic belief that magic and spirituality are technologies that must be utilized to prepare and develop the planet for the coming age.

"Well, we're all on the same side." She's hip to their codified lifestyle and too determined to get them to her club to let their critical tone or angry-looking fashion choices get in the way. At Berkeley there were kids plenty more strung out than these guys. Besides, if she can turn one TOPY into a Toon Towner, thousands could follow. Kurt has the same intention. Toon Town would be an excellent venue to distribute TOPY literature.

Everyone's trying to turn everyone else on to basically the same thing. Diana takes their names down for the ever-expanding guest list (Preston won't be happy about that) and moves on.

## The Protocol of Empathy

Back at Kurt's apartment later that day, the group prepares to go to Toon Town for the evening. They'll check out the club, it's decided, and give out some of their latest propaganda. A new member of the group—a runaway teenager who was found at a concert last weekend—wonders why everyone is so preoccupied with spreading the word. Kurt is quick to answer him.

"That's what TOPY's always existed for: to help people realize that this society is in a crisis point. People have to wake up instead of sleeping in front of the TV, which is a window on information which you don't even realize is subliminal 'cause the intentions aren't even known to all the people."

Kurt's tiny black-and-white television set has the word *virus* scrawled across its screen in indelible marker, a constant reminder to all viewers that the media is carrying potentially infectious subliminal ideas.

"It's the programming that's dangerous. The television networks create programs which program the reality of the viewer. Each viewer is defined by nothing more than his programming."

So, TOPY members replace regular, power-depleting television programming with information of their own: magick.

"Majick is a map of the external reality. Pagans who've understood this throughout history have stayed away from the church, and used the occult as a type of underground communication. Symbols which were agreed upon."

The revelation of the subcultural latticework vanishes as Kurt's girlfriend suddenly enters.

"I got an electric shock," she announces, with a certain amount of wonderment in relating the incident. "And it made my finger go numb. I was plugging in my hair dryer to the socket, and my finger's numb. I don't know what to do! It hurts like hell. I mean, it doesn't hurt at all, but . . . I got shocked and it affected me."

"Do you have any cigarettes, Kim?" Kurt asks her in an even tone.

"Yeah," she answers. "Do you want one? Want some pot?"

She goes out, still staring at her thumb, to search for tobacco and/or cannabis. Although these kids are far out on a technopagan limb, their familial interactions look as traditionally patriarchal as the Bunkers. In one sense they seem to have taken cyber paganism the farthest. Their model of the human being is really that of the computer with will. But in another way, they appear to have adopted a more sexist and radically traditional value system than their parents could have had. The Coyotes have all become pack animals, roaming the streets for adventure, while the Kalis stay at home, shop for clothes, or mix potions.

When Kurt does get to the topic of socializing, he speaks about it in a language more suited to computer modem protocol than human interaction:

"When computers talk, there's a basic handshake that happens between two terminals. The computer is analogous to the human biosystem, or a neural linguistic coalitive technological system." Kim sits up on Kurt's knee as he continues. She lights Kurt's cigarette for him and puts it into his mouth.

"Empathy is caused by frequencies being shared by people, and when they interlock their frequencies, they cause a certain level of syncopation. The closer that that level of syncopation is together, the closer that those frequencies are locked in the higher level of communication that you're experiencing. Interlocking can happen in what we now call protocol: the terms that are agreed by the two users."

The highest level of protocol between two users is, of course, sexual intercourse, an act of creativity that TOPY members are trying to demystify. Since they see sex as the connective energy in all interactions, the word *of* has been replaced in TOPY-spell by the word *ov*, representative of "ovum," the sexual energy, which needs to be liberated from society's restrictions and reintegrated with the will. In a practical sense, this means using the sexual energy for the practice of majick.

"Your dick is a majick wand if you know how to use it," one roommate loves to say. As another of the many leaflets around the house insists in block type:

> We are thee gardeners ov thee abyss. Working to reclaim a strangled paradise choked with unwilled weeds, subconscious manifestations ov fear and self-hate. We embrace this fear and our shadow to assimilate all that we think we are not. Realigning ourselves on thee lattice ov power. Change is our strength. We turn the soil to expose thee roots ov our conditioned behavioral responses. Identifying and dissimilating the thought structures that blind us ov our beauty and imprison us from our power. We thrash these weeds beyond recognition, beyond meaning, beyond existence to the consistency of nothingness. Returning them to their origin, thee abyss. Thee fertile void revealed is pure creative inspiration. In coum-union, we impregnate thee abyss; thee omninada; thee all nothingness, with thee seed ov creation. Cultivating, through will and self-love, thee infinite beauty and love that is Creation.

The creative energy in TOPY is always linked with the darkness. It is through recognition of the shadow (what Radzik considers the anima liberated by Ecstasy) that new life may see the light. The "fertile void revealed is pure creative inspiration," because an acknowledgment of the unconscious programming and darkness within us opens the possibility for their obliteration. Leaving them in the unconscious or repressing them turns them into monsters, which will sooner or later have to be dealt with in the form of Charlie Mansons, Chernobyl disasters, or worse.

Still, to most of Cyberia, the TOPY view is unnecessarily dark and its treatment of the human organism too mechanistic. They have an almost puritanical obeisance to the forces they believe are controlling the universe. House kids have a hard time understanding the TOPY's fear and paranoia, especially about their own deities.

Jody Radzik, for example, believes he once encountered the spirit of Kali directly. To him, there was nothing dark about her, he tells me as he spraypaints a graffiti picture of the goddess onto a billboard at a construction site in downtown Oakland:

"I can positively describe that experience as making love with God. I know that's what it was. Nobody can tell me different. I will argue until the day I die that that's what my experience was. It was a wonderful experience and it's led me to greater opening. Every now and then I do Ecstasy again because it brings me back to that incredible experience that I can't even begin to describe. It's there. It's there that I learned how to make love with God. It's how I offered myself as a sex slave to God, through MDMA, and it's brought me to really a wonderful experience of life."

Several TOPYs, who are walking by, stop to watch Radzik paint. "Whoah!" exclaims one girl. They stare in astonishment.

"Better be careful, man!" warns the largest of the guys, whose nose has at least three rings in it. "Kali is dangerous. She'll get you really hard. She's the Destroyer."

The TOPYs shake their heads and walk on in horror and disdain. Radzik looks up from his work and shouts after them with a wide smile: "Kali has her fist up my ass up to her elbow and she loves every minute of it!"

He puts the finishing touches on his masterpiece and mumbles under his breath: "Fucking art critics!"

# 4

# Cut and Paste: Artists in Cyberia

## chapter thirteen

Because Cyberia is still evolving, it is impossible to pin down a single cyberian aesthetic. The art of Cyberia is a work in progress, where the forefathers of each genre coexist and even collaborate with the most recent arrivals. The conflicts over which art and lifestyles are "truly" cyberian are less a symptom of divisiveness than they are an indication of the fact that this aesthetic is still in the process of un-folding. The artistic and religious debates between the TOPYs and house kids like Jody Radzik arise because all the different evolution-ary levels of Cyberia exist simultaneously.

While current state-of-the-art cyberians like Radzik or Mark Heley claim they have no agenda and believe they are acting against no one, their belief system was developed out of the ideas of people who did. Just as E-generation free-form love raves can be traced back to the radical "be-ins" of the confrontational sixties, house music and designer beings can be traced back to the arts and artists of a more admittedly countercultural movement.

As we attempt to determine exactly what it means to be a cyber-ian, and who is succeeding at it best, let's briefly trace the develop-ment of the cyberian aesthetic and ethic in music, literature, and the arts.

### Anti-Muzak

Cyberians most often credit Brian Eno with fathering the cyber music genre. His invention of the arty Ambient Music paved the way for Macintosh musicians by taking emphasis off of structure and placing it on texture. These aren't songs with beginnings and endings, but extended moments—almost static experiences. Inter-nally, Eno's music isn't a set of particular sounds one listens to but a space in which one breathes. Unlike traditional rock music, which can be considered male or active in the way it penetrates the lis-tener, Eno's Ambient Music envelops the listener in an atmosphere of sound. Inspired by Muzak, Eno's recordings use similar techniques to produce the opposite effects. In September 1978, Eno wrote the liner notes to his first Ambient record:

"Whereas the extant canned music companies proceed from the basis of regularizing environments by blanketing their acoustic and atmospheric idiosyncrasies, Ambient Music is intended to enhance these. Whereas conventional background music is produced by stripping away all sense of doubt and uncertainty (and thus all genuine interest) from the music, Ambient Music retains these qualities. And whereas their intention is to 'brighten' the environment by adding stimulus to it (thus supposedly alleviating the tedium of routine tasks and leveling out the natural ups and downs of the body rhythms) Ambient Music is intended to induce calm and space to think. Ambient Music must be able to accommodate many levels of listening attention without enforcing one in particular; it must be as ignorable as it is interesting."[1]

Eno quickly gained popularity on headier college campuses and even inspired famous precyberian Ambient tripping parties at Princeton University, where each room of a house called the Fourth World Center would be set up with a different decor and Eno record. His was the ideal music for fledgling collegiate cyberians in their first attempts to synthesize new intellectual discoveries like the fractal and chaos mathematics with the equally disorienting psychedelic perspective. This newness and uncertainty is precisely the territory of Eno's creativity.

"One of the motives for being an artist," he relates from personal experience, "is to recreate a condition where you're actually out of your depth, where you're uncertain, no longer controlling yourself, yet you're generating something, like surfing as opposed to digging a tunnel. Tunnel-digging activity is necessary, but what artists like, if they still like what they're doing, is the surfing."[2] The image of artist-as-surfer was born, soon to be iterated throughout popular culture.

Eno speaks of "riding the dynamics of the system" rather than attempting to control things with rules and principles[3]—good advice for those who would dare venture into the dangerous surf of future waters, but even more significant for his use of new mathematics terminology as a way of describing the artistic endeavor. His

musical compositions follow what he calls a "holographic" paradigm, where the whole remains unchanged but texture moves
about as individual timbres and resonances are altered. To some,
the music feels as cold, neutral, and boring as a Siber-Cyberia. To
others, it is a rich world of sound, bursting with boundless creativity
and imagination, uninhibited by the arbitrary demands of drama,
structure, and audience expectation. Eno epitomizes the art student
turned musician, and, true to form, he refuses to shape his compositions around the skeletal structure of standard songwriting.

His recording techniques become as much his guides as his tools,
and he "surfs" his pieces toward completion, cutting, pasting, dubbing, and overdubbing. His collaboration with David Byrne, *My Life
in the Bush of Ghosts,* best demonstrates his use of these techniques and was the inspiration for the industrial, house, and even
rap and hip-hop recording artists who followed. Like the house
song "Your Son Is Dead," these compositions form an anthropolog-
ical scrapbook, sampling voices and sounds from real life. The
record jacket lists the sound bytes used in each song, which include
a radio-show host, a Lebanese mountain singer, Algerian Muslims,
and even an unidentified New York City exorcist. Each voice is layered over different percussive and instrumental tracks, sometimes
modern sounds over tribal beats, or vice versa. The effect is a startling compression of time and culture, where the dance beat of the
music is the only regulated element in a barrage of bird, animal, industrial, television, radio, random, musical, and human noises. The
industrial noises were soon to become an entire genre of their own.

Eno has remained central to the creation of a cyberian aesthetic.
He gives regular interviews to *Mondo 2000* magazine and is often
spotted at virtual reality events and house parties. His forecast for
the future of his own and the rest of popular music mirrors the
evolution of the computer subculture, which abandoned the clean
lines of the Space Odyssey vision for the gritty, urban realism of
*Bladerunner* and, as we'll see, cyberpunk books like *Neuromancer.*
Eno says that the new music is "built up by overlaying unrelated
codes and bits and pieces of language, letting them collide to see
what new meanings and resonances emerge. It is music that throws
you off balance. It's not all tightly organized . . . a *network* rather
than a structure."

## Coyote 1

The TOPYs, of course, took the idea of a collision-based nett-work even further. "Industrial" pioneer and TOPY pater Genesis P. Orridge also bases his music on Muzak, attempting to create an even more violently antibrainwashing style of songwriting than Eno's. His original group, Throbbing Gristle, was the first major industrial band, and even his current industrial/house band, Psychic TV, incorporates industrial sounds to deprogram what he sees as a Muzak-hypnotized youth culture. In his treatise on fighting Muzak, P. Orridge testified:

"We openly declared we were inventing an anti-muzak that, instead of cushioning the sounds of a factory environment, made use of those very sounds to create rhythmic patterns and structures that incorporated the liberating effects of music by unexpected means. This approach is diametrically opposed to the position of official muzak, as supplied by the Muzak Corporation of America. Their intention is to disguise stress, to control and direct human activity in order to generate maximum productivity and minimum discontent."[4]

Throbbing Gristle's mission was a social reengineering effort to decode brainwashing stimuli from the oppressive status quo. This motivated them to create what they called "metabolic" music, for which cut-and-paste computer techniques were necessary. They took irritating machine noises, factory sounds, and other annoying postmodern samples and overlaid them using the computer to create a new kind of acoustic assault. They knew the new sound was unpleasant—so much so that they considered it a "nonentertainment-motivated music." Orridge was more interested in affecting the body directly through the textures of his sounds than he was in making any aesthetic statement through entertaining songs or ear-pleasing harmonic structures.

The bare-bones quality of his music was thought to go right past the analytic mind, de-composing the listener's expectations about music. Making use of Muzak's painstaking research into the effects of various frequencies and pulses on the physiology and psychology of listeners, Orridge picked his sounds on the basis of their ability to "decondition social restraints on thought and the body." Orridge claimed certain passages of his songs could induce orgasms. In industrial music, it was not important that listeners understood what was happening to them any more than it was in Muzak technology. The music needed only to deprogram the audience in any way available.

For his current, more house-oriented Psychic TV project, Orridge has made a more self-conscious effort to expose Muzak and the societal values it supports. The music still contains deconditioning elements, but is a more transparent parody of Muzak techniques. Listeners can feel the way the music works and enjoy it. It is less angry and abrasive because it no longer seeks to provoke fear and anxiety as its weapon against passivity-inducing Muzak. Instead, this lighter music invites thought and even humor by creating new and greater pleasures. Orridge is not merely fighting against Muzak; he is trying to do it better than they are. He not only deprograms his audience but reprograms as well, and makes listeners fully aware of the conditioning techniques of modern society in the process. This creates what Orridge calls "a distorted mirror reflecting Muzak back on itself." He believes he can show his listeners and followers—through self-consciously cut-and-paste house music—that the technologies in place around them can be successfully analyzed and reversed. They contain, in code, "the seeds of their own destruction and hopefully the structure that nurtures it."

Cut-and-paste technology, applied to music, becomes a political statement. While beginning as a confrontational assault on programming, it developed into a race to beat Muzak at its own game. Muzak teaches that the world is smooth and safe. There is no such thing as a discontinuity. If a shopper in the grocery store experiences a discontinuity, he may take a moment to reevaluate his purchases: "Did I buy that because I wanted it, or was I still influenced by the commercial I saw yesterday?" If a voter experiences a discontinuity, the incumbency is challenged. Muzak's continuous soundtrack promotes the notion that we are in a world that behaves in an orderly, linear fashion. Cut-and-paste music like Psychic TV is an exercise in discontinuity. But rather than angrily shattering people's illusions about a continuous reality, it brings its listeners into a heightened state of pleasure. The teaching technique is bliss induction directly through the sound technology:

"We've been saying that pleasure has become a weapon now. You know, confrontation just doesn't work. They know all about that game, the authorities, the conglomerates, and even the super-markets, they know all those scams. So straight-on confrontation isn't necessarily the most effective tactic at the moment. Ironically, what used to be the most conservative thing, which was dance music, is now the most radical. And that's where the most radical ideas are being put across, and the most jarring combinations of sounds and sources as well."[5]

## Filtering Down to the Posse

Many musical groups in various corners of Cyberia take their cue from the industrial and early house eras. We link up with our own crowd in the form of a house band Jody Radzik promotes, Goat Guys from Hell. The guys in this group got to know one another at Barrington, a cooperative house for some of the most artsy and in-tellectual students at Berkeley. This was the sort of place you could easily find forty people tripping to Eno records or Psychic TV and, needless to say, a household the university was happy to have an excuse to shut down after one student committed suicide on the premises.

But even after their building was confiscated, a core group re-mained true to the Barrington ideals modeled after the philosophies of musical pioneers like G.P. Orridge. As the band GGFH first formed, they chose to use anti-Muzak recording techniques similar to those by Psychic TV, but for less overtly political purposes. The closer we get to today's house music and pure cyberian enthusiasm, in fact, the farther we get from any external agenda. To GGFH, the enemy is not the authorities, but the repression of the darkness within ourselves.

But as I sit at Pico Paco Tacos with GGFH members Ghost, a slightly scary-looking big white guy in rapper clothes, and Brian, a toonish, long-haired Iro-Celtic keyboardist, I learn that implicit in their sampling techniques are some strong points of view about our society. Brian (the Celt) takes a break from his veggie burrito to explain:

"We take American culture in all its fucked-up-ness, its expres-sions of violence and sensationalism of violence—and stick it back

in its face. Our culture tries to suppress and repress the negative impulses and then people like Ricky Ramirez go off and do these sick
things. Then the culture feeds on the sick things and trivializes or
sensationalizes them."

As a Spanish-language muzaky version of "I've Got You Under
My Skin" plays on a radio in the kitchen, more tacos arrive, along
with Jody Radzik, who begins to iterate his take on the band:
"GGFH is the shadow of our culture. These guys are channeling the
global shadow. Their album is a kind of Jungian therapy on a social
level." Ghost shrugs. Brian nods, but doesn't fully agree:

"The guys that we're talking about are people like Ricky Ramirez,
being sentenced to death saying, 'See you at Disneyland,' or mass
murderers at McDonald's." He swallows his food and continues in a
more collegiate dialect: "The polar opposites in our culture are very
interesting to us."

Radzik's enthusiasm prevents him from allowing his prodigy to
speak further. "The more of a good person you think you are, the
more of a model citizen you think you are, the bigger the evil shit
you've got stored away back there. You can never purge it. You've
got to accept it. You allow for it, and then it becomes harmless. The
cultural repression of the shadow is what is leading to the high level
of violence in the world today."

The juxtapositions of these polar opposites—post office order
and chaotic bloody death, McDonald's clowns and automatic
weapons, Ramirez and Disneyland—are the subject matter of
GGFH. This is why their style, then, is correspondingly polar and
depends on the cut-and-paste computer techniques that can bring
disparate elements together. Melody takes a back seat to texture,
and again we see musicians creating atmospheres and timeless
moments instead of structured pieces with heroic journeys. The
music has moved from an LSD sensibility to one of Ecstasy.

Likewise, Brian's composition process is a feel-your-way-through-
it experience. He'll begin with a sampled sound, then tweak knobs
and dials until he's developed a texture. Like Eno, he thinks of
sound waves as currents to be surfed, and consciously gives himself
over to the sound, working as a mere conduit for its full expression.
("The sound simply demands to be treated a certain way.") But this
Brian's surfboard is language and image from popular culture: "We

find samples and cut-ups that fit with the atmosphere of the sound. We've got one that's very dreamy so we used a sample of Tim Leary saying 'flow to the pulse of life.' Another is a real hard dance beat, so it has Madonna sampled saying 'fuck me'—which I think is really cool because if you wanted to put Madonna into two words, 'fuck me' is pretty good."

Radzik can't resist making another comparison: "It's like me! I've sampled all these different religions, and created my own belief system. That includes psychedelics."

House music is never remembered for its melody but for a particular texture—what genre songwriters call "the main ingredient." Like Eno, house composers start with the sound, then surf the system that forms around it. The songwriting process is not exactly random—it depends on the composer's taste and the samples he's assembled, but the machinery does take on a life of its own. Cyber artists like GGFH experience a shamanic journey as they create and layer a given piece. Although listeners might detect only one basic set of textures, each moment of the song can be decompressed like a DMT trip into any number of more linear experiences.

## Climax

Sarah Drew, girlfriend of *Mondo* chief R.U. Sirius, is a house musician/performance artist who herself needs to be decompressed in order to be understood. The final frontier of house artist, she's a consciously self-mutated psychedelic cyborg. Eno developed the idea of music as a texture; Orridge exploited it; GGFH plays with it; Sarah Drew lives it.

"She just showed up at the door one day," recalls R.U. Sirius about Sarah's arrival at the Bay Area and the *Mondo 2000* headquarters. "And I just said. 'Okay. Yeah. Looks good to me!' I guess it was a sexual thing."

Sarah—a beautiful young woman from an extremely wealthy family—turned on to psychedelics and the notion of designer reality as a child. Her social status gave her the luxury and time to choose exactly who—and what—she wanted to be. By the time Sarah entered college, her life had become an ongoing art project. When she saw a *Mondo* magazine, she knew it was something she wanted to be part of—not simply to get on the staff, but to *become Mondo 2000*.

First step: to link her body with the brain from which *Mondo* emanates. Within a few weeks, she and R.U. Sirius were a couple, so to speak, and they lived together in a room in the *Mondo 2000* mansion, publisher Queen Mu's cyberdelic answer to the Hefner estate.

We're at the aftermath of a party. It is about three in the morning, and almost everyone is in the same altered state. The remaining guests include Walter Kirn, a *GQ* reporter doing a piece on computers and psychedelics, to whom Sarah is speaking in a psychedelic gibberish. The poor boy is having a hard time telling whether Sarah's trying to seduce him or drive him insane.

She's been talking about a past DMT experience, then suddenly she cuts herself off in midsentence and pins the journalist against the refrigerator, making a rapid "ch-ch-ch-ch-ch" sound while widening her eyes. Perhaps she is describing the frame-within-a-frame-within-a-frame zoom-out feeling on psychedelics, when one suddenly experiences a broad and sudden shift in perspective. Or maybe she's pretending to be a snake. A few other heads turn as she looks into Walter's eyes, flips back her long brown hair, and, her mouth an inch from his, again spits out "ch-ch-ch-ch-ch."

One cyberian newcomer explains to the mesmerized New Yorker that Sarah means to express the feeling of many scenes receding suddenly and the accompanying realization of the kind one gets when he conceives an idea from hundreds of points of view at once. But the veterans know what's really going on: Sarah is a media personality. She's a multimedia manifestation of the magazine itself. She's leaped off the page. She's a house song. She's a human cyborg.

At about four o'clock, Sarah turns off the lights for the half-dozen survivors of the psychedelic excursion and plays a cassette of freshly recorded music called Infinite Personality Complex.

The listeners close their eyes and the stereo speakers explode with a vocal fission. Moaning, keening, and howling make up most of the sound, but it is so deep, so rich, so layered—or at least so damn loud—that it creates a definite bodily response. To listen to her music is to have the experience of your brain being dehydrated and reconstituted many times per second. "Come inside my little yoni," her lyrics iterate over themselves. Somehow, Sarah Drew's music is the real thing. This is a woman on the very edge of something, and even if that something is sanity itself, her work and persona merit exploration.

By dawn, everyone has gone to bed except Sarah, Walter (who is no longer in this thing for the story), and R.U. Sirius, who watches the whole scene with detached amusement, utterly unafraid of losing his girlfriend to the journalist.

As Walter talks to Sarah, she manifests totally. Sarah *is* a magazine article. She "groks" what he says, making an *mm* sound again and again as she nods her head. This is not a normal, conversational acknowledgment she's making, but a forced feedback loop of rapidly accelerating mms—as if the faster Sarah mms, the more she's understanding, and the more she's prodding him on to explore deeper into the phenomenon he's describing. He's simply trying to tell her he's attracted to her.

But Sarah is a cyborg, and finally answers his question with a long discourse about virtual space. Our current forms of communication—verbal and physical—are obsolete, she explains. Someday she will be able to project, through thought, a holographic image into the air, into which someone will project his own holographic mental image.

"Then we would literally see what the other means," she borrows from Terence McKenna, "and see what we both mean together." It would be the ultimate in intimacy, she tells him, touching his arm gently, because they would become linked into one being.

The reporter has had enough. "But wouldn't it be much easier to just *fuck?*"

Six months later, having moved to the next evolutionary level, Sarah recalls what she was going through in the Infinite Personality period. "I remember I would reach into my mind and . . . ch-ch-ch-ch-ch-ch. It was the way I had of expressing what I was experiencing at that time. Sometimes I'm a very, very, very high conduit. It was like a huge information download."

For Sarah, the relationship of DNA, computers, psychedelics, and music is not conceptual but organic. According to Drew, her Infinite Personality Complex served as a "highly dense information loop." But, like her work, her own DNA was mutating—evolving into a denser informational structure. As an artist, she became capable of downloading the time-wave-zero fractal through her own resonating DNA, and then translating it into music. Meanwhile, she was

also becoming a human, biological manifestation of the downloading process, evolving—like her society—by becoming more intimately linked to technology.

"I was becoming what you can call a cyborg. It was time for me
to make that synthesis. In this kind of work, you are the becoming—
not an artist separate from the medium. Then you can even be in
multiple places at once. Ch ch-ch-ch-ch-ch-ch!"

Artist as art object goes way back, but not artist as cyborg or information loop time traveler. The other particular advantage of becoming a cyborg is, of course, that it enables the artist to interact
fully with her computer and other high-tech recording equipment.
Sarah's current house project is an adaptation of the Bacchae, for
which she's using an EMU synthesizer/sampler. She makes a moan
or a whisper into a microphone that the EMU records digitally. Then
she replays, overdubs, and manipulates the sounds with computers.
Finally, she ends up with a house recording that, again, re-creates a
timeless, skinless sexual experience through computers.

"It starts out with soft, light sounds and whisperings, then moves
into a sort of ecstasy. As it starts to build, the breathing becomes
the rhythms, and the rhythms become the breathing. It's the sound
of ecstasy happening. And I have a male, Dionysian figure, going
into orgasm as he's being torn apart. And it ends up in a climax. All
in five minutes."

In addition, using the 3-D "holographic" sound techniques developed for virtual reality systems, Sarah creates a three-dimensional
acoustic space where the audience can experience sounds as real,
physical presences. The whispers seem to come from all sides. This
is not just a "sens-u-round" effect but a genuine cyberian effort
in structure, style, and meaning. "I'm talking about a holographic
sense of presence and movement," she insists. "We can take
people through time that way by creating a space with sound.
It'll move people back in time."

By creating a space with sound, Sarah makes a time machine in
which she can transport her audience—not by bringing them into a
different space but by changing the space that they're already in.
The implication of her music is that time does not really exist, since
it can be compressed into a single moment. The moment itself, of
course, is Dionysian; orgiastic bliss is the only inroad to timelessness.
Because Sarah creates her sound space out of her own voice and

cyborg presence, she feels her music is a way of taking her audience into herself. Her ultimate sexual statement is to make love to her entire audience and create in them the bliss response.

Despite her flirtatious manner and flippancy about orgasm, Sarah takes human sexuality quite seriously. As several recording engineers carry equipment into Sarah's basement studio to mix the final tracks for her Bacchae record, she makes a startling admission: she'll probably perform with "low energy" today because she had an abortion yesterday. For lack of anything better to say, one of the engineers asks her how it was.

"I took acid before I went in," she says, "because I really wanted to experience it. It was a purge."

To average ears, this sounds like intense, artsy beatnik nonsense, but Sarah's unflinching commitment to experiencing and understanding her passage through time has earned her recognition as one of the most fully realized participants in Cyberia. Everyone in the scene who knows Sarah—and almost everybody does—is a little frightened of her, but also just a wee bit in awe.

She is most definitely for real, and however bizarre she gets, everything she says and does is in earnest. Even her affectations— weird sounds, strange hats, pseudointellectual accent, and name dropping—are done innocently, almost like a child trying on costumes to test the reality of each. Sarah's life is absolutely a work in progress, and her pieces are indistinguishable from her self.

"To have an abortion on acid," muses R.U. Sirius the day afterward. "It hasn't seemed to affect her too much. It was intense, and she cried, but one of the things I like about her is she can have these incredibly intense experiences, and she expects them."

The discontinuity training is complete. Cyberian music has evolved into a cyborg.

## chapter fourteen

The literature of Cyberia underwent a similar evolution. What began as a dark, negative worldview later developed into a multimedia celebration of timelessness and designer reality. Today, the literature of Cyberia—like its music—has become personified by cyberians themselves, who adopt into their own lives the ethos of a fictional designer reality.

### The Interzone

"Beat" hero William Burroughs didn't start the cyberpunk movement in literature, but he foresaw it, most notably in his novel *Naked Lunch* (1959). Although written long before video games or the personal computer existed, Burroughs's works utilize a precybernetic hallucinatory dimension called the Interzone, where machines mutate into creatures, and people can be controlled telepathically by "senders" who communicate via psychedelics introduced into the victims' bloodstreams.

Burroughs' description of the psychic interface prophesizes a virtual reality nightmare: Senders gain "control of physical movements, mental processes, emotional responses, and apparent sensory impressions by means of bioelectrical signals injected into the nervous system of the subject. . . . The biocontrol apparatus [is] the prototype of one-way telepathic control." Once indoctrinated, the drug user becomes an unwilling agent for one of the Interzone's two main rivaling powers. The battle is fought entirely in the hallucinatory dimension, and involves "jacking in" (as William Gibson will later call it) through intelligent mutated typewriters.

Burroughs' famed "prismatic" style of writing—almost a literary equivalent of Brian Eno's Ambient Music—reads more like jazz than the narrative works of his contemporaries. Each word or turn of phrase can lead the reader down an entirely new avenue of thought or plot, imitating the experience of an interdimensional hypertext adventure. But as a pioneer of nonmimetic hallucinatory and even pornographic literature, Burroughs suffered condemnation from the courts and, worse, occasional addiction to the chemicals that offered him access to the far reaches of his consciousness. Unlike the cyberian authors of today, Burroughs was not free simply to romp in the uncharted regions of hyperspace, but instead—like early psychedelic explorers—was forced to evaluate his experiences against the accepted, "sane" reality of the very noncyberian world in which he lived. The morphogenetic field, as it were, was not yet fully formed.

This made Burroughs feel alone and suspect he was mentally ill. In a letter to Allen Ginsberg, he wrote that he hoped the writing of *Naked Lunch* would somehow "cure" him of his homosexuality. As David Cronenberg, who later made a film adaptation of the book, comments, "even at that time . . . even these guys, the hippest of the hip, were still capable of thinking of themselves as sick guys who could be cured by some act of art or will or drugs."[6]

Burroughs' early pre-Cyberia, as a result, became as dark, paranoid, and pessimistic as the author himself. It was three decades before cyberian literature could shake off this tone. In the current climate, Burroughs has been able to adopt a more full-blown cyber aesthetic that, while still cynically expressed, calls for the liberation of humanity from the constraints of the body through radical technologically enhanced mutation:

"Evolution did not come to a reverent halt with homo sapiens. An evolutionary step that involves biologic alterations is irreversible. We now must take such a step if we are to survive at all. And it had better be good. . . . We have the technology to recreate a flawed artifact, and to produce improved and variegated models of the body designed for space conditions. I have predicted that the transition from time into space will involve biologic alteration. Such alterations are already manifest."[7]

It wasn't until the 1990s (and close to his own nineties) that Burroughs gained access to other forms of media, which more readily accepted his bizarre cyberian aesthetic. Filmmaker Gus Van Sant (*Drugstore Cowboy; My Own Private Idaho*) collaborated with Burroughs on a video version of the satiric poem "Thanksgiving Prayer," which later appeared in freeze-frame form in *Mondo 2000*.

But long before Burroughs himself successfully crossed over into other media, his aesthetic and his worldview had found their way there.

## Jacking in to the Matrix

Cyberpunk proper was born out of a pessimistic view similar to that of William Burroughs. The people, stories, and milieu of William Gibson's books are generally credited with spawning an entirely new aesthetic in the science fiction novel, and cross-pollinating with films like *Bladerunner, Max Headroom,* and *Batman.* Taking its cue from comic books, skateboard magazines, and video games more than from the lineage of great sci-fi writers like Asimov and Bradbury, William Gibson's landmark novel *Neuromancer* is a gritty portrait of a future world not too unlike our own, with computer hackers called "cowboys," black market genetic surgeons, underground terrorist-punkers called Moderns who wear chameleonlike camouflage suits, contraband software, drugs, and body parts, and personality imprints of dead hackers called "constructs" who jet as disembodied consciousness through the huge computer net called "the matrix." The invention of the matrix, even as a literary construct, marks the birth of cyberpunk fiction. Here, the matrix describes itself to Case, Gibson's reluctant cowboy hero:

"The matrix has its roots in primitive arcade games," said the voice-over, "in the early graphics programs and military experimentation with cranial jacks." On the Sony, a two-dimensional space war faded behind a forest of mathematically generated ferns, demonstrating the spacial possibilities of logarithmic spirals; cold blue military footage burned through, lab animals wired into test systems, helmets feeding into fire control circuits of tanks and war planes. "Cyberspace. A consensual hallucination experienced daily by billions of legitimate operators, in every nation, by children being taught mathematical concepts. . . . A graphic representation of data abstracted from the banks of every computer in the human system. Unthinkable complexity. Lines of light ranged in the nonspace of the mind, clusters and constellations of data. Like city lights . . . receding . . ."[8]

The matrix is a fictional extension of our own worldwide computer net, represented graphically to the user, much like VR or a video game, and experienced via dermatrodes, which send impulses through the skin directly into the brain. After years away from cyberspace, Case is given the precious opportunity to hack through the matrix once again. Gibson's description voiced the ultimate hacker fantasy for the first time:

He closed his eyes.

Found the ridged face of the power stud.

And in the bloodlit dark behind his eyes, silver phosphenes boiling in from the edge of space, hypnagogic images jerking past like film compiled from random frames. Symbols, figures, faces, a blurred, fragmented mandala of visual information.

Please, he prayed, *now—*

A gray disk, the color of Chiba sky.

*Now—*

Disk beginning to rotate, faster, becoming a sphere of paler gray. Expanding—

And flowed, flowered for him, fluid neon origami trick, the unfolding of his distanceless home, his country, transparent 3D chessboard extending to infinity. Inner eye opening to the stepped scarlet pyramid of the Eastern Seaboard Fission Authority burning beyond the green cubes of Mitsubishi Bank of America, and high and very far away he saw the spiral arms of military systems, forever beyond his reach.

And somewhere he was laughing, in a white-painted loft, distant fingers caressing the deck, tears of release streaking his face." [9]

The invention of cyberspace as a real place is the most heralded of the cyberpunk genre's contributions to fiction and the arts. William Gibson and his colleague/collaborator Bruce Sterling paint vivid portraits of a seamy urban squalor contrasted by an ultra-high-tech web of electronic sinews, traveled by mercenary hackers, digital cowboys, artificial intelligences, and disembodied minds.

These authors acknowledge the discrepancy between the promise of technological miracles, such as imprinting consciousness onto a silicon chip, and their application in a real world still obsessed with power, money, and sex. Their books are the literary equivalent of industrial music, exploring a world where machines and technology have filled every available corner, and regular people are forced to figure out a way to turn these technologies against the manipulators of society.

Contributing to the pessimistic quality of these works is another idea shared with the industrial movement—that human beings are basically programmable. "I saw his profile," one character remarks about another. "He's a kind of compulsive Judas. Can't get off sexually unless he knows he's betraying the object of his desire. That's what the file says." And we know that means he can't act otherwise. Characters must behave absolutely true to their programming, having no choice but to follow the instructions of their emotional templates. Even Molly, the closest thing to a love-interest in *Neuromancer,* leaves her boyfriend with a written, self-defeating apology: "ITS THE WAY IM WIRED I GUESS."[10]

Like Burroughs' reluctant hero in *Naked Lunch,* Case suffers from addictions, and is thus exploited by higher powers. He must pay for the joy of jacking in by becoming an agent for a dark, interdimensional corporation. Also like Burroughs' prismatic style, the feeling of these books is more textural than structural. Like fantasy role-playing, computer games, or Nintendo adventures, these books are to be appreciated for the ride. Take the opening of Gibson and Sterling's novel, *The Difference Engine:*

Composite image, optically encoded by escort-craft of the trans-Channel airship *Lord Brunel:* aerial view of suburban Cherbourg, October 14, 1905.

A villa, a garden, a balcony.

Erase the balcony's wrought-iron curves, exposing a bath-chair and its occupant. Reflected sunset glints from the nickel-plate of the chair's wheel-spokes.

The occupant, owner of the villa, rests her arthritic hands upon fabric woven by a Jacquard loom.

These hands consist of tendons, tissue, jointed bone. Through quiet processes of time and information, threads within the human cells have woven themselves into a woman.

Her name is Sybil Gerard.[11]

Like the characters in *Fantastic Voyage,* we move through a multi-tiered fractal reality, enjoying the lens of a camera, the dexterity of a computer design program, the precision of a microscope, the information access of a historical database, the intimacy of a shared consciousness, and, finally, the distance and objectivity of a narrative voice that can identify this entity by its name. The way in which we move through the text says as much if not more about the cyberpunk worldview than does its particular post-sci-fi aesthetic. Writers like Gibson and Sterling hate to be called "cyberpunk" because they know their writing is not just an atmosphere or flavor.

While this branch of fiction may have launched the cyberpunk milieu, it also embodies some of the principles of the current renaissance in its thematic implications.

Even the above passage from *The Difference Engine* demonstrates a sense of holographic reality, where identity is defined by the consensual hallucination of a being's component parts. Similarly, like a DMT trip, a shamanic journey, or a hypertext computer program, reality in these books unfolds in a nonlinear fashion. A minor point may explode into the primary adventure at hand, or a character may appear, drop a clue or warning, and then vanish. Furthermore, these stories boldly contrast the old with the new, and the biological with the technical, reminding us that the evolution of society does not progress in a smooth, curvilinear fashion.

Sterling's *Schismatrix*, for example, pits the technical against the organic in a world war between Mechanists, who have mastered surgical manipulation of the human body through advanced implant technology, and Shapers, who accomplish similar biological manipulation through conscious control over their own DNA coding. This is the same metaphorical struggle that systems mathematician Ralph Abraham has explored throughout human history, between the organic spiritual forces—which he calls Chaos, Gaia, and Eros—and the more mechanistic forces embodied by technology, patriarchal domination, and monotheism. In fact, Sterling's own worldview is based on a nonlinear systems mathematics model.

"Society is a complex system," he writes for an article in *Whole Earth Review* "and there's no sort of A-yields-B business here. It's an iteration. A yields B one day and then AB is going to yield something else the next day, and it's going to yield something else the next and there's 365 days in a year, and it takes 20 years for anything to happen."[12]

Just as these writers incorporate the latest principles of chaos math, new technology, and computer colonization into their stories and milieu, they are also fascinated by exploring what these breakthroughs imply about the nature of human experience. William Gibson knew nothing about computers when he wrote *Neuromancer*. Most of the details came from fantasy: "If I'd actually known anything about computers, I doubt if I'd been able to do it."[13] He was motivated instead by watching kids in video arcades:

"I could see in the physical intensity of their postures how rapt these kids were. It was like one of those closed systems out of a Pynchon novel: you had this feedback loop, with photons coming off the screen into the kids' eyes, the neurons moving through their bodies, electrons moving through the computer. And these kids clearly believed in the space these games projected. Everyone who works with computers seems to develop an intuitive faith that there's some kind of actual space behind the screen."[14]

Gibson's inspiration is Thomas Pynchon, not Benoit Mandelbrot, and his focus is human functioning, not computer programming. The space behind the screen—the consensual hallucination—is Cyberia in its first modern incarnation. Gibson and his cohorts are cyberpunk writers not because they're interested in hackers but because they are able to understand the totality of human experience as a kind of neural net. Their stories, rooted partially in traditional, linear fiction and common sense, mine the inconsistencies of modern culture's consensual hallucinations in the hope of discovering what it truly means to be a human being. Their permutations on consciousness—a cowboy's run in the matrix, an artificial intelligence, an imprinted personality—are not celebrations of technology but a thought experiment aimed at conceptualizing the experience of life.

As ushers rather than participants in Cyberia, Gibson and Sterling are not optimistic about the future of such experience. Most criticism of their work stems from the authors' rather nihilistic conclusions about mankind's relationship to technology and the environment. Gibson's characters in Neuromancer enjoy their bodies and the matrix, but more out of addictive impulsiveness than true passion.

Gibson admits, "One of the reasons, I think, that I use computers in that way is that I got really interested in these obsessive things. I hadn't heard anybody talk about anything with that intensity since the Sixties. It was like listening to people talk about drugs."[15] The cyberian vision according to these, the original cyberpunk authors, is a doomed one, where the only truth to be distilled is that a person's consciousness has no spirit.

In a phone conversation, Bruce Sterling shares his similar worldview over the shouts and laughter of his children: "If you realize that the world is nonlinear and random, then it means that you can be completely annihilated by chaos for no particular reason at all.

These things happen. There's no cosmic justice. And that's a disquieting thing to have to face. It's damaging to people's self-esteem."

Both Sterling and Gibson experienced the "cyberian vision," but their conclusions are dark and hopeless. Rather than trashing the old death-based paradigm, they simply incorporate chaos, computers, and randomness into a fairly mechanistic model. Sterling believes in systems math, cultural viruses, and the promise of the net, but, like Bruce Eisner, he doesn't see technology as inherently liberating. "I worry about quotidian things like the greenhouse effect and topsoil depletion and desertification and exploding populations and species extinction. It's not gonna matter if you've got five thousand meg on your desktop if outside your door it's like a hundred twelve degrees Fahrenheit for three weeks in a row."

While they weren't ready to make the leap into cyberian consciousness, Gibson and Sterling were crucial to the formation of Cyberia, and their works took the first step toward imagining a reality beyond time or locational space. These writers have refused, however, to entertain the notion of human beings surviving the apocalypse, or even of real awareness outside the body. Hyperspace is a hallucination, and death is certainly real and permanent. Even Case's friend, the one disembodied consciousness in *Neuromancer,* knows he's not real: his only wish is to be terminated.

It has been left to younger, as-yet less recognized writers, like WELL denizen Mark Laidlaw, to invent characters whose celebration of Cyberia outweigh the futility of life in a decaying world. One of his stories, "Probability Pipeline," which he wrote in collaboration with cyber novelist and mathematician Rudy Rucker, is about two friends, Delbert, a surfer, and Zep, a surfboard designer, who invents the ultimate board, or "stick": one that, utilizing chaos mathematics, can create monster waves.

"Dig it, Del, I'm not going to say this twice. The ocean is a chaotic dynamical system with sensitive dependence on initial conditions. Macro info keeps being folded in while micro info keeps being excavated. . . . I'm telling you, dude. Say I'm interested in predicting or influencing the waves over the next few minutes. Waves don't move all that fast, so anything that can influence the surf here in the next few minutes is going to depend on the surfspace values within a neighboring area of, say, one square kilometer. I'm only going to fine-grain down to the millimeter level, you wave, so we're looking at, uh, one trillion sample points. Million squared. Don't interrupt again, Delbert, or I won't build you the chaotic attractor."

"You're going to build me a new stick?"

"I got the idea when you hypnotized me last night. Only I'd forgotten till just now. Ten fractal surf levels at a trillion sample points. We model that with an imipolex CA, we use a nerve-patch modem outset unit to send the rider's surfest desires down a co-ax inside the leash, the CA does a chaotic back simulation of the fractal inset, the board does a jiggly-doo, and . . . "

"TSUUUNAMIIIIII!" screamed Delbert, leaping up on the bench and striking a boss surfer pose.[16]

Laidlaw and Rucker's world is closer to the cyberian sentiment because the characters are not politicians, criminals, or unwilling participants in a global, interdimensional battle. They are surfers, riding the wave of chaos purely for pleasure. To them, the truth of Cyberia is a sea of waves—chaotic, maybe, but a playground more than anything else. The surfers' conclusions about chaos are absolutely cyberian: sport, pleasure, and adventure are the only logical responses to a fractal universe. Like the first house musicians who came after Genesis P. Orridge's hostile industrial genre, dispensing with leather and chains and adopting the fashions of surfwear and skateboarding, these writers have taken the first leap toward ecstasy by incorporating surf culture into their works.

Laidlaw first thought of writing the story, he explains to me in the basement office of his San Francisco Mission District home, "at Rudy's house, where he had a Mandelbrot book with a picture of a wave. I looked at it, and realized that a surfboard can take you into this stuff." Laidlaw rejects the negative implications of Gibson's hardwired world and refuses to believe that things are winding down.

"The apocalypse? I see that as egotism!" Likewise, abandoning the rules of traditional structure ("plot," Laidlaw explains, "merely affords comfort in a hopeless situation"), Laidlaw follows his own character's advice, and surfs his way through the storytelling.

"Get rad. Be an adventurist. You'll be part of the system, man," explains the character Zep, and eventually that's what happens. Like Green Fire, who on his visionquests must control his imagination lest his fantasies become real, Del accidentally sends too many paranoid thought signals through his surfboard/chaotic attractor to the nuclear power plant at the ocean shore and blows it up; but, as luck would have it, he, Zep, and their girl Jen escape in an inter-dimensional leap:

The two waves intermingled in a chaotic mindscape abstraction. Up and up they flew, the fin scraping sparks from the edges of the unknown. Zep saw stars swimming under them, a great spiral of stars.

Everything was still, so still.

And then Del's hand shot out. Across the galactic wheel a gleaming figure shared their space. It was coming straight at them. Rider of the tides of night, carver of blackhole beaches and neutron tubes. Bent low on his luminous board—graceful, poised, inhuman.

"Stoked," said Jen. "God's a surfer!"[17]

The only real weapon against the fearful vision of a cold siber-Cyberia is joy. Appreciation of the space gives the surfer his bearings and balance in Cyberia.

This is why art and literature are seen as so crucial to coping there: they serve as celebratory announcements from a world moving into hyperspace. No matter how dark or pessimistic their milieus, these authors still delight in revealing the textures and possibilities of a world free of physical constraints, boring predictability, and linear events.

## Toasters, Band-Aids, Blood

Comic book artists, who already prided themselves on their non-linear storytelling techniques, were the first to adopt the milieu of cyberian literature into another medium. Coming from a tradition of superheroes and clearcut battles between good and evil, comics tend to focus on the more primitive aspects of Cyberia, and are usually steeped in dualism, terror, and violence. While younger comic artists have ventured into a post-nihilistic vision of Cyberia, the first to bring cyberian aesthetics into the world of superheroes, like the original cyberpunk authors, depicted worlds as dark as they could draw them.

Batman, the brooding caped crusader, was one of the first of the traditional comic book characters to enjoy a cyberpunk rebirth, when Frank Miller created *The Dark Knight Returns* series in the 1980s. As Miller surely realized, Batman is a particularly fascinating superhero to bring to Cyberia because he is a mere mortal and, like us, he must use human skills to cope with the postmodern apocalypse. The mature Batman, as wrought by Miller, is fraught with inconsistencies, self-doubt, and resentment toward a society gone awry. He is the same Batman who fought criminals in earlier, simpler decades, who now, as an older man, finds himself utterly unequipped for the challenges of Cyberia.

Miller's *Dark Knight* series interpolates a human superhero into the modern social-media scheme. Commentators in frames the shape of TV sets interpret each of Batman's actions as they occur. Newsmedia criticism running throughout the story reminds the audience that Batman's world has become a datasphere: Each of his actions affects more than just the particular criminal he has beaten up—it has an iterative influence on the viewing public.

For example, after one act of vigilantism, a Ted Koppel-like newsman conducts a TV interview with a social scientist about Batman's media identity. The psychologist responds:

Picture the public psyche as a vast, moist membrane—through the media, Batman has struck this membrane a vicious blow, and it has recoiled. Hence your misleading statistics. But you see, Ted, the membrane is flexible. Here the more significant effects of the blow become calculable, even predictable. To wit—every anti-social act can be traced to irresponsible media input. Given this, the presence of such an aberrant, violent force in the media can only lead to anti-social programming.[18]

The iterative quality of the media within the comic book story creates a particularly cyberian "looking glass" milieu that has caught on with other comic book writers as a free-for-all visual sampling of diary entries, computer printouts, television reports, advertisements, narratives from other characters as well as regular dialogue and narration. In addition, the comic books make their impact by sampling brand names, media identities, and cultural icons from the present, the past, and an imagined future. Comics, always an ideal form for visual collage, here become vehicles for self-consciously gathered iconic samples. This chaos of imagery, in a world Batman would prefer to dominate with order and control, is precisely what causes his anguish.

In the *Batman* comics we witness the ultimate battle of icons, as Batman and Joker conduct a cyberian war of images in a present-day datasphere. They no longer battle physically but idealistically, and their weapons are the press and television coverage. This becomes particularly ironic when the reader pauses to remember that Batman and the Joker are comic book characters themselves—of course they would behave this way. They *are* their media identities, which is why their manifestation in the datasphere is so important to them. Their battle is a metaconflict, framed within a cut-and-paste media.

So poor Batman, a character out of the patriarchy (he is, after all, avenging the murder of his father), finds himself caught in a nightmare as he tries to control postmodern chaos. In Frank Miller's words, "Batman imposes his order on the world; he is an absolute control freak. The Joker is Batman's most maddening opponent. He represents the chaos Batman despises, the chaos that killed his parents."[19] Living in a comic book world, it's no wonder that Batman is going crazy while the Joker seems to gain strength over the years.

This is why the experience of Miller's world is more like visiting an early acid house club than reading a traditional comic book. Miller initiates a reexploration of the nonlinear and sampling potential of the comic-book medium, pairing facing pages that at first glance seem unrelated but actually comment on each other deeply. A large, full-page abstract drawing of Batman may be juxtaposed with small cells of action scenes, television analysis, random comments, song lyrics, or newsprint. As the eye wanders in any direction it chooses, the reader's disorientation mirrors Batman's confusion at fighting for good in a world where there are no longer clear, clean lines to define one's position. The comic-book reader relaxes only when he is able to accept the chaotic, nonlinear quality of Miller's text and enjoy it for the ride. Then, the meaning of Batman's story becomes clear, hovering somewhere between the page and the viewer's mind.

Even more disorienting and cyber-extreme is the work of Bill Sienkiewicz, whose *Stray Toasters* series epitomizes the darkest side of the cyberpunk comic style. The story—a mystery about a boy who, we learn, has been made part machine—is depicted in a multimedia comic-book style, with frames that include photographs of nails, plastic, fringe, packing bubbles, toaster parts, leather, Band-Aids, and blood. This world of sadomasochism, crime, torture, and corruption makes *Neuromancer* seem bright by comparison. There is very little logic to the behaviors and storyline here—it's almost as if straying from the nightmarish randomness of events and emotions would sacrifice the nonlinear consistency. In essence, *Stray Toasters* is a world of textures, where the soft, hard, organic, and electronic make up a visual dreamscape through which both the characters and the readers are moved about at random. As Bruce Sterling would no doubt agree, an accidental or even an intentional electrocution could come at any turn of a page.

Finally, though, cyber-style comics have emerged that are as hypertextual as Miller or Sienkiewicz's, but far more optimistic. Like the characters of Marc Laidlaw and Rudy Rucker, the Teenage Mutant Ninja Turtles are fun-loving, pizza-eating surfer dudes, for whom enjoying life (while, perhaps, learning of their origin and fighting evil) is of prime importance. They are just as cyberpunk and nonlinear as Batman or the Joker, but their experience of life is playful. While the characters and stories in the subsequent films and TV cartoons are, admittedly, fairly cardboard, the original comic books produced out of a suburban garage by Eastman and Laird are cyberpunk's answer to *The Hitchhiker's Guide to the Galaxy*. Four turtles, minding their own business, fall off a truck and into a puddle of ooze that turns them into human-size talking turtles. They are trained by a rat to become ninja warriors, and then they go on an interdimensional quest to the place where the transformative ooze originated. Throughout their adventures, the turtles maintain a lighthearted attitude, surfing their way through battles and chases.

The violence is real and the world is corrupt, but the turtles maintain hope and cheer. The comic itself, like the Toon Town atmosphere, is a sweet self-parody, sampling nearly all of the comic-book-genre styles. But instead of creating a nightmarish panoply, Eastman and Laird use these elements to build a giant playground. Challenges are games, truly evil enemies are "bad guys," and the rewards are simple—pizza and a party. The *Teenage Mutant Ninja Turtles* series offers the only optimistic response to a nonlinear and chaotic world: to become softer, sweeter, more adventurous for its own sake, and not to take life too seriously.

## Signal Compression and Mind Expansion

The multimedia quality of cyber comic books spills over into cyberian video production, which has begun to reinterpret its own dynamic in relation to the fantasy games, novels, and comics. While these media borrow from video's quick-cut electronic immediacy, videographers now borrow back from the cyberpunk style and ethics to create a new graphic environment—one that interacts much more intimately with the viewer's body and consciousness than does the printed page.

At any Toon Town house event, television monitors throughout the club flash the computer-generated imagery of Rose X, a company created by Britt Welin and Ken Adams, a young married couple who moved to Petaluma, California, to be close to their mentor, Terence McKenna. Global Village enthusiasts, they hope their videos will help to awaken a network of like-minded people in remote regions throughout the nation. Their vision, inspired in part by McKenna, is of a psychedelic Cyberia, where techniques of consciousness, computers, and television co-evolve.

Like McKenna, Ken and Britt believe that psychedelics and human beings share a morphic, co-evolutionary relationship, but they are quick to include technology in the organic dance. As they smoke a joint and splice wires in their garage-studio, Ken explains the video-psychedelic evolutionary model.

"Psychedelic experiences are almost like voices from your dream state. They call you and they seduce you. People are also constantly seduced by psychedelic techniques on TV that have to do with fluid editing and accelerated vision processing. People love that stuff because it strikes them in a very ancient place, something that spirals back down into the past for everybody whether or not they're using psychedelics. It's there already."

Like MTV videos that substitute texture for story and quick cuts for plot points, Rose X videos work on an almost subliminal level. Meaning is gleaned from the succession of images more than their linear relationship. Viewers process information moment to moment, thus the amount processed increases with the number of cuts, even if the data is less structured. Rose X takes these techniques a step further by intentionally appealing to the viewer's ability to experience a kind of morphic resonance with the patterns and data flashing on the screen. Even their subject matter—their most popular videos are talks by Terence McKenna and Ralph Abraham—is intended to awaken dormant zones of human consciousness.

Britt, a perky, dark blonde with a southern accent, pops in a "video collage" and details her take on the relationship of technology, psychedelics, and consciousness. The images swirl on a giant video screen flanked by banks of computer equipment and wires. It's difficult to isolate what's around the screen from what's being projected onto it.

"We work in a psychedelic state when we're able to. And then we have a different relationship to our technology. We're into a concept called 'technoanimism,' where we really think of technology itself as an animistic dynamic that filters through the individual machines, bringing an overspirit to them—an animistic spirit that's way beyond what humans are comprehending on their own level."

Britt, like Sarah Drew from the music world, has developed herself into a cyborg. Both women unite with their technology in order to channel information they believe is new to humanity. Just as house musicians start with a sound, then go where the sound takes them, Britt allows her video and computer equipment to lead her into artistic discoveries. "When you are functioning at a high psychedelic level and you go into a cyberspace environment, you lose your parameters and you find yourself entirely within the electronic world. It breeds its own surprises."

Unlike most men in the cyber-arts scene, who tend to think of themselves as dominators of technology, Ken, like Britt, strives to become "one" with the machine. "Our video-computer system's set up to ease us into a level of intimacy where we can use it in a transparent sense. If I enter into a trance relationship with it, then it ends up having a spiritlike existence."

Rose X's current project, a feature-length video call *Strange Attractor,* emerges out of their interest in the relationship of technology to organic interdimensional consciousness. In the story, a reversal of the Adam and Eve myth, Rose is a "strange attractor'"—a person who, through lucid dreaming, can access the vast network of artificial environments normally entered through computers or virtual reality. On one of her journeys into cyberspace, she befriends another strange attractor—a young man who has gotten lost in the consensual hallucination. Her task is to rescue this lost soul by getting him to experience his body—through virtual sex—or his spirit—by getting him to eat a psychoactive apple. On the way, she is helped by an interdimensional sect who use organic methods to access Cyberia, and thwarted by an evil race of authorities, who hope to control interdimensional travel and trap the human race forever in its earthly, single-dimensional reality.

The battle is typically cyberpunk, but here the forces of chaos are the good guys, and those who put a lid on interdimensional travel are the bad guys. The good guys are true cyberians, who use ancient techniques, psychedelics, and computers in a nondiscriminatory cybersampling of whatever works. Britt and Ken believe Eve was right, and that had Adam followed his own impulses rather than God's orders, everything would have been okay.

Unlike Burroughs and other earlier voyagers, Britt embraces the ambiguous impulses that can feel so unsettling:

"Westerners tend to try to suppress them and ignore them, probably out of fear of insanity. If there are voices or beings in your mind that you don't seem to have any control over—that can be a terrifying prospect."

Similarly, rather than fearing technology's influence over them, they lovingly embrace their machinery as an equal partner in the race toward hyperspace. The printed, "official" version of Britt and Ken's psychedelic and technological agenda equates the experience of drugs with the promise of technology and the lost art of ecstasy:

"Strange but efficient organic forms appearing and disappearing resemble visions before sleep when two worlds touch. This is computer video signal compression. Like peyote, like psilocybin, silicon has songs to sing, stories to tell you won't hear anywhere else."

Likewise, the Rose X company is true to cyberian ideals of tribal, open interaction—a new garage-band ethic based on pooling resources and hacking what's out there. Britt trained herself on the Amiga Video Toaster after she convinced her employer to buy one. Ken bought his with money from an NEA grant. But even without elaborate social hacking, the Video Toaster's low cost makes it as available now as a guitar and amplifier were in the sixties. The device links the personal computer to the television, giving the viewing public its first opportunity to talk back to the screen.

Low-cost guerrilla production techniques have also led artists toward the cut-and-paste aesthetic. No longer concerned with making things look "real," videographers like Ken and Britt do most of their work in postproduction, manipulating images they shoot or scrounge. Like house music recording artists, they employ sampling, overlaying, and dubbing. Ken is proud that his work never tries to imitate a physical reality and is especially critical of filmmakers who waste precious resources on costly special effects. Video art in Cyberia is cut-and-paste impressionism. Just as comic-book artists include television images or even wires and blood in their cells, videographers include pictures of the Iraq bombings, virtual reality scenes, and even old sitcoms.

"We're much more like a cyberpunk comic book. We don't want it to look like it takes place in a natural setting. We want it to all be self-contained in a conceptual space that's primarily videographic—like virtual reality. It'll be the reality of the imagination. We've quit trying to mimic reality; we try to mimic our imagination, which is the root of all reality anyway."

Again, the final stage in the development of a cyberian genre is the designer being, mated both with technology and with psychedelics in the hope of creating a new territory for human consciousness. But what the designers of the new literary milieu may not realize is that around the world, thirsty young minds absorb these ideas and attempt to put them into effect in their own lives. The fully evolved cyberian artists aren't making any art at all. They're living it.

# chapter fifteen

## Playing Roles

Ron Post, aka Nick Walker, is a gamemaster and aikido instructor from suburban New Jersey. In his world, fantasy and reality are in constant flux. Having fully accepted ontological relativism as a principle of existence, Ron and his posse of "gamers" live the way they play, and play as a way of life. It's not that life is just a game, but that gaming is as good a model as any for developing the skills necessary to journey successfully through the experience of reality. It is a constant reminder that the rules are not fixed and that those who recognize this fact have the best time. Ron, his "adopted" brother Russel (they named themselves after the comic-book characters Ron and Russel Post), and about a dozen other twenty-something-year-olds gather each week at Ron's house to play fantasy role-playing games. Like the psychedelic trips of the most dedicated shamanic warriors, these games are not mere entertainment. They are advanced training exercises for cyberian warriors.

Fantasy role playing games, unlike traditional board games, are unstructured and nonlinear. There is no clear path to follow. Instead, the game works like an acting exercise, where the players improvise the story as they go along. There is no way to "win" because the only object is to create, with the other players, the best story possible. Still, players must keep their characters alive, and having fun often means getting into trouble and then trying to get out again.

Ron's game is based in GURPS, the Generic Universal Role Playing System, by Steve Jackson; it is a basic set of numerical and dice-roll rules governing the play of fantasy games. In addition, Jackson sells "modules," which are specific guidelines for gaming in different worlds. These modules specify realistic rules for play in worlds dominated by magic, combat, high-tech, even cyberpunk—a module that depicts the future of computer hacking so convincingly that the U.S. Secret Service seized it from Jackson's office believing it was a dangerous, subversive document.

I meet "the Posts" at Ron's house, which is next to the train overpass in South New Brunswick. It's the sort of day where everyone blames the sweltering heat on the greenhouse effect—too many weather records are being broken for too many days straight. The gamers sit on the front steps of Ron's house with their shirts off, except for the two girls. The group defies the stereotypically nerdy image of role players—this is an attractive bunch; they don't need gaming just to have a group of friends. Ron smiles and shakes my hand. His build is slight but well defined, which I imagine is due to hours of aikido practice. His hard-edged, pointy face and almost sinister voice counterbalance his quirky friendliness. He laughs at the cookies and wine I've brought as an offering of sorts, recognizing the gesture as one of unnecessary respect. He hands off the gifts to one of the other gamers and, as several begin to devour the food (these are not wealthy kids), Ron takes me upstairs to his room.

On his drafting table are the map and documents for Amarantis, the game Ron spent about a year designing for his group to play. It's a world with a story as complex as any novel or trilogy—but one that will be experienced by only about a dozen kids. Amarantis is a continent that floats interdimensionally—that is, the land mass at its eastern coast changes over time. It could be one civilization one year and a completely different one the next. The western coast of the continent is called the "edge." It's a sharp drop into no one knows what—not even Ron, the creator of this world. He'll decide what's there if anyone ventures out over it. The "tech level" of this world is relatively low—crossbows are about as advanced as the weaponry gets, but there is magic. The power and accuracy of magic on Amarantis fluctuate with what Ron calls the "weather," which refers not to atmospheric conditions but to the magical climate. The world is of particular interest to the IDC (the InterDimensional Council, which regulates such things), whose members recognize it as a nexus point for interdimensional mischief. Amarantis also has metaphorical influence over the rest of the fictional universe and even on other fantasy game worlds. What happens here—in a fractal way—is rippled out through the rest of that universe's time and space. If the IDC can maintain decorum here, they can maintain it throughout the cosmos.

Ron wants me to play along today, so we must invent a character. I am to enter Amarantis as an IDC cadet, who has escaped the academy via its interdimensional transport system. But first we must create my character's profile. My strengths and weaknesses are determined by a point system out of the GURPS manual. Each character has the same number of total points, but they are distributed differently. The more points a character has dedicated to agility, for example, the more tasks he can perform which require this asset.

During play, rolls of the dice are matched against skills levels to determine whether a character wins a fight, picks a lock, or learns to fly. If a character has spent too many points on wit and not enough on brute strength, he better not get cornered by a monster. GURPS has come up with numerical values for almost every skill imaginable, from quarterstaff combat to spaceship repair. Players may also acquire disabilities—like a missing arm or an uncontrollable lust for sex—which gives them points to use elsewhere. As in *Neuromancer,* characters must behave according to their profiles. Ron rewards players who, while maintaining their weaknesses, still manage to play skillfully.

For all the mathematics of character creation, the playing of the game itself is quite relaxed and chaotic. When Ron and I emerge from his bedroom we find today's players sitting in the living room, shirts still off, ready for action. Ron sets up a table for himself in the corner with his map, a notebook of information, and a box of index cards for every character in Amarantis.

What's going on here, essentially, is the creation of a fantasy story, where game rules and character points dictate the progression of the plot. A player thinks up an idea and is allowed to run with it as far as he can go until a conflict arises. Each character has an agenda, but these agendas do not get satisfied to the point where the game can end. For example, an agenda might be to extend the power of a large corporation, to destabilize the government of a city, or, as in my character's case, to spread goodwill throughout the universe.

Ron declares my arrival: "Suddenly, in a blaze of light, a large metal obelisk crashes through the floor of the stage. Smoke and sparks fly everywhere. The obelisk opens to reveal . . . " And there I am, in the middle of the floor show in an Amarantis night club. After I excuse away my arrival as a space-surfing accident—which no one believes—Russel, who plays a corporate businessman, invites everyone over to the Bacchic temple, a religious organization and megacorporation, to join the revelry already in progress. When we go there, Russel proceeds to seduce a young dancer (whose show I interrupted) with the promise of career advancement. As he takes her to his bedroom, I wander around the castlelike church. I hope to steal Russel's prize possession: a flying dragon.

Rolls of the dice decide my fate. The other players, especially Russel, watch on in horror, powerless: his character is in bed with the dancer and can't hear or see me even though the real Russel can. Other players worry for me—they know things about Russel's immense powers that I don't. But my character has a weakness for taking risks, and, disappointed by the lack of enthusiasm for my message of peace and harmony, I feel my only choice is to head straight for the "edge" and thus either certain doom or certain awakening. I find the dragon in an open courtyard. If I can get it to fly I'll have an easy getaway, but the creature is unbridled. I use my skill of resourcefulness—"scrounging," as it's called in the game— to find a rope to fashion into a bridle. I roll the three dice—two 2's and a 1. The other players moan. I'm a lucky roller, and the dice indicate that I easily find the rope. But the hard part is flying the creature. My dexterity is the skill that Ron pits against the dice. He calls this task a "D minus 8"—very hard. I need to roll a 10 or lower to succeed. I roll a 9. Amazing. Players cheer as gamemaster Ron describes the dragon taking off into the night. I use the stars to navigate west, toward the edge. Russel stares at me from across the room and chills go up my spine. He reaches for the GURPS Magic Module to find a spell to get his dragon back . . . and to destroy me. He plans on using corporate/church money to hire a powerful professional wizard.

"Is the Wizard's Hall open this late?" he asks Ron.

I look at Ron, who smiles knowingly at me. He had advised me to take "magic-protection" as a strength, and I reluctantly had done so. Thanks to Ron's insistence in adding this feature to my character, none of Russel's spells will work on me. I'm on my way to the edge.

FRP's (fantasy role-playing games) are surprisingly engrossing. They share the hypertext, any-door-can-open feeling of the computer net. And, like on a computer bulletin board, FRP's do not require that participants play in the same room or even the same city. Play is not based in linear time and space. A character's decision might be mailed in, phoned in, enacted live, or decided ahead of time. Also, there is no "object" to the game. There is no finish line, no grand finale, no winner or loser. The only object would be, through the illusion of conflict, for players to create the most fascinating story they can, and keep it going for as long as possible. As with cyberian music and fiction, role-playing games are based on the texture and quality of the playing experience. They are the ultimate designer realities, and, like VR, the shamanic visionquest, or a hacking run, the adventurer moves from point to point in a path as nonlinear as consciousness itself. The priorities of FRPs reflect the liberation of gamers from the mechanistic boundaries imposed on them by a society obsessed with taking sides, winning, finishing, and evaluating.

## Edge Games

These kids are not society's dropouts. Indeed, they are extremely bright people. Ron and Russel met at a school for gifted yet under-achieving high-schoolers in the Princeton area. They were smarter than their teachers, and knew it, which made them pretty uncontrollable and unprogrammable. Their brilliance was both their weakness and their strength. Because the subjects in school bored them, they turned to fantasy games that gave their minds the intellectual experience for which they thirsted. Of course, their elders never understood.

"Parental reaction is negative towards anything that teaches kids to think in original or creative ways," Russel reflects. "Playing the games is an exercise in looking at different realities—not being stuck in a single reality. It gives you courage to see how you're following many rules blindly in real reality."

Russel explains his childhood to me as we share a shoplifted cigarette beneath the train overpass. He has learned that the rules of this world are not fixed, and both he and Ron live according to the principles of uncertainty and change. Like the heroes in a cyberpunk novel, they are social hackers who live between the lines of the system and challenge anything that seems fixed. When Russel is hungry and has no money, he steals food from the supermarket . . . but he doesn't believe he'll get caught. Geniuses take precautions that regular shoplifters don't, I'm told, and survival to them becomes yet another "edge game."

What is the edge? "The edge is the imaginary or imposed limit beyond which you're not supposed to go," says Russel. "Where you'll get yourself really hurt. Pushing or testing the boundaries. Usually we find out the boundaries aren't really there. It's a matter of putting yourself through the test of your own fear."

Ron and Russel's comfortable suburban upbringing offered them few opportunities to test their tolerance for fear. The boys were forced to create their own edge in the form of behavioral games, so that they could experience darker, scarier realities. These edge games ranged from stealing things from school and playing elaborate hoaxes on teachers to assuming new identities and living in these invented roles for weeks at a time. Once, after taking LSD, Ron, Russel, and their friend Alan went to the mall to play an edge game they called "space pirates." Ron and Russel played interdimensional travelers, and Alan, who was temporarily estranged from them for social reasons, played a CIA-like spy trying to catch them. By the end of the acid trip and the game, Alan was crying hysterically in his mother's kitchen, and the Post brothers had to decide "whether we were going to help Alan get himself back together from this and rebuild things, or let him crumble into the kitchen floor and become permanently alienated."

Unlike the western border of the continent of Amarantis, to Russel and Ron the edge is no fantasy. Even Sarah Drew's abortion on acid could be called an edge game. The consequences of playing too close can be extremely real and painful. Ron spends as much time as possible on the edge, but he takes the risks seriously. "If you fuck up on the edge, you die. Edge games involve real risk. Physical or even legal risk. Try this: Take a subway or a city street, walk around, and make eye contact with everyone you meet, and stare them down. See how far you can take it. You'll come up to someone who won't look away."

Part of the training is to incorporate these lessons into daily life.

All of life is seen as a fantasy role-playing game in which the stakes are physically real but the lessons go beyond physical reality. Unlike the characters of a cyberpunk book, human beings are not limited to their original programming. Instead, born gamers, humans have the ability to adopt new skills, attitudes, and agendas. They just need to be aware of the rules of designer reality in order to do so. Fantasy role-playing and edge games in real life are ways of developing a flexible character profile that can adapt to many kinds of situations. As Ron explains: "The object in role-playing games is playing with characters whose traits you might want to bring into your own life. You can pick up their most useful traits, and discard their unuseful ones from yourself." One consciously chooses his own character traits in order to become a designer being.

Ron slowly slips into the Zen-master tone he probably uses with his students at the dojo. As the gamemaster, too, he serves as a psychologist and spiritual teacher, rewarding and punishing players' behaviors, creating situations that challenge their particular weaknesses, and counseling them on life strategies. Like a guided visualization or the ultimate group therapy, a gaming session is psychodramatic. Moreover, adopting this as a life strategy leads gamers to very cyberian conclusions about human existence.

"I regard any behavior we indulge in as a game," Ron says, waxing Jungian. "The soul is beyond not only three-dimensional space but beyond the illusion of linear time. Any method we use to move through three- or four-dimensional space is a game. It doesn't matter how seriously we take it, or how serious its consequences are."

Ron's wife of just two weeks looks over at him, a little concerned. He qualifies his flippant take on designer reality: "To play with something is not necessarily to trivialize it. Anything you do in your life is a role-playing game. The soul does not know language—any personality or language we use for thinking is essentially taking on a role."

To Ron, everything on the explicate order is basically a game—arbitrarily arranged and decided. Ron and Russel have adopted the cyberian literary paradigm into real life. Fantasy role-playing served as a bridge between the stories of cyberpunk and the reality of lives in Cyberia. They reject duality wholesale, seeing existence instead as a free-flowing set of interpretations.

Again, though, like surfers, they do not see themselves as working against anything. They do not want to destroy the system of games and role-playing that defines the human experience. They want only to become more fully conscious of the system itself.

Ron admits that they may have an occasional brush with the law, but, "we're not rebels. There's nothing to rebel against. The world is a playground. You just make up what to play today."

These people don't just trip, translate, and download. They live with a cyberian awareness full-time. Unlike earlier thinkers, who enjoyed philosophizing that life is a series of equations (mathematician Alfred North Whitehead's observation that "understanding is the aperception of patterns as such"), or Terence McKenna, who can experience "visual language" while on DMT, Ron guides his moment-to-moment existence by these principles.

"I'm aware that time is an illusion and that everything happens at once." Ron puts his arm around his young wife, who tries not to take her husband too seriously. "I've got to perceive by making things into a pattern or a language. But I can choose which pattern I'm going to observe."

Role-playing and edge games are yet another way to download the datastream accessed through shamanic journeys and DMT trips. But instead of moving into a completely unfiltered perception of this space and then integrating it piecemeal into normal consciousness, the gamer acknowledges the impossibility of experiencing reality without an interpretive grid, and chooses to gain full control over creation of those templates. Once all templates or characters become interchangeable, the gamer can "infer" reality, because he has the ability to see it from any point of view he chooses.

"The whole idea of gaming is to play different patterns and see which ones you like. I like playing the game where I live in a benevolent universe, where everything that happens to me is a lesson to help enlighten me further. I find that a productive game. But there are other games. Paranoia is a really good edge game. Or one can play predator: I live in a benevolent universe and I'm the *other* team."

That's probably why society has begun to react against designer beings: They don't play by the rules. Cyberian art, literature, game-playing, and even club life are tolerated when they can be interpreted as passing entertainment or fringe behavior. Once the ethos of these fictional worlds trickles down into popular culture and human behavior, the threat of the cyberian imagination becomes *real*. And society, so far, is unwilling to cope with a reality that can be designed.

# 5

# Warfare in Cyberia:
## Ways and Memes

# chapter sixteen

## Cracking the Ice

Like a prison escape in which the inmates crawl through the ventilation ducts toward freedom, rebels in Cyberia use the established pathways and networks of our postmodern society in unconventional ways and often toward subversive goals. Just as the American rail system created a society of hobos who understood the train schedule better than the conductors did, the hardwiring of our world through information and media networks has bred hackers capable of moving about the datasphere almost at will. The nets that were designed to hold people captive to the outworn modalities of a consumer society are made from the same fibers cyberians are now using in their attempt to climb out of what they see as a bottomless pit of economic strife, ecological disaster, intellectual bankruptcy, and moral oblivion.

Warfare in Cyberia is conducted on an entirely new battleground; it is a struggle not over territory or boundaries but over the very definitions of these terms. It's like a conflict between cartographers, who understand the ocean as a grid of longitude and latitude lines, and surfers, who understand it as a dance of chaotic waves. The resistance to renaissance comes out of the refusal to cope with or even believe in the possibility of a world free of precyberian materialism and its systems of logic, linearity, and duality. But, as cyberians argue, these systems could not have come into existence without dangerous patriarchal domination and the subversion of thousands of years of nondualistic spirituality and feminine, earth-based lifestyles.

Pieced together from the thoughts and works of philosophers like Terence McKenna and Ralph Abraham, the ancient history of renaissance and antirenaissance from the cyberian perspective goes something like this: People lived in tribes, hunting, gathering, following animal-herd migrations for ready food supplies, enjoying free sex, and worshipping the elements. As they followed the herds, these nomads also ate the psychedelic mushrooms that grew on the animals' dung, and this kept any ego or dominator tendencies in check. The moment when people settled down in agricultural communities was the moment when everything went wrong. Instead of enjoying the earth's natural bounty, people worked the soil for food—an act considered by extremists to represent the rape of Gaia and the taming of nature. Psychedelics fell out of the daily diet because people weren't following herds anymore. They had time to sit around and invent things to make life easier, like the wheel, and so came the notions of periodicity and time.

Time was a particular problem, because if anything was certain to these people, it was the fact that after a certain amount of time, everybody dies. The only way to live on after death is through offspring—but ancient men did not know who their offspring were. Only women knew for sure which children were their own. In previous, psychedelics-influenced tribes, the idea of one's own personal children mattered less, because everyone identified with the tribe. Now, with developed egos, men became uncomfortable with free love; thus patriarchal domination was born. Men began to possess women so that they would know which children were their own. The ideas of "property," "yours," "mine," and a host of other dualities were created. In an attempt to deny the inevitability of death, a society of possessors was born, which developed into a race of conquerors and finally evolved into our own nation of consumers.

Others blame the invention of time for the past six thousand years of materialist thought. Fearing the unknown (and, most of all, death), ancient man created time as a way to gauge and control his unpredictable reality. Time provided a framework in which unpredictable events could appear less threatening within an overall "order" of things. Of course the measured increments were not the time itself (any more than the ticks of a watch say anything about the space between them when the real seconds go by), but they provided a kind of schedule by which man could move through life and decay toward death in an orderly fashion. Whenever man came upon something he did not understand, he put over it a grid, with which he could cope. The ocean and its seemingly random sets of waves is defined by a grid of lines, as are the heavens, the cities, and the rest of reality. The ultimate lines were drawn to categorize and control human behavior. They are called laws, which religions and eventually governments emerged to write and enforce.

According to cyberian logic, the grids of reality are creations. They are not necessarily real. The Troubadours believed this. People burned at the stake as witches in the fourteenth century died for this. Scientists with revolutionary ideas must commit to this. Anyone who has taken a psychedelic drug experiences this. Fantasy gamers play with this. Hackers who crack the "ice" of well-protected computer networks prove this. Anyone who has adopted the cyberian vision lives this.

The refusal to recognize the lines drawn by "dominator society" is a worse threat to that society than is the act of consciously stepping over them. The exploitation of these lines and boxes for fun is like playing hopscotch on the tablets of the Ten Commandments. The appropriation of the strings of society's would-be puppeteers in order to tie their fingers and liberate the marionettes is a declaration of war.

Such a war is now being waged, and on many levels at once. The cyberian vision is a heretical negation of the rules by which Western society has chosen to organize itself. Those who depend on this organization for power vehemently protect the status quo by enforcing the laws. This is not a traditional battle between conservative and liberal ideologies, which are debates over where to put the lines and how thick to draw them. Today's renaissance has led to a war between those who see lines as real boundaries, and those who see them as monkey bars. They can be climbed on.

Cyberian warriors are dangerous to the "line people" because they can move in mysterious ways. Like ninjas, they can creep up walls and disappear out of sight because they don't have to follow the rules. Cyberian activities are invisible and render the time and money spent on prison bars and locks worthless. The inmates disappear through the vents.

As Marshall McLuhan and even George Orwell predicted, the forces in "power" have developed many networks with which they hope to control, manipulate, or at least capitalize on the behaviors and desires of the population. Television and the associated media have bred a generation of conditioned consumers eager to purchase whatever products are advertised. Further, to protect the sovereignty of capitalist nations and to promote the flow of cash, the defense and banking industries have erected communications networks that hardwire the globe together. Through satellites, computers, and telecommunications, a new infrastructure—the pathways of the datasphere—has superimposed itself over the existing grids like a metagrid, enforcing underlying materialism, cause and effect, duality and control.

But cyberians may yet prove that this hardwiring has been done a little too well. Rather than create an easy-to-monitor world, the end of the industrial era left us with an almost infinite series of electronic passages. The passages proved the perfect playground for the dendrites of expanding young consciousnesses, and the perfect back doors to the power centers of the modern world. A modem, a PC, and the intent to destabilize might prove a more serious threat to the established order than any military invasion. Nowhere is the fear of Cyberia more evident than in the legislation of computer laws and the investigation and prosecution of hackers, crackers, and data-ocean pirates.

## Forging Electronic Frontiers

There are as many points of view about hacker ethics, responsibility, and prosecution as there are players. Just how close to digital anarchy we move depends as much on the way we perceive law and order in the datasphere as it does on what's actually going on. While many young people with modems and personal computers are innocently exploring networks as they would the secret passages in an interactive fantasy game, others are maliciously destroying every system they can get into. Still other computer users are breaking in to networks with purpose: to gain free telephone connections, to copy information and code, or to uncover corporate and governmental scandals. No single attitude toward computer hacking and cracking will suffice.

Unfortunately, the legal and law-enforcement communities understand very little about computers and their users. Fear and ignorance prevail in computer crime-prosecution, which is why kids who "steal" a dollar's worth of data from the electronic world suffer harsher prosecution than do kids who steal bicycles or even cars from the physical world. Raids have been disastrous: Bumbling agents confiscate equipment from nonsuspects, destroy legally obtained and original data, and even, on one occasion, held at gunpoint a suspected hacker's uninvolved young sister. After a series of investigations and botched, destructive arrests and raids (which proved more about law enforcement's inability to manage computer use, abuse, and crime than it did about the way hackers work, play, and think), two interested parties—Mitch Kapor, founder of Lotus, and John Barlow, Grateful Dead lyricist and computer-culture journalist—founded the Electronic Frontiers Foundation.

The EFF hopes to serve as a bridge of logic between computer users and law enforcement so that cyberspace might be colonized in a more orderly, less antagonistic fashion. In Barlow's words, the seemingly brutal tactics of arresting officers and investigators "isn't so much a planned and concerted effort to subvert the Constitution as the natural process that takes place whenever there are people who are afraid and ignorant, and when there are issues that are ambiguous regarding constitutional rights."[1]

The EFF has served as a legal aid group defending hackers whom they believe are unjustly prosecuted and promoting laws they feel better regulate cyberspace. But while the EFF attempts to bring law and order to the new frontier, many hackers still feel that Barlow and Kapor are on "the other side" and unnecessarily burdening virgin cyberspace with the failed legal systems of previous eras.

Barlow admits that words and laws can never adequately define something as undefinable as Cyberia: "I'm trying to build a working scale model of a fog bank out of bricks. I'm using a building material that is utterly unsuited to the representation of the thing I'm trying to describe."

And while even the most enlightened articulators of Cyberia find themselves tongue-tied when speaking about the new frontier, other, less-informed individuals think they have the final word. The media's need to explain the hacker scene to the general public has oversimplified these issues and taken us even farther from understanding them. Finally, young hackers and crackers feed their developing egos with overdramatized reports on their daring, and any original cyberian urge to explore cyberspace is quickly overshadowed by their notoriety as outlaws.

Phiber Optik, for example, a twenty-year-old hacker from New York, plea-bargained against charges that he and his friends stole access to "900" telephone services. When he was arrested, his television, books, telephone, and even his Walkman were confiscated along with his computer gear. While he sees the media as chiefly responsible for the current misconceptions about the role of hackers in cyberspace, he appears to take delight in the media attention that his exploits have brought him.

"People tend to think that the government has a lot to fear from a rebellious hacker lashing out and destroying something, but we think we have a lot more to fear from the government because it's within their power to take away everything we own and throw us in jail. I think if people realize we aren't a dissident element at all, they would see that the government is the bad one."

Phiber claims that the reason why hackers like himself break into systems is to explore them, but that the media, controlled by big business, presents them as dangerous. "The term they love to use is 'threat to society.' All they see are the laws. All they see is a blip on the computer screen, and they figure the person broke the law. They don't know who or how old he is. They get a warrant and arrest him. It's a very inhuman thing."

But this is the very argument that most law-enforcement people use against hackers like Phiber Optik: that the kids don't get a real sense of the damage they might be inflicting because their victims are not real people—just blips on a screen.

Gail Thackery served as an assistant attorney general for Arizona and is now attorney for Maricopa County. She has worked on computer crime for two decades with dozens of police agencies around the country. She was one of the prosecuting attorneys in the Sun Devil cases, so to many hackers she is considered "the enemy," but her views on the legislation of computer laws and the prosecution of offenders are, perhaps surprisingly, based on the same utopian objective of a completely open system.

"I see a ruthless streak in some kids," says Thackery, using the same argument as Phiber. "Unlike a street robbery, if you do a computer theft, your victim is unseen. It's a fiction. It's an easy transition from Atari role-modeling games to computer games to going out in the network and doing it in real life."

The first hacker with whom she came in contact was a university student who in 1973 "took over" a class. Intended for social workers who were afraid of computers, the class was designed to acquaint them with cyberspace. "What happened," explains Thackery, "was this kid had planted a Trojan horse program. When the students logged on for their final exam, out came, instead of the exam, a six-foot-long typewriter-art nude woman. And these poor technophobic social workers were pounding keys. They went cuckoo. Their graduation was delayed, and in some cases it delayed their certification, raises, and new titles."

Thackery sees young hackers as too emotionally immature to cope with a world at their fingertips. They are intellectually savvy enough to create brilliant arguments about their innocent motivations, but in private they tell a different story. "I always look at their downloads from bulletin boards. They give legal advice, or chat and talk about getting busted, or even recite statutes. Kids gang up saying, 'Here's a new system. Let's trash this sucker! Let's have a contest and see who can trash it first!' They display real callous, deliberate, criminal kinds of talk."

Gail's approach to law enforcement is not to imprison these young people but to deprogram them. She feels they have become addicted to their computers and use them to vent their frustrations in an obsessive, masturbatory way. Just as a drug user can become addicted to the substances that provide him access to a world in which he feels happier and more powerful, a young computer user, who may spend his days as a powerless geek in school, suddenly gains a new, powerful identity in cyberspace. Like participants in role-playing games, who might shoplift or play edge games under the protective veils of their characters, hackers find new, seemingly invulnerable virtual personas.

"After we took one kid's computer away," Gail says, speaking more like a social worker than a prosecuting attorney, "his parents said the change is like night and day. He's doing better in school, he's got more friends, he's even gone out for the ball team. It's like all of a sudden this repressed human arises from the ashes of the hacker."

The hacker argument, of course, is that another brilliant young cyberian may have been reconditioned into boring passivity.

Thackery argues that it's a victory for the renaissance. "I have a philosophical, idealistic view of where computers started to head, and where the vandals actually kicked us off the rails. We wanted everybody to have a Dick Tracy wristradio, and at this point I know so many people, victims who have had their relationship to technology ruined. All you have to do is have your ATM hacked by a thief and you start deciding technology's not worth it."

So, in the final analysis, Gail Thackery is as cyberian as the most truly radical of the hackers. These are the ones who hack not for a specific purpose or out of resentment but for the joy of surfing an open datastream. The padlocking of the electronic canals is the result of society's inability to cope with freedom. Corporate and governmental leaders fear the potential change or instability in the balance of power, while macho, pubescent hackers act out the worst that their ego-imprisoned personalities can muster. In both analyses, the utopian promise of Cyberia is usurped by a lust for domination and a deeply felt resentment.

Several months after speaking with Thackery, I get a phone call late at night. She is crying; she's furious and needs someone to listen.

"Phiber's been busted again! Dammit!" She goes on to explain that the Secret Service in New York, along with the FBI and the Justice Department, have just arrested Phiber and several of his friends, including Outlaw and Renegade Hacker—the famed MOD (Masters of Deception) group. She takes it as a personal defeat:

"I always think when we catch these kids, we've been given a chance to show them a better way to spend their lives," her voice cracks in despair, "to finish school, get real jobs, stay out of trouble because it's a big bad world out there. Now Phiber's gonna go to jail. A kid's going to jail! I thought we made a dent but we blew it! I saw it coming."

What Gail had observed was undue media attention and praise for a boy who deserved better—he deserved scorn and derision. According to Gail, the positive reinforcement bestowed on him by reporters, computer-company owners, and sixties' heroes since his first arrest steered him toward more crime and antisocial behavior.

"Phiber was the only hacker to go on *Geraldo*. Where's Geraldo now? Nowhere! The kid's an embarrassment to him now!" Gail is fuming—"flaming," as they say on the WELL. Looking at it from a cyberian vantagepoint, Phiber became a victim of the fact that observers always affect the object they are observing. Media observation—from the likes of Geraldo or even me—threw Phiber farther off course than he already was. His problems were iterated and amplified by the media attention.

"What really irks me," adds Gail, "is guys like Kapor [Mitch Kapor, founder of Lotus] and Jobs [founder of Apple] misleading these kids by not scolding them for hacking. They shouldn't pat them on the shoulder! Kapor has no idea what's really going on out there today. When he was hacking, things were very different. It was a few pieces of code or a university prank. They're scared to tell these kids the truth because of their liberal guilt."

She calls them hypocrites: "These guys certainly protect their own software. The money that's funding the EFF is the same money that's paying for Lotus's attorneys, and they protect their proprietary rights, believe me! Guys like Kapor and Jobs are fighting an old sixties' battle, and getting kids put in jail with their misleading touchy-feely rhetoric. The kids shouldn't be made to fight these battles for them. It's the kids who are on the front line!"

Gail explains that the young hackers blindly follow the wisdom of the original computer hackers—but that this is a logic no longer appropriate on today's violent computer frontier. Organized crime and Colombian drug cartels now hire young hackers to provide them with secure, untraceable communications and intelligence.

"Now these kids are being used by drug dealers! They are being prostituted, but it's the kids who go to jail! Where's the EFF now?"

Cyberia is not real yet, but the problems facing it are. On one hand, fledgling cyberians are still rooted in the political activism and cultural extremism of the 1960s and '70s, and eager to please the people they consider their forefathers—Tim Leary, Steven Jobs, Mitch Kapor, William Burroughs—by wholeheartedly embracing their lifestyles and priorities. Kids who attempt to emulate William Burroughs will probably become addicted to drugs, and kids who take Steven Jobs' words at face value may end up prosecuted for computer crime. On the other hand, the technologies and pathways that young, brilliant cyberians forge are irresistible both to themselves and their would-be exploiters. Ego invades hyperspace.

Maybe the detractors are right. Maybe the cyberian technologies are not intrinsically liberating. While they do allow for cultural change through principles such as feedback and iteration, it appears that they can almost as quickly be subverted by those who are unready or unwilling to accept the liberation they could offer. But others present convincing arguments that the operating principles of Cyberia eventually will win out and create a more just Global Village.

# chapter seventeen

As we slouch farther toward the chaos attractor at the end of time, we find most of our networks, electronic or otherwise, working against their original aims or being diverted toward different ends. Subnetworks and metanetworks grow like mold over the original medium. Be it a symptom of social decay, cyberian genesis, or both, the growth of new colonialism around and within our old systems and structures brings a peculiar sort of darkness-before-dawnishness to the close of this millennium.

Compare our subculture of cyberians to Hogan's Heroes carrying out rebellious acts under the noses of guards and through underground tunnels in the prison camp. Perhaps the most telling sign of our times is that the United States has a greater percentage of its population in jail than does any other country, and is breeding a criminal subculture further and further removed from accepted social scheme.

It was in prison that legendary phone phreaque Cap'n Crunch (who got his name for using a two-note whistle he found in a box of Cap'n Crunch cereal to make free long-distance phone calls) was forced to join the ranks of the criminal subculture. His real name is John Draper, and I find him at Toon Town operating a computer-video interface.

After several meteoric climbs to the top of the programming profession, Draper is in the low phase of an endless rags-to-riches-to-rags curve that has defined the past twenty or so years of his life. It seems as though every time he develops a brilliant new program, an investigation links one of his friends, or friends of his friends, to something illegal, and then Draper's equipment—along with his livelihood—gets confiscated, delaying his progress and costing him his contract. The large, gray-haired, bespectacled cyber veteran suggests that we duck into the brain-machine room to speak about his prison experience.

"In order for me to survive in jail, I had to make myself valuable enough so they wouldn't harass me or molest me. So I had to tell everybody how to make calls, how to get in to the system, and what to do when they got in there. We'd have little classes. Out of pure survival I was forced to tell all and, believe me, I did."

Draper believes that thousands of telephone and computer crimes resulted from his prison classes. When his technologies got in the hands of inmates serving time for embezzlement or fraud, they in turn developed some of the most advanced industrial hacking done today.

Draper's experiences mirror the ways in which cyberian counter-culture movements form in society at large. For intellectual, emotional, or even physical survival, clusters of people—not always linked by geography—form posses characterized by the specific networks holding them together. This, then, initiates a bottom-up iteration of cyberian ideals.

One startling example is the growing community of "Mole People," who inhabit the forgotten tunnels of New York's subway system. The New York City Transit Authority estimates that about five thousand people live on the first level, but that accounts for only one-third of the tunnel system. Other officials estimate that closer to twenty-five thousand people live in the entire system, which goes much farther down than police or transit workers dare trek, and consists of hundreds of miles of abandoned tunnels built in the 1890s. The ash-colored denizens of the subways elect their own mayors, furnish their underground apartments, find electricity, and in some cases install running water. Sounding more like an urban myth than a real population, mole people claim that their children, born in the tunnels, have never seen the light of day. Others speak of patrols, organized by mole leaders to prevent their detection by making sure that outsiders who stray into their camp-sites and villages never stray out again. Whether or not this is an exaggeration, we do know that numerous television news crews who have attempted to reach the lower tunnels were pelted with rocks and forced to retreat.

"It's for security," explains J.C., who was asked by the mayor of his Mole community to explain their philosophy of life to Jenny Toth, a New York journalist who befriended the Mole People in 1990. "Society lives up in a dome and locks all its doors so it's safe from the outside. We're locked out down here. They ignore us. They've forgotten what it is to survive. They value money, we value survival. We take care of each other."[2] Alienation, disorientation, and, most of all, necessity, form new bonds of community cooperation not experienced above ground.

A man who lives hundreds of feet under Grand Central Station explains: "You go down there, play with some wires, and you got light. And before you know it, there are twelve to fifteen people down there with you. They become like neighborhoods; you're friends with everyone. You know the girls at the end and the family in the middle. When someone gets sick, we put our money together to get medicine. Most people team up. You can just about make it that way."[3]

This bottom-up networking is analogous to the formation of the Global Electronic Village, which also depends on bonds of mutual interest and like-minded politics. Each system is made up of people whose needs are not met or are even thwarted by established channels and each system exploits an existing network, using it for a purpose that was not intended. These kinds of communities make up an increasingly important component in the overall dynamical system of society. Programmer Marc de Groot compares this social landscape with the conclusions of systems math:

"The classic example of the feedback loop is the thermostat, which controls itself. I think we're becoming aware of the fact that the most common type of causality is feedback, and not linear or top-down. The effect goes back and affects the cause, and the cause affects the effect. We have a society where power becomes decentralized, we get feedback loops, where change can come from below. People in power will try to eliminate those threats."

The fears about cyberian evolution may stem from a partial awareness of these new channels of feedback and iteration. Those who believe they are currently in power attempt to squash the iterators, but find that their efforts are ineffectual. Like mutating bacteria or even cockroaches, feedback loops will foster adaptive changes faster than new antibiotics or bug sprays can be developed to combat them. Meanwhile, the formerly powerless who now see themselves as vitally influencing the course of history through feedback and iteration become obsessed with their causes and addicted to their techniques. But however obsessed or addicted they get,

and however fearfully or violently society reacts, feedback and iteration slowly and inevitably turn the wheel of revolution, anyway.

## Negative Feedback Iteration

Feedback loops are mathematics' way of phrasing revolution and
are as natural a part of existence as plankton, volcanoes, or thyroid
glands. The negative feedback loops to a mechanistic, consumption-
based culture are irate labor, eccoterrorists, and consciousness-
expansion advocates, who conduct their iterations through cheap
communications, printing, and video production.

Take Chris Carlsson, for example, editor of *Processed World,* a
magazine that he says is "about the underside of the information
age and the misery of daily life in a perverse society based on the
buying and selling of human time." Carlsson looks more like a college professor than an office worker; he's a brilliant, ex-sixties radical who dropped out of the rat race to make his living as an office
temp data processor in the San Francisco financial district.

On a lazy Sunday morning, Carlsson explains the intricacies of his
historical-philosophical perspective as he changes the screen in his
pipe and the grounds in his espresso pot. He believes that we are
currently living in a "socially constructed perversion," an unnatural
reality that will be forced to change. According to Carlsson, our society is addicted to consumption, and this addiction leads us to do
things and support systems that benefit only the dollar, not the individual. The systems themselves are constructed, like Muzak, to
squash the notion of personal power.

"It's hard to imagine how else it could be. The only questions you
are asked in this society are, 'What do you want to buy?' and, 'What
are you going to do for money?' You don't get to say, 'What do I
want out of life and how can I contribute to the totality?' There's no
mechanism at all in our society that promotes some sort of role for
the individual."

The "processed world" is a place where the bottom line is all that
matters. Workers are paid as little as possible to produce goods that
break as quickly as possible, or serve no function whatsoever other
than to turn a buck. For this final phase in the era of credit and
GNP expansion, there can never be enough stuff—if there were, the
corporations would go out of business. The motivation is to sell; the

standard of living, the environment, cultural growth, and meaning to life do not enter into the equation.

Chemical companies who want to sell chemicals, for example, thrive on weak crops and cattle; they hope to create a chemically dependent agriculture. "Thus, the first application of gene-splicing technology will be bovine growth hormone," Carlsson says. "Not that we need more milk in this country; we have a surplus!" But the growth hormone will increase a cow's output of milk. Farmer Jones will need to keep up with Farmer Smith, so he, too, will buy the hormone. Unfortunately, the hormone also weakens the cows' knees, which requires that the farmers purchase more antibiotics as well as other drugs, bringing more dollars to the chemical companies. Another example: It is to the chemical company's advantage to lobby against sterile fruit flies as a way of combating the medfly crisis in California. By "persuading" the government to use pesticides, chemical companies weaken the plants they are "saving," and thus create further dependence on fertilizers and medications—more money, less effectiveness, greater pollution.

Carlsson does not blame the "people in charge" for our predicament. "The chairman of the board doesn't feel like he has any power. He's just as trapped in. Nothing matters to the stockholders but how the balance sheet looks." Further, as the work environment increasingly dehumanizes, the system loses precious feedback channels with which it can correct itself. The dollar oversimplifies the complexities of a working society (and its needs—as we'll see later in this chapter—have simplified the global ecology to disastrous levels). As the workplace gets more automated, workers become merely a part of the spreadsheet: their input and output are monitored, regulated, and controlled by computer. As jobs are replaced by machines (which do the work more efficiently), workers are demoted rather than promoted. Any special skills they developed over time now become obsolete.

The way out, according to Carlsson, is subversion and sabotage.

"When you sell your time, you are giving up your right to decide what's worth doing. The goal of the working class should be to abolish what they do! Not being against technology, but being against the way it's being used. Human beings can find subversive uses for things like computers and photocopy machines. They were not made to enhance our ability to communicate, and yet they do. They provide everybody with a chance to speak through the printed medium. The work experience tells the worker that he has no say, and that what he is doing is a complete waste of time. But this profound emptiness and discontent is not evident on TV. Everything in society erodes your self-esteem."

*Processed World* magazine hopes to enhance the worker's self-esteem by appealing to his intellect and giving him tips on how to subvert the workplace. It's a homespun publication that articulates the experience of office workers so that they may realize they're not going crazy and their situations are not unique. It serves also as a forum for workers to share their observations on consumer society, abuses at work and techniques for fighting back. Slogans like "sabotage . . . it's as simple as pulling a plug" and joke ads for "cobalt-magnet data-zappers" for erasing office hard disks accompany the articles and testimonials written by reader/workers about ways to disable the workplace and thus disrupt the "evil" practices of big companies.

The computer is the primary instrument of sabotage in the workplace. The techniques that industrial hackers use against competitive companies are now being used by workers against their own companies. Usually—as throughout Cyberia—the routes to the greatest destruction have already been established unwittingly by the company bosses in the hope of better monitoring and controlling their employees.

On a tour of the data entry department at a major insurance firm, a computer serviceman and office saboteur explains the way things can get reversed. "Our office managers monitor the workers through a special intercom feature in the worker's telephone," he whispers as we stroll through the tract-deskscape. "I know this because I installed the phone system, and I taught the office managers how to use it, and I know that they do use it, because I monitor *them!*" We arrive at the desk of another worker, who plays video games on his computer. When he hits the escape key, a dummy spreadsheet covers the screen.

"Show him how the phone works," my escort requests.

The worker punches some keys on his phone and hands me the receiver. Someone is dictating a memo about how to order paper.

"That's the floor manager's office," the worker says, smiling proudly as he takes back the receiver and carefully hangs it up.

My guide boasts about the achievement. "You can repair this phone system through a modem to act like a bugging device—useful for bosses to spy on their workers. But if you modify the software—which is easy enough to do through the modem by remote control without ever entering the boss's office—you can take advantage of the same feature in reverse!"

"He did it right from my desk with my computer!" adds the worker, thankfully.

As we walk, most of the workers smile knowingly at my guide. They all are in this together. In the lingo of office sabotage, he confides proudly, "We've got this place pretty well locked up."

Sabotage, like computer hacking, can be seen as both a natural iteration and a destructive urge. True, it makes people feel more powerful and sends a warning signal—in the form of negative feedback—to the system as a whole. But it's also an opportunity for people to vent their frustration in general. A child who feels powerless and unpopular suddenly gains strength and status with a computer modem. An anonymous worker who cannot see any purpose to his life gets an ego boost when his well-planned prank disables an entire company.

Whether the motives are cyberian idealism or masturbatory ego gratification, these actions still serve as iterative feedback. We cannot dismiss these efforts as neurotic impulse or childish power fantasy just because their perpetrators cannot justify themselves with cyberian rhetoric. Even the most obsessive or pathological urges of saboteurs, when viewed in a cyberian context, appear to be the natural reactions of an iterative system against the conditions threatening its existence.

The most pressing of these conditions, of course, are the ones currently destroying the biosphere. As James Lovelock observed, Gaia defends herself through iterative feedback loops like plankton, algae, trees, and insects, which help maintain a balanced earth environment and conditions suitable for biological life. One such iterative loop may be the radical environmental group Earth First! These self-proclaimed "eccoterrorists," like their founder, the burly Arizonan Dave Foreman, have developed an extraordinarily virulent sociopolitical virus called "ecotage" or "ecodefense."

Ecotage is a terrorist approach to the defense of the environment. Rather than conduct protests, stage blockades, or influence legislation through lobbying, eccoterrorists perform neat, quick, surgical maneuvers that thwart the aims of those who would violate the environment. These actions, called "monkeywrenching," take the form of burying spikes in trees so that they may not be cut down; disabling vehicles; pulling down signs or electric wires; destroying heavy machinery or aircraft; spiking roads or woods to make them impassable; triggering animal traps; and, most important, getting away with it. Their acts are never random, but carefully planned to make the greatest impact with the least effort and risk. Cutting two cables on a helicopter rotor the evening before an insecticide spray, for example, does more damage than stealing the distributor caps out of forty jeeps in a company's parking lot. A few low-cost, well-planned ecotage attacks can make an entire deforestation project unprofitable and lead to its cancellation.

As Foreman explains in his *Ecodefense: A Field Guide to Monkeywrenching*—a kind of *Anarchist's Cookbook* with a purpose—monkeywrenching is powerful because it is nonviolent (no forms of life are targeted, only machines), not organized (impossible to be infiltrated), individual, specifically targeted, timely, dispersed throughout the country, diverse, fun, essentially nonpolitical, simple, deliberate, and ethical.[4] Of course the ethics are arguable. Businesses have a "legal" right to destroy the environment (especially if they've paid big bills lobbying for that right). The monkeywrenchers feel that the current political system is merely a gear in the destruction machine, and that the only tactic left is direct action.

Bob and Kali (yes, she's a TOPY member) are eccoterrorists from the Northwest. They have limited their activities (or at least the ones they're willing to talk about) to "billboard trashing and revision." Their hope is to preserve national parks and reverse the propaganda campaigns of would-be environmental violators. Kali, who works as a waitress in an interstate highway rest stop, is an odd mix of American sweetheart blonde and ankle-braceleted Deadhead—on her way from the counter to the tables she can be heard humming "Sugar Magnolia" through her Colgate smile. Her unthreatening demeanor allows her to listen in on and even provoke truckers' and construction workers' conversations about ongoing projects. Her boyfriend, Bob, then gives this information to more serious monkeywrenchers in their area over his school's computer network.

Bob is an art-studio assistant at the state university farther up the highway. He was motivated to take action against billboarding on his long drives down to the diner to pick Kali up from work each evening. "There's more and more billboards every week. There was a law passed to limit the number of billboards, but every time we pass a good law like that, the opposite thing happens in reality." Taking his pseudonym Bob from the "savior" of the Church of the Subgenius, a satirical cyberian cult, the young man has a tongue-in-cheek attitude toward his monkeywrenching and delights in the efficiency of his visual wit.

"One two-dollar can of spray paint can reverse a hundred-thousand dollar media campaign. You use their own words against them, expose their lies with humor." Using his own version of a device diagramed in Foreman's *Field Guide*, Bob puts a can of spray paint on top of a long metal rod with a string and trigger in the handle. From the ground, he can alter or add to a billboard many feet above his reach. Following Foreman's advice, he keeps the tool dismantled and hidden in a locked compartment of his truck, and varies the locations and times of his "hits" so that he won't get caught. "The book says answer the billboards. That's what we do. It's like they leave space for our comments." Among Bob's favorites are painting tombstones on the horizons of Marlboro Country and changing campaign slogans from "elect" to eRect."

Both Bob and Kali support the activities of more aggressive monkeywrenchers, but fear keeps them from going on those missions. "Not everyone's gotta risk their lives," Kali explains. "They've gotten chased by guys with bats."

"But what they're doing is essential," Bob adds. "It's a completely natural response. When the body gets sick, it makes more white blood cells. These guys are like that. We're like that, too, to an extent."

From a cyberian perspective, eccoterrorists are natural generators of negative feedback in the great Gaian organism. Even Brendan O'Regan, the reserved and mild-mannered vice president for research at the Institute of Noetic Sciences, acknowledges the place of ecotage as a valuable meme against the violation of the planet:

"Even if you disagree with the tactic, they're pointing out that industry is generating a kind of anarchy toward the environment. Eccoterrorists generate an anarchy back. There is an extreme that is driving it. Ecotage is sabotage on behalf of the environment. It's done rationalizing that due process of law and ethical concern is not being followed by the owners of the system, so 'fuck them.' And a lot of this stuff will be happening in concert with and through technologies like the fax, copiers, the computer network. It's chaos against chaos."

The systems set in place by the "establishment," as long as we're using blanket terminology, created a new series of feedback loops and iterators which allowed us to communicate and become aware of the natural ones destroyed by deforestation and environmental tyranny. Large organizations like Greenpeace depend on computer hackers and satellite experts both to set up their own communications networks and to intercept law enforcement communications about planned actions. Illegal television broadcasting vans, which have already been used in Germany, are currently under construction in the Bay Area; they will be capable of substituting scheduled programming with radical propaganda, or even superimposing text over regular transmissions.

Ecoterrorists are never antitechnology. They see high tech as a tool for faster and more effective feedback and iteration. For this reason, the developers of the Gaia hypothesis do not predict doom for our planet—especially from the development of inventions that appear unnatural. They realize the place of technology in the bigger picture, and even its value in regulating the biosphere. As James Lovelock, originator of the Gaia hypothesis, assures us:

"In the end we may achieve a sensible and economic technology and be more in harmony with the rest of Gaia. There can be no voluntary resignation from technology. We are so inextricably part of the technosphere that giving it up is as unrealistic as jumping off a ship in mid-Atlantic to swim the rest of the journey in glorious independence."[5]

Howard Rheingold, a social theorist, editor of the *Whole Earth Review* and author of computer culture books including *Virtual*

*Reality,* also admits: "It might be correct that technology was the wrong choice a long time ago and that it led to a really fucked up situation. But I don't see a way of getting out of this—without most of the people on Earth dying—without learning how to manage technology."

The danger here, of course, is in overestimating our potential to see our situation clearly and to implement technology toward the ends necessary. An oversimplification of the issues is as dangerous to our survival and, even more, our liberation, as is the reduction and simplification of our biosphere through the elimination of the millions of species upon which Gaia depends for feedback and iteration.

# chapter eighteen

## May the Best Meme Win

It's by using the technologies and pathways laid down by promoters of control that cyberians believe they must conduct their revolution. The massive television network, for example, whose original purpose was to sell products and—except for a brief period during the Vietnam War—to manufacture public consent for political lunacy, has now been coopted as a feedback mechanism by low-end home video cameramen. Coined "Video Vigilantes" on a *Newsweek* cover, private citizens are bringing reality to the media. When a group of cops use excessive force on a suspect, chances are pretty good that someone with a camcorder will capture the images on tape, and CNN will have broadcast it around the world within a couple of hours. In addition, groups such as Deep Dish TV now use public access cable channels to disseminate convincing video of a reality quite different from the one presented on the network newscasts.

"The gun used to be the great equalizer," explains Jack Nachbar, professor of popular culture at Bowling Green University, in reference to camcorders. "You can say this is like the new six gun, in a way. It can really empower ordinary people."[6] Police departments now bring their own video cameras to demonstrations by groups like DIVA (Damned Interfering Video Activists) in order to make a recording of their own side of the story. The new war—like Batman's media battle against the Joker—is fought not with conventional weapons but with images in the datasphere. The ultimate weapon in Cyberia is not the sword or even the pen but the media virus.

The media virus is any idea that infiltrates the host organism of modern society. It can be a real thing, like Mark Heley's Smart Bar, which functions on an organic level yet also acts as a potent concept capable of changing the way we feel about drugs, health care, and intelligence. A virus can also be a pure thought or idea, like

"Gaia" or "morphic resonance," which, when spread, changes our model of reality. The term *virus* itself is a sort of metamedia virus, depicting society as an immunodeficient host organism vulnerable to attack from "better" thoughts and messages. A virus contains genetic codes, what cyberians call "memes," which replicate throughout the system as long as the information or coding is useful or even just attractive. Cyberian activists are marketing experts who launch media campaigns instead of military ones, and wage their battles in the territory of cyberspace. How the computer nets, news, MTV, fashion magazines, and talk show hosts cover a virus will determine how far and wide it spreads.

The public relations game is played openly and directly in Cyberia. As we've seen, people like Jody Radzik, Earth Girl, and Diana see their marketing careers as absolutely compatible with their subversive roles. They are one and the same because the product they market—house culture—is a media virus. "The fuel that's going to generate the growth of this culture is going to be trendiness and hipness," Radzik says. "We're using the cultural marketing thing against itself." So, to be hipper and trendier, people buy Radzik's clothing and are exposed to the memes of house culture: fractals, chaos, ecstasy and Ecstasy, shamanism, and acceptance. Making love groovy.

But older, more practical generations cannot be so easily swayed by fashion or hipness. Cyberians who hope to appeal to this market segment use different sorts of viruses—ones that are masked behind traditional values, work ethics, and medical models. Michael Hutchinson, author of *The Book of Floating, Megabrain,* and *Sex and Power,* makes his living distributing information about brain machines and other stress-reduction devices. He is a tough and determined New Yorker dressed in local Marin County garb: pastels, khaki, and tennis shoes. Similarly, the cyberian motives behind his "stress-reduction" systems are dressed in quite innocent-sounding packaging.

"When we took acid in the sixties," Hutchinson admits, "we felt our discovery could change the world. A lot of the spirit at the time was, 'Hey, let's dump this stuff in the reservoir and turn on America . . . the world! We can get everybody high and there won't be any war!'"

But it's hard to get people to drop acid. Getting them to put a set of goggles on their eyes is a whole lot easier and can even be justified medically. Numerous studies have demonstrated that the flashing lights and sounds produced by brain machines can relax people, invigorate them, and even relieve them from substance abuse, clinical depression, and anxiety. The machines work by coaxing the brain to relax into lower frequencies, bringing a person into deep meditative states of consciousness. This can feel like a mild psychedelic trip according to Hutchinson, and has many of the same transformational qualities.

"The subconscious material tends to bubble to the surface, but you are so relaxed by the machine that you're able to cope with whatever comes up. Over a period of time, people can release their demons in a very gentle way. If it were as intense as an acid trip, it would scare people away." Hutchinson smiles. In a way he is glad to admit that brain machines are really transformational wolves in therapeutic sheep's clothing. "There's something really subversive to what we're working on here. We've convinced businesses to use these devices for stress reduction, schools for better learning curves, doctors for drug rehabilitation. The hidden agenda is that we actually get them into these deep brain states and produce real personality transformation. That's the secret subtext. I think in the long run this machine's going to have a very revolutionary effect. If everybody in the world . . ."

His sentence trails off as he muses on global brain-machine enlightenment. But the Food and Drug Administration has other plans for these devices. Manufacturers may no longer make medical claims about the machines before they have received FDA approval— a process requiring millions of dollars. Hutchinson is convinced that there are powers behind the suppression of the brain machine virus.

"George Bush once said, 'The only enemy we have is unpredictability.' Authoritarian systems depend on their citizens to act with predictability. But anything that enhances states of consciousness is going to increase unpredictability. These machines lead people to new, unpredictable information about themselves. The behavior that results is unpredictable, and, in that sense, these tools are dangerous. Big Brother is threatened when people take the tools of intelligence into their own hands."

This is why Hutchinson spends his efforts educating people about brain machines rather than distributing the machines himself. His newsletters detail where to purchase machines, how they work, why they're good, and how to make them. "Mass education is mass production," he says. "Even if the machines are outlawed, the circuit diagrams we've printed will keep the technology accessible."

Finally, though, the most cyberian element of the brain virus machine is the idea, or meme, that human beings should feel free to intentionally alter their consciousnesses through technology. As the virus gains acceptance, the cyberian ideal of a designer reality moves closer to being actualized.

## Meme Factory

For the survival of a virus, what promoters call "placement" is everything. An appearance on *The Tonight Show* might make a radical idea seem too commonplace, but an article in *Meditation* might associate it with the nauseatingly "new" age. A meme's placement is as important to a media virus as the protein shell that encases the DNA coding of a biological virus. It provides safe passage and linkage to the target cell, so that the programming within the virus may be injected inside successfully. One such protein shell is Queen Mu and R.U. Sirius's *Mondo 2000.*

Originally birthed as *High Frontiers,* a 'zine about drugs, altered states of consciousness, and associated philosophies, the publication spent a brief incarnation as *Reality Hackers,* concerning itself with computer issues and activism as Cyberia's interests became decidedly more high tech. Now known to all simply as *Mondo,* the two or so issues that make their way down from the Berkeley Hills editorial coven each year virtually reinvent the parameters of Cyberia every time they hit the stands. If a virus makes it onto the pages of *Mondo,* then it has made it onto the map. Cyberia's spotlight, *Mondo* brings together new philosophy, arts, politics, and technology, defining an aesthetic and an agenda for those who may not yet be fully online. *Mondo* is the magazine equivalent of a house club. But more than gathering members of a geographical region into a social unit, *Mondo* gathers members of a more nebulous region into a like-minded battalion of memes. Its readers are its writers are its subjects.

Jas Morgan, a pre-med student in Athens, Georgia, knew there was something more to reality but didn't know where to find it. As for most true cyberians, drugs, music, and media had not made Jas dumb or less motivated—they had only made it imperative for him to break out of the fixed reality in which he had found himself by the end of high school. (He once placed one of his straight-A report cards on his parents' kitchen table next to a small bag of pot and a note saying "We'll talk.")

Like many other fledgling cyberians scattered around the United States, Jas had few sources of information with which to confirm his suspicions about life. He listened to alternative FM radio late into the night and read all of Timothy Leary's books twice. Jas had been particularly inspired by Leary's repeated advice to the turned-on: "Find the others." When Jas came upon an issue of *High Frontiers,* he knew he'd found them.

*High Frontiers* was the first magazine to put a particular selection of memes together in the same place. Ideas that had never been associated with one another before—except in pot-smoke-filled dorm rooms—could now be seen as coexistent or even interdependent. The discontinuous viral strands of an emerging culture found a home. Leary wrote about computers and psychedelics. Terence McKenna wrote about rain-forest preservation and shamanism. Musicians wrote about politics, computer programmers wrote about God, and psychopharmacologists wrote about chaos. This witches' brew of a magazine put a pleasant hex on Jas Morgan, who found himself knocking on the door of publisher/"Domined-itrix" Queen Mu's modest mansion overlooking Berkeley, and, he says, being appointed music editor on the spot. The Mondo House, as it's admiringly called by those who don't live there, is the hilltop castle/kibbutz/home-for-living-memes where the magazine is writ-ten, edited, and, for the most part, lived. Dispensing with the for-mality of an objectified reality, the magazine accepts for publication whichever memes make the most sense at the time. The man who decides what makes sense and what doesn't is R.U. Sirius, aka Ken Goffman, the editor in chief and humanoid mascot.

Jas moved in and quickly became *Mondo*'s jet-setting socialite, especially after Queen Mu's own schedule got too crowded for her to continue publicizing the magazine by herself. His good looks and preppy manner served as an excellent cover for his otherwise "illicit" agenda, and he helped get the magazine long-awaited recognition from across the Bay (the city of San Francisco) and the Southland (Los Angeles). But as Jas developed the magazine's cosmopolitan image, R.U. Sirius developed Jas' image of reality. Jas quickly learned to see his long-standing suspicions about consensus reality as truths, and his access to new information, people (Abbie Hoffman's ex-wife became his girlfriend), and chemicals gave him the lingo and database to talk up a storm.

"Every time I want a CD, I have to go out and spend fifteen dollars to get one when it would be really nice just to dial up on the computer, or, better, say something to the computer and get the new release and pay a penny for it. And to not have it take up physical space and to not have all these people in the CD plant physically turning them out to earn money to eat. I want a culture where everybody's equally *rich*. People will work out of their homes or out of sort of neotribal centers with each other, the way the scientists work together and brainstorm. Everyone worries about motivation. Don't worry—people wouldn't just sit around stoned watching TV."

He ponders that possibility for a moment. "Maybe people *will* want to take a year off, smoke some grass and watch TV. But then they'll get bored and they'll discover more and more of themselves."

The boys and girls at *Mondo* have made a profession of quitting the work force, spacing out, and sitting around talking like this. (Since my shared experience with the *Mondo* kids, publisher Queen Mu has worked to make the magazine more respectable. Most references to drugs are gone, and the original band of resident renegades—who Mu now calls "groupees"—has slowly been replaced by more traditional writers and editors as the magazine tries to compete with the tremendously successful *Wired* magazine. But, in its heyday, *Mondo* was as vibrant as "The Factory," Andy Warhol's loft/commune/film studio of 1960s New York City. *Mondo* the magazine and *Mondo* the social setting provided a forum for new ideas, fashion, music, and behavior.)

Like their counterparts in Warhol's New York, the kids I meet at this, the original wild-hearted *Mondo 2000*, have dedicated their lives to discussing and embodying fringe concepts. Their editorial decisions are made on the "if it sounds interesting to us, then it'll be interesting to them" philosophy, and their popularity has given them the authority to make a meme interesting to "them" simply by putting it in print.

Much of the clan found itself working with R.U. Sirius. Someone shows up at the door, talks the right talk, and he's in. The current posse numbers about twenty. At the center of this circus is R.U. Sirius himself. He's Cyberia's Gomez Addams, and he makes one wonder if he is a blood relation to the menagerie surrounding him or merely an eccentric voyeur. It's hard to say whether Sirius is the generator of Cyberia or its preeminent detached observer, or both. Maybe his success proves that the ultimate immersion in hyperspace is a self-styled metaparticipation, where one's surroundings, friends, and lovers are all part of the information matrix, and potential text for the next issue. While some social groups would condemn this way of treating one's intimates, these Cyberians thrive off it. They are human memes, and they depend on media recognition for their survival.

"We're living with most of our time absorbed in the media," Ken speculates on life in the media whirlwind. "Who we are is expressed by what we show to the world through media extensions. If you're not mentioned in the press, you don't exist on a certain level. You don't exist within the fabric of the Global Village unless you're communicating outwards."

So, by that logic, Sirius decides what exists and what doesn't. He has editorial privilege over reality. "Oppose it if you want," he tells me as we drive back from a Toon Town event to the *Mondo* house late one night, "but you're already existing in relation to the datastream like the polyp to the coral reef or the ant to the anthill or the bee to the beehive. There's just no getting away from it." Moreover, Sirius is Cyberia's genetic engineer, designing the reality of the media space through the selection of memes.

R.U. Sirius's saving grace—when he needs one to defend himself against those who say he's playing God—is that he doesn't choose the memes for his magazine with any conscious purpose or agenda. The reason he left Toon Town so early (before 2:00 A.M) is that, in his opinion, they present their memes too dogmatically. "Mark

Heley and the house scene are a bit religious about what they're doing. *Mondo 2000* doesn't have an ideology. The only thing we're pushing is freedom in this new territory. The only way to freedom is not to have an agenda. Protest is not a creative act, really."

The memes that R.U. Sirius chooses for his magazine, though, are politically volatile issues: sex, drugs, revolutionary science, technology, philosophy, and rock and roll. Just putting these ideas into one publication is a declaration of an information war. Sirius claims that one fan of theirs, a technical consultant for the CIA and the NSA, always sees the magazine on the desks of agents and investigators. "He told us 'they all love you guys. They read you to try to figure out what's going on.' Why that's pretty pathetic. I told him we're just making it up."

In spite of his lampoonish attitude, Sirius admits that his magazine reflects and promotes social change, even though it has no particular causes. "We're not here to offer solutions to how to make the trains run on time. We're coming from a place of relative social irresponsibility, actually. But we're also offering vision and expansion to those who want it. We don't have to answer political questions. We just have to say 'here we are.'"

And with that we arrive at R.U.'s house. Sirius has a little trouble getting out of the car. "I'm kicking brain drugs right now," he apologizes. "I was experiencing some back pain so I'm staying away from them, for now." Yet, he manages to round off his exit from the vehicle with a little flourish of his cape. He moves like a magician—a slightly awkward magician—as if each action is not only the action but a presentation of that action, too. No meaning. Just showmanship.

As he walks the short footpath to house, he comes upon journalist Walter Kirn, who is urinating off the front porch into the bushes below.

"We have a bathroom, Walter." Sirius may be the only person in Cyberia who can deliver this line without sarcasm.

Walter apologizes quickly. "This was actually part of an experiment," he says, zipping up, and thinking twice about offering his hand to shake. He proceeds to explain that he's been waiting to get in for almost an hour. He thought he saw movement inside, but no one answered the bell. Then he began to wait. And wait. Then he remembered something odd: "That whenever I take a piss, something unusual happens. It acts as a strange attractor in chaos math. When I introduce the seemingly random, odd action into the situation, the entire dynamical system changes. I don't really believe it, but it seems to work."

Sirius stares at Kirn for a moment. This is not the same journalist who arrived in Berkeley last week. He's been converted.

"So you peed us here, I guess."

Walter laughs at how ludicrous it all sounds. "It was worth a try."

"Apparently so," concludes Sirius, opening the door to the house with that strange hobbitlike grace of his.

Why no one heard Kirn's ringing and knocking will remain a mystery. About a dozen brilliant cyberians sit chatting in the large, vaulted-ceiling living room. The cast includes Eric Gullichsen (the VR designer responsible for Sense8—the first low-cost system), two performance artists, one of Tim Leary's assistants, one member of an all-girl band, plus Sarah Drew, Jas Morgan, a few other members of the editorial staff, and a few people who'd like to be. This is not the official Mondo staff, and on any night an entirely different set of people might be here.

One resident concocts coffee in the kitchen (hopefully strong enough to oust the most sedentary of couch potatoes from their cushions), as a guy who no one really knows sits at the table carefully reading the ingredients on the cans of Durk and Sandy mind foods that are strewn about. Back in the living room, the never-ending visionary exchange-cum-editorial meeting prattles on, inspiring, boring—abstract enough to confuse anyone whose brain chemistry profile doesn't match the rest of the room's at the moment, yet concrete enough to find its way onto the pages of the next issue, which still has a couple of openings. The VR designer might get his next project idea at the suggestion of a writer who'd like to cover the as-yet nonexistent "what if . . . ?" technology. Or a performance artist might create a new piece based on an adaptation of the VR designer's hypothetical interactive video proposal. This is at once fun, spaced, intense, psychedelic, and, perhaps most of all, business.

"It's interesting to see what happens to the body on psychedelics," someone is saying. "The perceptions of it. Some of it can be quite alien-looking. Some of it's very fluffy and soft and wonderful. Sort of gives you some hints of what the physical evolution of the body is going to be like."

"And the senses. Especially hearing and sound," adds Sarah, looking deep into the eyes of one of her admirers. She's this Factory's Edie Sedgwick except with a shrewd mind and a caring soul. "Think if, instead of developing TV, we had taken sound reproduction into art. It would have created a different society." No one picks up on the idea, but Sarah has nothing to worry about. A huge spread on her music is already slated for the next issue.

Sirius sits down next to Sarah, and her suitors back off a little. Kirn watches the couple interact, silently gauging their level of intimacy. Perhaps Sirius is only a cyber Warhol, after all. Sarah might be his art project more than his lover. Meanwhile, others wait for Sirius to direct the conversation. Is he in the mood to hear ideas? How was Toon Town? Did he think of the theme for the next issue?

Journalist-turned-starmaker R.U. Sirius is the head "head" at *Mondo,* and he serves as the arbiter of memes to his growing clan. It is Sirius, with Mu's approval, who finally decides if a meme is worth printing, and his ability to stay removed from "the movement" gives him the humorist's-eye view of a world in which he does not fully participate, yet absolutely epitomizes. Having made it through the 1960s with his mind intact, Sirius shows amazing tolerance for the eager beavers and fist wavers who come through the *Mondo* house every day. In some ways the truest cyberian of all, "R.U. Sirius" asks just that question to everyone and everything that presents itself to him. His smirkishly psychedelic "wink wink" tone makes him impervious to calamity. His "no agenda" policy infuriates some, but it coats the memes in his glossy magazine with an unthreatening candy shell. Hell, some of the strongest acid in the sixties came on Mickey Mouse blotter.

Sirius sits in a rocker and smiles in silence awhile. He knows these people are his willing subjects—not as peasants to king, but as audio samples to a house musician. As Sirius said earlier that day, "I like to accumulate weird people around me. I'm sort of a cut-and-paste artist." He waits for someone to provide a few bites.

"We were talking about the end of time," one of the performance artists finally says. "About who will make it and who won't."

"Through the great attractor at the end of time, she means," continues another. "Into the next dimension."

"Only paying *Mondo 2000* subscribers will make it into hyperspace," Sirius snickers, "and, of course, underpaid contributors."

Everyone laughs. The mock implication is that they will be rewarded in the next dimension for their hard work and dedication to *Mondo* now—especially writers who don't ask for too much money. Sirius puts on a more genuinely serious tone, maybe for the benefit of Kirn, who still jots occasional notes into his reporter's notebook. This is media talking about metamedia to other media.

"I'm not sure how this is all going to come to pass, really." Sirius says slowly, so that Kirn's pen can keep up with his him. "Whether all of humanity will pop through as a huge group, or as just a small part, is hard to speculate. I don't think it'll be rich, dried-up Republican white men who come through it in the end. It's more likely to be people who can cope with personal technologies, and who do it in their garages. You have to have your own DNA lab in your basement."

"I've got this theory about New Age people and television." Jas sits up in his chair, gearing up for a pitch. The relaxed setting in no way minimizes the personal and professional stakes. To them, this is an editorial meeting.

"New Age people are very much like the *Mondo* or the psychedelic people are—they just go outdoors and camping because they are scared of technology. That's because growing up in the sixties, parents would take TV time away as a punishment. Plus, TV became an electronic babysitter, and took on an authoritarian role. And I think a certain amount of TV had to be watched at the time in order to get the full mutation necessary to become one of us. They didn't get enough, so they became New Age people with mild phobias towards technology."

There's a pause. Most eyes in the room turn to Sirius for his judgment on the theory, which could range anywhere from a sigh to an editorial assignment. Would the idea become a new philosophical virus?

"Hmmph. Could be . . . " He smiles. Nothing more.

Jas goes downstairs, covering the fact that he feels defeated. Someone lights a cigarette. More coffee is served. (The *real* editorial meeting is scheduled for Monday morning.) The guy in the kitchen has passed out. Someone pops in a videocassette. Walter, wondering now what he liked about Sarah, checks his watch. Somehow, it's hard to imagine this gathering as our century's equivalent of the troubadours.

But maybe this *is* the real Cyberia. It's not tackling complex computer problems, absorbing new psychedelic substances, or living through designer shamanic journeys. It's not learning the terminology of media viruses, chaos math, or house music. It's figuring out how two people can sell smart drugs in the same town without driving each other crazy. It's learning how to match the intentions of Silicon Valley's most prosperous corporations with the values of the psychedelics users who've made them that way. It's turning a nightclub into the modern equivalent of a Mayan temple without getting busted by the police. It's checking your bank statement to see if your ATM has been cracked, and figuring out how to punish the kid who did it without turning him into a hardened criminal. It's not getting too annoyed by the agendas of people who say they have none, or by the inane, empty platitudes of those who say they do. It's learning to package the truth about our culture into media-friendly, bite-size pieces, and then finding an editor willing to put them in print because they strike him as amusing.

Coping in Cyberia means using our currently limited human language, bodies, emotions, and social realities to usher in something that's supposed to be free of those limitations. Things like virtual reality, smart bars, hypertext, the WELL, role-playing games, DMT, Ecstasy, house, fractals, sampling, anti-Muzak, technoshamanism, ecoterrorism, morphogenesis, video cyborgs, Toon Town, and *Mondo 2000* are what slowly pull our society—even our world— past the event horizon of the great attractor at the end of time. But just like these, the next earth-shattering meme to hit the news-stands or computer nets may be the result of a failed relationship, a drug bust, an abortion on acid, or even a piss over the side of the porch.

Cyberia is frightening to everyone. Not just to technophobes, rich businessmen, midwestern farmers, and suburban housewives, but, most of all, to the boys and girls hoping to ride the crest of the informational wave.

Surf's up.

# notes

## Part I — Computers: Revenge of the Nerds

1. Facts from *Mondo 2000,* winter 1991.
2. Ralph Abraham, in *Gentlemen's Quarterly,* "Valley of the Nerds," by Walter Kirn, July 1991.
3. Kirn, "Valley of the Nerds."
4. John Perry Barlow, "Crime and Puzzlement," *Whole Earth Review,* fall 1990.
5. Jaron Lanier, in an interview with George Gleason, 1991.
6. Warren Robinett, "Electronic Expansion of Human Perception," in *Whole Earth Review,* number 72, fall 1991.
7. Lanier interview with Gleason.
8. Tim Leary, *Tim Leary's Greatest Hits,* (Los Angeles: Knoware, 1991).
9. Leary, *Greatest Hits.*
10. Lanier interview with Gleason.

## Part II — Drugs: The Substances of Designer Reality

1. Terence McKenna, *Food of the Gods: The Search for the Original Tree of Knowledge: A Radical History of Plants, Drugs and Human Evolution,* (New York: Bantam, 1992), p. 6.
2. Thomas Pynchon, in Bruce Eisner, *Ecstasy: The MDMA Story* (Berkeley: Ronin, 1989).
3. Eisner, *Ecstasy,* p. 1.
4. Terence McKenna, *Food of the Gods,* p. 261.
5. Gracie and Zarkov, *Notes from Underground: A "Gracie and Zarkov" Reader* (privately published in 1984, c/o *Mondo 2000* magazine).
6. Earth Girl, in *Rolling Stone,* Sept 5, 1991, "Get Smart" by Gary Wolf.
7. Michael Hutchinson and John Morganthaler, *Megabrain Report,* vol 1 number 1, p. 18.

## Part III — Technoshamanism: The Transition Team

1. Fraser Clark in a self-interview, advance copy submitted to *Mondo 2000* in 1991.

## Part IV — Cut and Paste: Artists in Cyberia

1. Brian Eno, liner notes to *Ambient Music,* September 1978.

2. ———, in Anthony Korner, "Aurora Musicalis," *Artforum* 24:10, summer 1986, in *Brian Eno: His Music and the Vertical Color of Sound* by Eric Tamm (Boston: Faber and Faber, 1989).

3. Eric Tamm, *Brian Eno: His Music and the Vertical Color of Sound* (Boston: Faber and Faber, 1989), p. 94.

4. Genesis P. Orridge, in *Mondo 2000,* issue #3, winter 1991.

5. Orridge, *Mondo.*

6. David Cronenberg, interviewed in "Too Extreme . . . Until Now," *Los Angeles Times,* May 12, 1991.

7. William Burroughs, from *Giorno Poetry Systems,* in "Whole Earth Review," summer 1989, n. 63 p. 54.

8. William Gibson, *Neuromancer* (New York: Ace Science Fiction, 1984), p. 52.

9. Gibson, *Neuromancer,* p. 52.

10. Gibson, *Neuromancer,* p. 267.

11. Gibson and Sterling, *The Difference Engine* (New York: Bantam, 1991), p. 1.

12. Bruce Sterling, interview in *Whole Earth Review,* winter 1988, n. 61, p. 11.

13. William Gibson, interview in *Mississippi Review,* vol 16.

14. Gibson, *Mississippi Review.*

15. Gibson, *Mississippi Review.*

16. Rudy Rucker and Mark Laidlaw, "Probability Pipeline" in *Synergy #2,* George Zebrowski, editor, (San Diego, CA: Harcourt Brace Jovanovich, 1987).

17. Rucker, *Pipeline.*

18. Frank Miller, *Batman: The Dark Knight* (New York: DC Comics, 1986).

19. Frank Miller, Interviewed in "Batman and the Twilight of the Idols" by Christopher Sharrett in Roberta E. Pearson and William Uricchio, eds., *The Many Lives of the Batman: Critical Approaches to a Superhero and His Media* (New York: Routledge, 1991).

## Part V — Warfare in Cyberia: Ways and Memes

1. John Barlow, in *Mondo 2000,* winter 1991, p. 46.

2. Jenny Toth, "The Mole People," *Exposure Magazine,* December 1990.

3. Toth, "Mole People."

4. Dave Foreman, *Ecodefense: A Field Guide to Monkeywrenching,* second edition (Tucson: Ned Ludd Books, 1987), pp. 14–17.

5. J. E. Lovelock, *Gaia: A New Look at Life on Earth* (New York: Oxford University Press, 1979), pp. 117 and 138.

6. Jack Nachbar in "Video Vigilantes," *Newsweek,* July 22, 1991.

# selected bibliography

Abraham, Ralph. *Chaos, Gaia, Eros: The Orphic Trinity in Myth and Science.* San Francisco: HarperSanFrancisco, draft from 1990.

Argüelles, José. *The Mayan Factor: Path Beyond Technology.* Santa Fe: Bear and Company, 1987.

*bOING-bOING* magazine. Boulder: 1990–92.

Briggs, John P., and David F. Peat. *Looking Glass Universe: The Emerging Science of Wholeness.* New York: Simon & Schuster, 1984.

———. *Turbulent Mirror: An Illustrated Guide to Chaos Theory and the Science of Wholeness.* New York: Harper & Row, 1989.

Carlsson, Chris, ed. *Bad Attitude: The Processed World Anthology.* New York: Verso Books, 1990.

Dean, Ward, and John Morgenthaler. *Smart Drugs & Nutrients: How to Improve Your Memory and Increase Your Intelligence Using the Latest Discoveries in Neuroscience.* Santa Cruz: B & J Publications, 1991.

Eisner, Bruce. *Ecstasy: The MDMA Story.* Berkeley: Ronin, 1989.

Foreman, David. *Ecodefense: A Field Guide to Monkeywrenching,* second edition. Tucson: Ned Ludd Books, 1987.

Gibson, William. *Neuromancer.* New York: Ace Science Fiction, 1984.

——— and Bruce Sterling. *The Difference Engine.* New York: Bantam, 1991.

Gleick, James. *Chaos: Making of a New Science.* New York: Penguin, 1987.

Graboi, Nina. *One Foot in the Future: A Woman's Spiritual Journey.* Santa Cruz: Aerial Press, 1991.

Gracie & Zarkov. *Notes From Underground: A "Gracie and Zarkov" Reader.* Privately published, 1984. c/o *Mondo 2000* magazine.

Harman, Willis. *Global Mind Change: The Promise of the Last Years of the Twentieth Century.* Indianapolis: Knowledge Systems, 1988

Laidlaw, Marc. *Dad's Nuke.* New York: Donald I. Fine, 1985.

Lovelock, J.E. *Gaia: A New Look at Life on Earth.* New York: Oxford University Press, 1979.

McKenna, Dennis J. and Terence K. *The Invisible Landscape: Mind, Hallucinogens and the I Ching.* New York: Seabury Press, 1975.

McKenna, Terrence. *Food of the Gods: The Search for the Original Tree of Knowledge: A Radical History of Plants, Drugs and Human Evolution.* New York: Bantam, 1992.

Miller, Frank. *Batman: The Dark Knight.* New York: DC Comics, 1986.

*Mondo 2000* magazine, issues 1–5. Berkeley: Fun City MegaMedia, 1988–91.

Pearson, Roberta E., and William Uricchio, eds. *The Many Lives of the Batman: Critical Approaches to a Superhero and His Media.* New York: Routledge, 1991.

Pelton, Ross. *Mind Food and Smart Pills: A Sourcebook for the Vitamins, Herbs, & Drugs that Can Increase Intelligence, Improve Memory, & Prevent Brain Aging.* New York: Doubleday, 1989.

Rheingold, Howard. *Virtual Reality: The Revolutionary Technology of Computer-Generated Artificial Worlds—and How It Promises and Threatens to Transform Business and Society.* New York: Summit, 1991.

Rucker, Rudy, R.U. Sirius and Queen Mu. *Mondo 2000: A User's Guide to the New Edge.* New York: HarperPerennial, 1992.

Sheldrake, Rupert. *The Presence of the Past: Morphic Resonance and the Habits of Nature.* New York: Vintage, 1989.

———. *The Rebirth of Nature: The Greening of Science and God.* London: Random Century, 1990.

Sienkiewicz, Bill. *Stray Toasters.* New York: Epic Comics, 1989.

Sterling, Bruce. *Islands in the Net.* Ace Books, 1989.

Stevens, Jay. *Storming Heaven: LSD and the American Dream.* New York: Harper & Row, 1988.

Tamm, Eric. *Brian Eno: His Music and the Vertical Color of Sound.* Boston: Faber and Faber, 1989.

Watts, Alan W. *The Joyous Cosmology: Adventures in the Chemistry of Consciousness.* New York: Vintage, 1962.

Wolfe, Tom. *The Electric Kool-Aid Acid Test.* New York: Farrar, 1968.

# index